INVESTABLE!

# INVESTABLE!

## When Pandemic Risk Meets Speculative Finance

A Cautionary Tale

SUSAN ERIKSON

The MIT Press
Cambridge, Massachusetts
London, England

The MIT Press
Massachusetts Institute of Technology
77 Massachusetts Avenue, Cambridge, MA 02139
mitpress.mit.edu

The MIT Press gratefully acknowledges the support of Simon Fraser University, which provided funds toward the publication of this book.

The MIT Press would like to thank the anonymous peer reviewers who provided comments on drafts of this book. The generous work of academic experts is essential for establishing the authority and quality of our publications. We acknowledge with gratitude the contributions of these otherwise uncredited readers.

This book was set in Adobe Garamond Pro by New Best-set Typesetters Ltd. Printed and bound in the United States of America.

Library of Congress Cataloging-in-Publication Data

Names: Erikson, Susan, author.
Title: Investable! : when pandemic risk meets speculative finance / Susan Erikson.
Description: Cambridge, Massachusetts : The MIT Press, [2025] | Includes bibliographical references and index.
Identifiers: LCCN 2024034738 (print) | LCCN 2024034739 (ebook) | ISBN 9780262549356 (paperback) | ISBN 9780262380164 (epub) | ISBN 9780262380171 (pdf)
Subjects: LCSH: Medical care—Finance. | Bonds. | Pandemics—Economic aspects. | Medical economics.
Classification: LCC RA410.5 .E747 2025 (print) | LCC RA410.5 (ebook) | DDC 338.4/73621—dc23/eng/20241228
LC record available at https://lccn.loc.gov/2024034738
LC ebook record available at https://lccn.loc.gov/2024034739

10   9   8   7   6   5   4   3   2   1

Cover art: *Red Man Watching White Man Trying to Fix Hole in the Sky* (1990) by Lawrence Paul Yuxweluptun, courtesy of the National Gallery of Canada.

EU product safety and compliance information contact is: mitp-eu-gpsr@mit.edu

To SRH: For making me laugh and, especially, all the rest

# Contents

## Publisher's Note

Seven figures in this book are images of data presented in tabular form.

When preserving the image as an artifact was the priority, we presented the image as a numbered figure in the main text and as a corresponding text table that appears in the appendix. When the data in the image was the priority, we presented the data as a text table in the main text and as a corresponding figure that appears in the appendix.

# Acknowledgments

I am a professor who wanted to write a book for a smart audience, but not necessarily an academic one. How *do* people write books that other people want to read? I floundered. Then Evelyn Duffy, the founder of Open Boat Editing and editor of journalist Bob Woodward's last six books, said yes to working with me as a developmental editor. Evelyn, a queen of dry wit, gave me notes that were exceptionally keen and fair, gently moving me away from my bad habits and nerdy impulses. Soon after, Matthew Browne, now at Harvard Education Press, also said yes. Throughout, Matt had a steady, kind, intelligent way of calming my racing mind and pointing me in the right directions. Their yeses gave me hope that this book might be a good idea.

I started writing this book in the early days of the COVID-19 pandemic. Lockdown isolation did not improve my confidence, but good friends, family, and colleagues did. Christel, Stephen Brown, Amy Maxon Johnstone, Michael Orsini, Liz Roberts, Susan Shepler, and especially Claire Wendland were on speed dial for fortification and excellent advice. Richard Rottenburg's long-standing support is a forever debt. Carole Browner, Liz Cooper, Abou Farman, René Gerrets, Sue Goldswain, Lukas Henne, Patricia Kingori, Rob Lorway, Bernarda Schram, Ting Lang Zhang, and especially Mette Svendsen gave me rounds of invaluable feedback that shifted my writing and analysis for the better. At key points, Leslie Armijo, Antoine de Bengy Puyvallée, Emilie Cloatre, Jeff Erikson, Mariane Ferme, Janice Grahm, Klaus Høyer, Leigh Johnson, Nora Kenworthy, Lenore Manderson, Melissa Parker, Koen Peeters, Robert Redfield, and especially Felix Stein and

Katerini Storeng offered incisive insights. In a class of its own was the patient way Gary Parker helped me understand catastrophe bonds, especially their yield calculations. Steve Evans was a go-to reference for my embarrassingly elementary questions about insurance-linked securities; he produces public-facing ILS data and analysis of inestimable value. By example and through conversation, Vincanne Adams, Sama Banya, Erian Baxter, Rose Marie Beck, Solomon Berewa, Toby Behrmann, Jeff Davis, Erich Dellers, Chuck Dileva, Hannah Dubois, Sakiko Fukuda-Parr, Donna Goldstein, Nina Hale, David Kananizadeh, Joseph Lamin, Melissa Leach, Misha Lowe, Haley MacGreggor, Laura Matt, Kate Meagher, Cindy Nofziger, Songi Park, David Raffa, Ursula Rao, Eva Schindele, Jamie Scott, Philippe Trahan, Sylvanus Spencer, and Lawrence Paul Yuxweluptun all helped me sort out, in many different ways, what was important to say about my research. Julie Livingston's and Vincent Duclos's provocations in Berlin got me to return to the question—Is this the world we want?—again and again. Erving Goffman's work inspired the "frontstage"/"backstage" organizational structure. Sam Corden, Tyler Loveless, and Dani Seiss of Open Boat Editing shepherded me through the book proposal phase in fine form. Kathleen Caruso, Katie Kerr, Katie Lewis, Nicholas DiSabatino, Stephanie Sakson, Matt Valades, and Anthony Zannino at the MIT Press provided generous production help. To the many, many people I cannot name for confidentiality reasons, I am so grateful for your trust and insights.

At Simon Fraser University, Tania Bubela showed me how much difference an insightful and compassionate administrator can make on an academic's research career and sanity; I am forever indebted. Conversations with Michael Hathaway, Kelley Lee, Sharon Mah, Megan McKenzie, Tamir Moustafa, Irene Pang, Stacy Pigg, Barbara Sanders, and Rochelle Tucker buoyed me in countless ways. Huge thanks to Don Taylor, Hazel Plante, and Mark Bodnar, library and publication experts of the first order. I've worked with amazing research assistants on this project; deepest thanks to Iveoma Udevi-Aruevoru, Augusta Abdulai, Earum Chaudhary, Pneet Grewal, Naima Osman, and fieldworker extraordinaire Sam Eglin. Baindu Kosia is one of a kind, and I learned so much from her. Adami and Mohamed rode the roads with me. My research was possible with Institutional, Insight

Development, and Insight grants from the Social Science and Humanities Research Council of Canada. After waning under the Conservatives, funding for medical anthropology research in Canada was revived in 2015 by the Liberal government, which upheld a vital tenet of good governance: for humans to live well together over time, critical analyses of emerging social norms are essential.

Books are a result of timely enablements, some going back in time. At a make-or-break point in my career, George DeMartino and Ilene Grabel showed me that academics can be both brilliant and upliftingly caring. Likewise, Charlie Piot and Anne Allison have been wind in my sails since graduate school. The sagacious Beate Schücking provided a home away from home and a steady stream of excellent advice. My Salone family—the wise and empathetic Kemoh Bartholemew Abdulai, with Hawa, Musu, Seibatu, and all their relations—watch out for me, spend *sababu* on me, and feed me, which every Sierra Leonean knows is love in its fullest measure. For a long time now, NEH and LEH have amused me with highly unorthodox means of distraction, wit, and good fun.

And, finally, and most of all, SRH, without whom everything would be so different and this book would be nothing but an itch, this book is dedicated to you for all you do and all you make possible every single day.

# Author's Note

The pandemic bonds—a financial device made up by one of the world's most powerful institutions, the World Bank[1]—can seem like a great idea for raising money to fight pandemics. Money is pooled ahead of time, rather than waiting for governments to pony up monies to stop a deadly infectious disease after it spreads. Private investors speculate on *the risk of pandemic*, putting their money into a special World Bank account, earning interest on the money they invest, what's called their principal. If a pandemic happens, investors lose their principal to organizations that fight disease, thwarting contagion before it escalates. If there's no pandemic, investors get their principal money back, in addition to interest. In a world where the risk of pandemic outbreak is ever-present, making *risk* the thing that investors buy is, at the very least, interesting. Soon after the idea for the pandemic bonds was first floated by the World Bank in 2014, I applied for a grant to study these kinds of investments and got it.

*Investable!* tells the story of the people who made the world's first pandemic bonds. Brought to life are the bankers, health experts, power brokers, risk vendors, bureaucrats, data nerds, modelers, and motorcycle crews who, in one way or another, contributed to the bonds' concept, design, sales, and data modeling. Sierra Leone, the small West African country of eight million people—regularly invoked as a lucky future recipient of the bonds' funds—also plays a starring role. It's a story about the excesses of capitalism and what humans do with money when governments are defunded and hollowed out and too little is invested in global public health goods.

I'm a professor, trained as an anthropologist, who never outgrew asking "why" all the time. When I finished high school, curiosity about the world beyond the confines of the small rural North American community where I grew up spurred me to go to college in a big US city. Upon graduation, a burning desire for travel and adventure prompted me to join a humanitarian organization that sent me as a twenty-two-year-old to eastern Sierra Leone, where I lived for two years. I followed that up with a brief career in global affairs, based in Washington, DC, but traveling regularly to Turkey and the former Yugoslavia, working with US Embassy officials and trade groups. All that made me pretty comfortable poking around for answers in big international institutions. That's useful for research I do, where, to mix a few metaphors, I get to draw back the curtain, poke around under the hood, try to turn every page, as the great Robert Caro said, and figure out how and why bold new health initiatives work—and don't.

As an anthropologist, I conduct research on the global political economy of human health, meaning I study how humans organize as groups to keep—or fail to keep—each other well. In other words, I analyze what people do—or don't do—about people getting sick. Rather than focusing on the viral, bacterial, or genetic origins of ill health, my attention is on the money and politics of sicknesses because, well, for one thing, impoverishment can make you sick. I study the stories that get told about the money and politics of health. Times being what they are, I pay special attention to the data and modeling techniques that direct where the money goes. That may sound dull as dirt, but data and modeling stories prove profoundly revealing. Deep behind the curtain, explained in the "backstage" chapters of this book, I show, for example, how pandemic bonds' data and modeling forecasts were geared more to investors losing their money than preventing loss of human life.

Since 2010, my research focuses on discovering what it means for human health to have a global tier of people with so much money that governments often turn to them to solve societal problems. I investigate whether private sector investor schematics are actually likely to deliver "more preparedness" and "better response" for people, especially the most vulnerable humans, as, for example, the World Bank claimed the pandemic bonds would. I've thought long and hard about the ideal mix of public and privately financed care, both in everyday kinds of ways and during crises. Here's what I found: There's more than enough money in the world to fund systems that would reduce human health suffering globally. But, increasingly, new care financing schemes favors private investors, *by design*. That was certainly the case of the pandemic bonds; they were designed with "What will investors buy?" front of mind.

Many of the university students drawn to my classes want to understand how investor capitalism is shaping human health. They already know that hedge fund investors buy up Vancouver apartment buildings, driving up their rents so high that at least one of them lived in their car and got internet access for their assignments in McDonald's or Starbucks parking lots. Many of them work part-time as essential workers, and they know firsthand what it means to have to sell their labor cheap. They know they are targeted to take on debt, and some have tried to make up the difference between what they spend and what they earn, with quick money schemes. They are a generation of young adults awash in opportunities to take on consumer debt and student loans, and to bet online.[2] In my classes, I see students wrestling with cultural norms that naturalize taking on debt and gambling their way to a better future. No surprise, then, that the mechanics of capitalism interest them. It's not a big leap for them to ask, *How did something like pandemic risk become investable?* And, seriously, *Why? How did we get here*, they ask, and *what does that mean for our futures?*

All economic systems have trade-offs. I grew up in North America, have lived in Europe, and, no question about it, like nice things. But I also worked in Yugoslavia while it transitioned to market-based socialism and lived in the former East Germany soon after the Berlin Wall crumbled. Living in Sierra Leone—a country courted and exploited by all kinds of economic interests—fleshed out for me the costs of *both* poverty and materialism. I've thought a lot about the opportunities afforded in capitalist systems and about how systems of private property ownership shape individual human lives, communities, and nation-states. The best systems organize their wealth for humans to live in communities with dignity and without despair, seeding individual opportunity while also providing quality support, like universal health, education, and pensioner care.

Societies have "tipping points," when their systems become out of balance. Societies can break, inflicting more human suffering. Many capitalist democracies around the world reel now from the instability of an economic system—capitalism—that has run hot for too long without the kinds of curbs on greed that people need to live together in peace and good health. Too much bodily suffering in the world right now has economic and political origins, not only bacterial or viral ones.

A big impetus for writing this book is to explain what health finance "innovation" looks like when the global capitalist system is out of balance. The pandemic bonds are an example of the type of financial devices that are offered up to meet societal shortfalls, using the same capitalist logics to fix the problem that caused the problem. Lawrence Paul Yuxweluptun, whose work graces the book's cover, captures this in his painting, *Red Man Watching White Man Trying to Fix Hole in the Sky*,[3] "as the white scientists use the same modes of knowledge that led to the problems in the first place."[4]

*  *  *

This book is about the pandemic bonds, but it is also about the value of using anthropological[5] method to follow the money and ask the question, Why *did* the pandemic bonds become a new type of capitalist quest in global health financing? Growing up as a solidly middle-class kid, I approached personal finance well into adulthood by making money through wage labor and getting a paycheck; if I wanted more money, I worked more. Making money from money was largely foreign to me. But I used anthropological research tools to understand how finance worked. Studying global health finance[6] became for me like the studying of communities in small villages by old-timey anthropologists. The pandemic bonds are cultural artifacts, studyable as objects of human workmanship, observable and repetitive action, and "the way we do things." And so, I got to work.

I traveled over 300,000 miles (480,000 kilometers) to write this book. Anthropologists like me who travel the world in search of answers have both the predisposition and opportunity to traipse. Studying the pandemic bonds meant literally going all over the place because the pandemic bonds were invented all over the place. Global ethnography[7]—the research method I used to study the bonds—is about going to where a thing takes you, spontaneously, intuitively. I "followed the thing"[8]—the pandemic bonds—and conducted research with people designing and selling them, and as well as in the places the bonds were supposed to help, like Sierra Leone. I trekked between North America, Europe, and West Africa, and hung out in Washington, DC; London; Munich; New York City; Freetown; and other cities. I followed special interests and logics as they led from one to another, moving between town-sized networks (the World Bank is 15,000 employees strong), Wall Street industries (like insurance-linked securities), and national bureaucracies (like Statistics Sierra Leone). I interviewed global investors wherever I found them, including up the street in my Vancouver neighborhood. I joined groups as best I could, residing in different places, working alongside people, taking part in conferences, meetings, bureaucratic office work, and data collection odysseys by motorcycle. I tracked the pandemic bonds from their big idea stage through their early design stages to the payout stage when COVID-19 triggered them in 2020.

I asked thousands of questions of hundreds of people: How do you see investor logics fitting with pandemic response logistics? What ideas about money dominate your workplace? What controls data flow? Who knows what? What shapes decision-making? Who's the real boss here? What topics are verboten? Who and what are left out, glorified, disparaged, gossiped about? The pandemic bonds were born of human networks, shared interests, and patterned activities of people in a worldwide social field; they can be studied like village genealogies. Along the way, I had a colossal amount of help from generous strangers and new acquaintances.

By chance, over decades, I've lived and worked in several of the countries and cities central to the pandemic bonds story. Sierra Leone, for one, was a country held up by the World Bank as a likely beneficiary of pandemic bonds financing. It has been a second home to me since my twenties. As an international humanitarian aid worker, I lived in the Eastern Province and worked in hospitals, clinics, and schools in the region that, coincidentally, later became the epicenter of both the 1991–2002 war and the 2014–2016 Ebola outbreak.*

I also lived in Germany, one of two primary country donor sponsors of the bonds and home to one of the reinsurance companies designing the bonds. Deutschland was the site of my PhD dissertation and postdoctoral research; I've lived there, all told, for seventeen months. The home of the bonds' data analytics firm was in Boston, where I spent four years at university. Washington, DC, home of the World Bank, was where I worked for big US government agencies for many years, cutting my teeth on international politics and policy, and witnessing the behind-the-scenes dramas of legislative and foreign policy deal-making. DC is also where, for over three years, I collaborated on projects with people at the World Bank, moving in and out of their H Street offices in an everyday kind of way.

Academic colleagues complain about how difficult it is for researchers to get into organizations like the World Bank to conduct research, and they are not wrong. Knowing people at the Bank from my earlier career helped my research. For this book, I met with over twenty people currently and formerly employed at the Bank who had varying degrees of involvement

---

*When I moved to a rural eastern Sierra Leonean town before the war, people made it clear to me that if I was to live there, I would be schooled. Rice is a staple food and neighborhood women taught me to correctly plant rice, pushing the tender green rice spouts deep enough into swamp mud for them to grow strong. They stressed the need for me to be chill when sharp-pincered ants marched through my kitchen, cleaning up every crumb in a two-inch-wide swath, like tiny teeming Roombas. (We won't be staying, just passing through.) I would need to let my neighbors cut down all the shade and mango trees around my house without protest because a neon-green snake had made its way into my bedroom from their branches. The thing I mistook for a wayward shoelace was a two-step mamba, so called, they said, because if it bites you, you've got two steps left. When Mende friends were troubled by domestic violence, the neighborhood women wanted assurances that I would seek out elder women's fixes; there was a hierarchy to getting it to stop. If I was going to assist midwives at prenatal clinics, charting fundal heights and newborn baby weights, I had to learn how to ask questions in ways that did not bring to mind a child a woman may have lost. I was not born knowing how to strain floating insects out of palm wine through my teeth, but I'm proof that humans are teachable and that it can become second nature. I was not in Salone during the war (1991–2002), but, since 2008, I have returned intermittently as an academic anthropologist. In 2014 when Ebola broke out, I was there with graduate students conducting research on health data use.

making up or reviewing the pandemic bonds, or who had opinions they were eager to share about the insider intrigue of the bonds. Several were in the proverbial room during key discussions. I met for face-to-face interviews and corresponded by email with folks from the three Bank units that did the heavy lifting to design the bonds. I interviewed them in Washington, at the Bank's Wolfensohn Atrium coffee shop, at their H Street and Treasury Building offices, at New York City and Washington restaurants and hotel lobbies, at conferences, on the phone, and by Zoom. I also met with World Bank officials from other units, some who had retired or left the Bank for other jobs. In Sierra Leone, I met with World Bank officials from DC who were in Freetown while they conducted what is still unselfconsciously called the annual "mission visit."

Anthropologists typically give pseudonyms to people and organizations in their books. But because the pandemic bonds were a highly visible and public-facing project offered by a publicly prominent international bank, protecting identities in this book is not exclusively within my control. No masking of identity was possible, for example, for the World Bank itself, or for Jim Yong Kim, who was the World Bank president when the pandemic bonds were created. Insiders, as they always do, will know who's who, but, still, throughout the book I anonymize as much as possible. I refer to the Bank employees who made up the bonds collectively as "designers," rather than identifying them by unit, and I use they/them/their pronouns when I'm quoting individuals whose gender would identify them. In direct quotes, I use substitutes for words that would reveal identities. Poignant quotable comments were left out because speakers could have been identified, or they were said to me during background-only interviews. Some quotes are edited slightly for brevity and clarity.

Anthropological research requires improvisation and being able to "sit"[9] with people. Or stand, as I learned one day in a restroom at a reinsurance conference in Germany. I had run into multiple dead-ends, unable to meet the people I hoped to interview. I was in methodological freefall. So I went to the restroom, which, as it turned out, was an auspicious place to meet a reinsurance executive. Waiting in line for the toilet in an uncommonly large room, I exchanged friendly glances with a fifty-something woman off to the side doing standing yoga stretches. I complimented her on her form. She asked me where I was from. We got to talking, and I shared my predicament. She had good friends in both reinsurance companies I was interested in; did I want her to introduce me to them? Why, yes, thank you very much! That one contact led to five hard-to-get interviews. My point is not that restrooms are full of people standing tadasana waiting to help anthropologists. Rather, being open to serendipitous moments of connection in unexpected places proved a useful approach for researching a complex financial device wherever I was in the world.

# Glossary and Acronyms

| | |
|---|---|
| **Capital** | An economic resource measured in terms of money |
| **Capital markets** | Where people come together to buy and sell assets and debt |
| **Global health** | Worldwide industry providing aid and technical training intended to improve human health outcomes |
| **International development** | Distinct industry and field of professional practices focused on fostering economic growth and civil society |

| | |
|---|---|
| **ART** | Alternative risk transfer |
| **The Bank** | The World Bank |
| **CCRIF** | Caribbean Catastrophe Risk Insurance Facility |
| **CDC** | U.S. Centers for Disease Control and Prevention |
| **Davos** | Swiss town that annually hosts the World Economic Forum |
| **DON** | World Health Organization's Disease Outbreak News |
| **FinTech** | Financial technology |
| **G20** | International country collaboration for the global economy |
| **GPU** | Graphics processing unit |
| **IBRD** | World Bank's International Bank for Reconstruction and Development |
| **IDA** | World Bank's International Development Association |
| **ILS** | Insurance-linked securities |
| **IMF** | International Monetary Fund |
| **NGO** | Nongovernmental organization |
| **P3** | Public-private partnership |

| | |
|---|---|
| **PEF** | Pandemic Emergency Financing Facility |
| **PHU** | Peripheral health unit |
| **PIH** | Partners in Health |
| **Prospectus** | Contractual specifications of the pandemic bonds |
| **SAL** | Structural adjustment loan |
| **SAP** | Structural adjustment program |
| **SEC** | U.S. Securities and Exchange Commission |
| **SEIR** | Susceptible-exposed-infectious-removed |
| **SIR** | Susceptible-infectious-removed |
| **UNICEF** | United Nations Children's Fund (formerly United Nations International Children's Emergency Fund) |
| **USAID** | United States Agency for International Development |
| **WB** | World Bank |
| **WEF** | World Economic Forum |
| **WHO** | World Health Organization |

## SETTING THE STAGE

*How did something like pandemic risk become investable?* And, seriously, *Why? How did we get here?* they ask. *What does that mean for our futures?*

Three stories to prepare for the stories that come after.

# 1 THE WORLD'S MOST CONTROVERSIAL INVESTMENT

Pandemic bonds were the brainchild of the World Bank. For anyone who knows the inner bureaucracy of the Bank[1]—a powerful supranational organization headquartered in Washington, DC—early talk[2] of the bonds championed a highly unlikely scenario: they would release money quickly, at the first signs of pandemic-level disease spread. In March 2015, Jim Yong Kim, the World Bank president at the time, declared in *Time* magazine, "Our goal is to create a new financial instrument that can rapidly disburse a large amount of funds within eight hours."[3] *Eight hours*, which he compared to the eight months it had taken the World Bank to disperse money to fight the West African Ebola outbreak in 2014. One of the Bank's pandemic bonds designing partners thought that the bonds' disbursement might more realistically take ten days.[4]

Eight hours. Ten days. Of course, after COVID-19 hit in early 2020,[5] the money took much longer to disburse. The promised payout began mid-May 2020, four and a half months after COVID-19's first official public health announcement by the Chinese government on December 31, 2019. That's 3,285 hours late, to use Kim's metric, or 137 days, well after the time when public health agencies might have contained the disease to a small area. Other aspects of the promised payout were also off. The money released was about 40 percent of the US$500 million Kim originally said would be available.[6] The bonds' geography was off too: poor countries in Africa, Asia, and Latin America were eligible to receive money, but Europe and North America were major sites of COVID-19 sickness, contagion, and death.

The designers who crafted the bonds imagined containing a small rural and remote outbreak, like when Ebola hit the "parrot's beak" region of Guinea, Sierra Leone, and Liberia in 2014. But COVID-19 was a different beast. By mid-May 2020 when the funds began to be dispersed, the world was already home to a full-blown global pandemic. Vast urban areas were hit hard. By official counts, which have proven low, more than four million people were already infected by that time. COVID-19 had spread to over 200 countries and territories, and already killed over 300,000 people.[7]

World Bank folks defended the basic idea of the bonds well after their late showing, one claiming in a 2021 email to me that "we insured against a coronavirus outbreak . . . I can't find other parties that had that level of foresight . . . [it] is definitely a useful precedent." Okay, but precedent to what exactly? What were the bonds supposed to *be*?

* * *

The existential fears of the early days of the COVID-19 pandemic have faded, but its lockdowns, the isolation, and confusion changed people's lives. Elders, essential workers, and health care providers died. Businesses went bust. Nation-states were worrisomely unmoored. Communities lost their footing. Because they weren't in school, children lost much more than days on the calendar. Economies are taking years to recover. And the fear of another pandemic in our lifetime is a constant risk.

But what if there was a silver bullet able to stop all that loss? That was the seductive promise of the World Bank's pandemic bonds. From Bank folks' perspective, the bonds were a no-brainer. Bonds are the Bank's bailiwick. They've have been the Bank's core business from its beginning. Less than 10 percent of World Bank's coffer comes from dues paid by its 184 country government members. The rest comes from private investors who invest in World Bank's bonds and their large stable of financial devices.

The Bank was not the bonds' only cheerleader. Soon after Kim started talking up the bonds in 2015, public endorsements of the pandemic bonds piled up in the media:

Saving the world, one bond at a time.

—*Euromoney*[8]

A little market medicine to prevent the next pandemic.
—*Financial Times*[9]

We have taken a momentous step that has the potential to save millions of lives and entire economies from one of the greatest systemic threats we face. . . . This creates an entirely new market for pandemic risk insurance.
—Jim Yong Kim, World Bank president[10]

Pandemic bonds have potential to be a win-win-win.
—Larry Summers, economist and former US Treasury Secretary[11]

By 2019, though, critiques of the bonds started emerging:

Financial goofiness. . . . An embarrassing mistake. . . . A dumb idea.
—The same Larry Summers[12]

Pandemic bonds: Designed to fail.
—*Nature*[13]

By 2020, as COVID-19 started its global spread and the bonds failed to pay out in months, much less hours, critiques of the bonds started outstripping endorsements, prompting *Bloomberg* reporters to hail them "the world's most controversial investment."[14] By my count, media critique of the bonds ran at about 2-to-1 against.

Pandemic bonds are the sick man of finance.
—*Reuters*[15]

World Bank scheme "waiting for people to die."
—*The Guardian*[16]

Months into the coronavirus outbreak, investors are still making returns off a novel pandemic bond intended to benefit poor countries.
—*Wall Street Journal*[17]

A bond that provides too little money too late—or none at all—is just financialization run amok.
—*The Conversation*[18]

Pandemic bonds are a type of catastrophe bond, or "cat bond." I first heard about cat bonds during a 2003 lunchtime talk at a storied school of international studies. The speaker was a Harvard-trained lawyer and PhD economist whom the dean introduced as "a brilliant man who adds value to any group." Five minutes in, the speaker bragged about a financial device he had introduced to the World Bank where he worked as a consultant. He said he had an answer to the problem of helping people affected by weather-related catastrophes. Turn the risk over to private investors. Investors, not governments, should pay for response, recovery, and rebuilding after disasters. Get private money, like the funds sitting in pensions, into risk pools, as a kind of insurance. Offer investors interest in return. *Make catastrophe investable.* Investors would be able to make money by speculating on where and when extreme weather events would happen next, he said. Catastrophe cleanup needed to get smarter by enticing well-endowed Samaritans to get richer.

Around me, the twenty-odd people in the room calmly munched on the food in front of them. But my stomach hurt. I was viscerally disturbed by what I heard. My mind filled with images of selling off units of human suffering to rich people who would buy them for a chance to make money. The audience—early career international affairs professors, some young business school visitors, and a few graduate students, all white—were not the Black and brown people the speaker said the financial device would save. The speaker argued it was the only way to help people who won't help themselves, hawking that common racist trope.

My unease mounted. At that time, I had already worked for about a decade as a global affairs expert, on the front lines of US humanitarian aid and trade programs in West Africa, the Balkans, and Central Asia. The speaker was wrong: even the poorest people plan for themselves and help others during disasters. No question that catastrophe recovery requires "staff, stuff, space, systems, and social support,"[19] all of which are expensive. Money is essential. But it is no panacea on its own. True problem-solving after catastrophe demands high levels of organization and political will. The best solutions are locally managed, not dictated by outsiders. On-the-ground, the kind of drive-by investment the speaker advocated can introduce more problems than it solves.

Plus, I was having a hard time imagining a reliable solution dependent on Wall Street[20] investors, a group not known for their stick-to-it-ness.

Cat bonds came across my radar again in 2007 when the *New York Times Magazine* published an article by writer Michael Lewis. In "In Nature's Casino,"[21] Lewis explains cat bonds this way: an investor "puts down his money and will lose it all if some specified bad thing happens within a predetermined number of years." If nothing happens, investors get all their money back, plus interest annually or semi-annually. When nothing happens, then investors profit. A catastrophe means investors lose their original payment, sometimes millions of dollars. Lewis's explanation and the speaker's assumptions synced: only money-making can incentivize people to address the big threats to humankind. Use private money, not public funds, for future catastrophes.

For catastrophe cleanup, the shift from public to private investor solutions emerged in the 1990s out of a little-known alcove of Wall Street, insurance-linked securities (ILS), which is a booming business today.[22] Pooling money from nation-states or using taxpayers' dollars effectively for catastrophe cleanup is not their job. Rather, the ILS remedy gives investors the chance to turn a profit when they put their money "at risk" for a few years. ILS instruments have grown in popularity because they give investors a chance to make money and insurance companies get a Plan B for sourcing other people's money when natural disasters like hurricanes, earthquakes, and floods hit and lots of claims get filed.

The World Bank issued its first ILS catastrophe bonds in 2014, though it had already been involved in designing them for about a decade. When the pandemic bonds were launched in 2017, they were considered an exciting innovation by many ILS insiders, providing new investment opportunities in a previously untapped domain—health. That was a Bank goal: to build an ILS market for pandemics, joining the established ILS markets for hurricanes, earthquakes, windstorms, and other nasty weather events.

Here's why we need to better understand the basic blueprint of devices like pandemic bonds: they help us understand how capitalist excesses—too much private money accumulated by too few people alongside too little public money—affect both global problem-solving and ordinary people. The bonds were rationalized as necessary because some governments are deemed too poor to pay for catastrophe cleanup. But many governments are too poor to pay for the common good after decades of structural adjustment, antigovernment, antitaxation campaigns. Taxes may be what we are supposed pay for civilized society, to paraphrase Oliver Wendell Holmes, but tax avoidance is currently high art[23] while austerity of public services is the order of the day. Financial devices like pandemic bonds are meant to fill the gaps.

There's another reason to understand devices like these. It's important to understand how money is accumulating for particular groups of people, because ith money comes power. There are special societal dangers—especially to human health—to impoverishing governments and allowing astronomical accumulations of wealth and power to sit in the hands of a small sliver of the world's population who can turn off the financial spigots whenever they feel like it.

### THE BONDS: THE SHORT STORY AND THEIR BIGGER SIGNIFICANCE

Here's the short story: using weather-risk catastrophe bonds as their exemplar, the world's first two ILS pandemic bonds were issued by the World Bank in July 2017. Officially called "Floating Rate Catastrophe Linked Capital At-Risk Notes" by the Bank, the bonds raised US$320 million from investors for pandemic response. Had there been no COVID-19 pandemic (or any other qualifying pandemic), investors would have gotten all their money back in July 2020 at what's called the bonds' "maturity date." But COVID-19 broke out months before the maturity date, triggering the bonds in April 2020 when preset criteria began being met—meaning that "enough" people had died, and other measurement thresholds were reached—to release money[24] for pandemic response in poor countries. From May to September 2020, US$194.86 million was disbursed in sixty-four countries.[25] That's a just-the-facts story of the bonds. (More details about the bonds than you'll probably want to know can be found in chapter 2.)

But the bigger significance of the bonds begs telling too. Emblematically, the bonds were about offloading costs usually borne by the public. This troubled me enough to study what anthropologists call the "local logics" of the bonds: By what reasoning did World Bank folks and others think that private investors could effectively hedge global pandemic risk and deliver sufficient pandemic response? What was their rationale? How had New Deal–style ideas about the role of government as *the* provider of social safety nets morph into a kind of private betting on pandemic? And the black-boxed mechanics of the bonds—the data and modeling—what did they have to do with pandemic financing? A retired Bank officer told me, "Traditionally, the Bank wouldn't have had private investors; we would have just had rich country donors for emergency response." How had *that* shift happened? Fifteen years into the twenty-first century, how had off-loading risk from public bodies into private hands become so normalized that the World Bank came to sell the bonds as the pandemic financing solution?

The bonds' promotors at the Bank and elsewhere seemed surprised the bonds prompted big existential questions, like "whether it's appropriate to tie responsibility for public health to private investment at all," as *Bloomberg* reporters put it.[26] The business of investment, after all, is to make money. Most bond advocates I interviewed didn't acknowledge that private investors are notoriously fickle and not obliged to consider the health of humans when they invest.

And yet. Even after investors lost money, even after the bonds' disbursements were late, debate continues backstage and out of sight about whether the pandemic bonds were irredeemably flawed or just needed better engineering and design parameters. Let's back up a bit and consider more of the story.

### GETTING RICH PEOPLE TO PAY FOR RISK

Risk[27] is everywhere and it's expensive. When I relocated for a job, I traded risks—wildfires for earthquakes. I left the threat of mountain wildfire for a more tremorous home base. Canada's Rain City—Vancouver—is on the coastal edge of the Pacific Ocean where tectonic plates meet in what one television series referred to as "Hell's Crust," where homeowners take out insurance on their insurance to hedge their huge earthquake deductibles. Though we collectively ignore it to get through the day, earthquake risk is a known known to western Canadians. But 2021 brought attention to three risks we had not prepared for—the COVID-19 pandemic; a devastating heat dome (temperatures of 120°F) that killed over 600 people in a week; and several atmospheric rivers (uncommonly heavy rain), one right after the other, that wiped out roads, bridges, and prime agricultural land. Risk is inescapable. To be alive is risky. Humans have been trying to mitigate risks—risks to business, life, and limb—since at least 1750 BCE when Babylon's Code of Hammurabi was codified.

Here's the thing about a risk: it doesn't always become a catastrophe. And between that space of will-it or won't-it is the room to make money and pocket the difference. Insurance companies are profitably built on the knowledge that people will pay for coverage against threats that never become full-blown crises.

With the pandemic bonds, the World Bank exploited that space. The Bank got investors to invest in pandemic risk at a time (before COVID-19) when few imagined a worldwide pandemic actually occurring. In 2015, on the heels of halcyon decades when millions of people couldn't imagine a pandemic affecting *them*, the Bank used the imagery of the three small West African countries of Sierra Leone, Liberia, and Guinea suffering from another Ebola-like outbreak to sell pandemic risk as an investment opportunity. Investment opportunities come in lots of sizes and designs. But the Bank's pandemic bonds weren't about getting retail investors to buy small business shares so that a whisky distillery had enough money to retool as a hand sanitizer factory or to fund public health messaging campaigns. No, for the pandemic bonds, the Bank wanted the "whales of Wall Street"—the big billion-dollars-in-assets folks with pension, endowment, and high-worth securities monies—to invest to invest in risk. And investors lined up, because, as one ILS executive put it at the time "there is a lot of capital looking for a productive home."

Belief that rich people can save the world with their money—runs strong, despite the fact that "fewer ha[ving] more"[28] notoriously destabilizes societies and brings down empires. "In the pandemic, it was the CEOs in many, many cases all over the world who were the heroes," a Silicon Valley CEO declared. They stepped up "to save the world."[29] Yes, private sector manufacturing of masks, diagnostic tests, and ventilators at scale was essential to the common good.[30] But with little fanfare, governments too scaled up, developing vaccines[31] and procuring medical supplies and equipment[32] for billions of people. No question, the world needs both sectors during pandemics!

But relying on investors has its limits. Saving the world was not what the pharmaceutical executives from Pfizer had front of mind, for example, when it refused to take its vaccine formula off-patent; its investors occupied their frontal cortexes. Public health was not served when Pfizer fought hard against waiving their patent for the broadscale manufacturing of generic coronavirus vaccines, stifling vaccine innovation that may have developed a better and less expensive vaccine. Pfizer doubled its revenue in 2021, making more money from its coronavirus vaccine alone—US$42.6 billion—than it did from the sale of all its products the year before.[33]

## IN PRAISE OF GOOD PANDEMIC GOVERNANCE

From a public health standpoint, the best infectious disease outbreak is the one you never hear about because it's already been contained. Historically, that's been done by governments. Quietly. Ploddingly. But in the decades before COVID-19 reconfigured our lives and sacked country economies, governance—the very *idea* of government—had taken quite a bashing. Decades upon decades of defunding and disparagement—"government is too slow, too stupid, too controlling, too fill-in-the-blank"—kept many of the world's governments from properly preparing for pandemics and monitoring disease outbreaks prior to 2020.

Before COVID-19, in some of the world's wealthiest countries, the government units set up to fight pandemics were intentionally weakened or decommissioned. In May 2019, just seven months before COVID-19 was first reported, Canada silenced its renowned decades-old early warning system for disease reconnaissance, citing budget cuts and "no pandemic scares in recent memory."[34] The United States shut down its pandemic response unit in 2018.[35] Before the first case of COVID-19, European countries prepared for flu,[36] but not coronavirus.

Asian and African governments paid more attention to averting pandemics. East Asian countries, after SARS, H1N1 and MERS outbreaks in the 2000s, established national legal frameworks and clear decision-making authority for pandemics.[37] When COVID-19 hit, some of these countries had staggeringly good health outcomes compared with North America and Europe.[38] The African Union, after the horrors of Ebola outbreaks in East, Central, and West Africa and in a move toward continental health decision-making and self-determination, created its own Centers for Disease Control in 2016.[39]

Governments' capacity to raise huge sums of money is one of the best things about them. "Nothing is privately insurable to the tune of two T[rillion] or whatever the final number will be [for COVID response]," an ILS executive said in 2021. During the COVID-19 pandemic, the "whatever" was the US$4.2 trillion the US government paid out as of January 2023 to quell the pandemic.[40] Yes, 4.2 *trillion*. The United States was not alone in its massive spending. Faced with COVID-19, governments around the world paid out billions and trillions of dollars, not only making diagnostics, vaccines, and treatments available at little or no cost, but also providing financial lifelines to businesses and people affected, unable or not allowed to work, something private investors did not do. Compare that sum with the World Bank dividing US$195.84 million of pandemic bonds investor's money among sixty-four countries for COVID-19 relief.[41] Or to the Bill and Melinda Gates Foundation, a private global health philanthropy that reportedly gave US$2 billion for COVID-19, with the first $1 billion paying to develop vaccines and diagnostic tests and the second billion spent on private sector initiatives, some which generated financial returns for Gates.[42]

During the pandemic, governments, even emaciated ones, showed what they *can* do when there is political will. The Sierra Leonean government, for example, had learned what not to do from the 2014–2016 Ebola pandemic.[43] When COVID-19 hit, it distributed COVID-19 tests in February 2020, which was about a month before the United States did.

In many countries during the pandemic, citizens quibbled about the role of government, but there is no question: governments stepped up, created vaccines, gave out masks and tests, and got shots in arms, much of it for free. COVID-19 is still with us, but when compared with pandemics in human history, it's been largely contained in miraculously short order. Despite epic and tragic human costs from the pandemic, governments outdid themselves. Billions of people around the world benefited from government-organized responses to the novel infectious disease. Government responses were not perfect. And many people found their governments hugely wanting. Some rejected government help outright. Others denied that COVID-19 existed at all. Yet most governments organized for the common good, and tried to take care of people, something private investors do not have the standing to do. COVID-19 laid bare the limitations of private investor backstopping of global health crises.

Yet calls for private investor solutions to big ticket challenges persist.

## HOW GOVERNMENTS GOT SO RELATIVELY POOR AND THE PRIVATE SECTOR SO RICH: A BRIEF HISTORY

Previous generations, haunted by memories of the economic deprivations of the Great Depression and two world wars, supported financial regulations that curbed greed, redistributed wealth, and lessened national economies' boom-bust cycles. In the United States, the 1933 Glass-Steagall Act separated ordinary folks' money from Wall Street banking to protect citizens' money from risky speculative schemes. There was widespread recognition that governments should organize and produce healthy and educated citizens as a matter of equity and human dignity. Over decades, human rights became codified.[44] Colonial regimes were challenged and overturned. Governments, even the newly postcolonial, were tacitly at the center of economic and development planning. In places that were well governed, tax monies were invested in community infrastructures, transportation, health, and education.

Social sentiment began to change in 1970s as neoliberalism[45]—a political order glorifying the transfer of economic control to the private sector—took hold in the world's wealthiest and most powerful countries. Neoliberal orthodoxy infused governments throughout the world with new ideas about the life-supporting force of "free markets." With that, came demands: Make it easier to make money. Excise the old curbs. Markets would discipline themselves. Human needs would be met because private companies would rise up with products and services to meet them. Essential goods and services like food, housing, and healthcare? It was assumed that private businesses and investors would provide. "All human action [would be brought] into the domain of the market."[46]

A new ideology about government emerged, asserting that less government is better. In the 1980s, US President Ronald Reagan and UK Prime Minister Margaret Thatcher mocked the idea that governments exist to help. Deregulation, government austerity, and tax cuts became potent neoliberal watchwords. Governance itself came under attack. Neoliberal tenets—that governments should be small, taxes should be low, and regulation should be minimal to foster private business growth—spread prodigiously worldwide, with a lot of help from the World Bank and its sister institution, the International Monetary Fund (IMF).

In the final decades of the twentieth century, there was widespread conviction globally that human well-being would be advanced by freeing people to take initiative and put at risk whatever they wanted to, including other people's money and social security. In this mindset, government is necessary only to facilitate the freedom to pursue individual ambitions, correct market failures, and enforce contracts. Fairness? Equity? Protections of human dignity? There were serious gaps in that master market plan.[47]

Today, neoliberalism may be in decline,[48] but it hasn't fallen completely apart,[49] and some of its more hidden financial structures remain vibrantly intact. In 1999, US legislators repealed the Glass-Steagall Act that had reined in capitalist excesses for over six decades. It was a US law, but it had had far-ranging effects on the global economy. That deregulation was partly responsible for the 2008 global financial crisis,[50] which is largely seen as the worst global financial crisis since the Great Depression. Passing the 2010 Dodd-Frank Reform and Consumer Protection Act,[51] US legislators attempted to again outlaw the riskiest plays with other people's money.

By the time Kim was named World Bank president in 2012, national economies and private fortunes were bouncing back after the 2008 financial crisis. The push for deregulation resumed. Dodd-Frank regulations were eased with the passage of a 2018 bill signed into law by US President Donald Trump. The financial sector became enfevered again with "innovation" that "disrupts"[52] the status quo. Novel financial devices like a pandemic bond, at home in the zeitgeist, seemed like progress. Financialization—a form of financial engineering that transforms work products, bodies, services, and risk itself—anything it can[53]—into investable, tradable, exchangeable, sometimes speculative financial instruments that are bought and sold was on the rise. So here we are, two decades into the twenty-first century. The aughts and the teens were wild rides because so many economic and political guardrails (like tax credits and voting rights) in the world's biggest economy were bandied back and forth in vicious cycles of law-making and repeal. And in that chaotic mix, some people grew unfathomably rich.[54] Countries were underfunded and maxed out. So, in the run-up to the sale of the pandemic bonds, the World Bank went to where the money was: private investors.

### BUT MONEY ALONE IS NEVER ENOUGH: THE DANGERS OF CARVING OFF RISK FROM RESPONSIBILITY

I can tell you, the [pandemic bond fund] is not the same as implementation, right? So it's not a mystery—it was never a mystery—you need staff, stuff, space, and systems.
—Paul Farmer, physician and anthropologist, in a public conversation with Kim about the pandemic bonds[55]

One of the least acknowledged aspects of the bonds was how risk was carved off from responsibility. Risk—the possibility of loss, injury, or death due to the hundreds of possible events in humans' lives—was made investible. Responsibility, on the other hand, remained a chore, a nuisance best left to someone else. Governments have been the "someone else" for hundreds of years; Wall Street folks aren't jumping in for that responsibility. Truth be told, no one wants the responsibility portfolio because there's too little money in it and it's so damn hard. But, in fact, that's a lot of what governments are *for*: taking care of the big-ticket threats that are not profitable.[56]

The skills and expertise it takes to make money on Wall Street are very different from the skills and expertise necessary for well-managed public health disease preparedness, detection, response, and aftercare. Investors aren't public health experts. The financial investment sector is not geared for *care*.[57] Good public health governance, though, is about holding the risk and responsibility for all the "what-ifs" and life-saving responses that humans need to survive deadly infectious disease and thrive in the thereafter. The World Bank's bonds were designed to fund, but not to prevent, deter, or implement pandemic response. From the outset, the bonds were designed to raise money from wealthy investors, and leave the care responsibilities to others. That splitting off of risk from responsibility, though, was hard to detect in the face of some pretty misleading World Bank press releases and promotional speeches from the president of the World Bank himself.

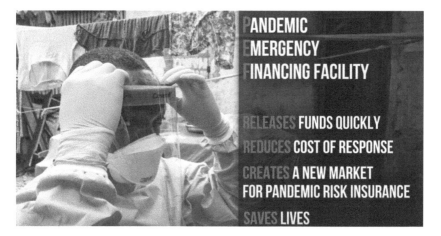

**Figure 1.1**
Screenshot from a World Bank Pandemic Emergency Financing Facility (PEF) video promoting the pandemic bonds. *Source:* World Bank, "World Bank Launches First Ever Pandemic Bonds to Support PEF," World Bank Treasury, June 28, 2017, YouTube Video, 3:48, https://www .youtube.com/watch?v=RgmBjDGHAAl. Copyright: The World Bank Group. All rights reserved.

## RECKONING WITH THE PANDEMIC BONDS

Surprising many people, including me, in July 2020 the *Financial Times* broke a story about the World Bank "ditch[ing a] second round of pandemic bonds."[58] Three months earlier, the Bank had advertised for a data modeler for pandemic bonds 2.0 (and they had chosen one). Two months before that, World Bank bonds designers had told me that "it doesn't really make that much sense to do one-offs," and that "We are keen to do a pandemic bonds 2.0 because we don't like to do one-offs." Despite changing their minds about pandemic bonds 2.0, the idea of pandemic bonds as a finance solution is not yet dead.

Nine months after the pandemic bonds paid out, one of the World Bank designers wrote me declaring the bonds a "big success," mentioning "future variations" and spelling out their expectations for future pandemic bond "children." It's fair to say that folks from global public health—the sector responsible for managing human health—and the folks from global finance saw the bonds quite differently. From a global public health standpoint, the bonds failed because they did not release money quickly enough to stop the pandemic, nor did they save lives or economies.[59] Many in the finance sector hold a different view. Sure, the bonds didn't work out as planned. But finance is like that. Trial and error. Rounds of failure can lead to success. Try, try, again.

"[They're] not a failure from my point of view," an investor said. "But certainly the payout mechanism should be rethought."[60] An insurance-linked securities executive agreed: "I don't know of any investors that are disappointed or have any complaints about what happened."[61] One of the World Bank bonds designers mused during a September 2020 public talk at a Canadian university, "Is there a future in this? Definitely yes. Will the future come more from the private sector insurance for private goods? Absolutely."

The bonds are likely to be tried again, in some version or another. When the news came that the World Bank was nixing pandemic bonds 2.0, some influential folks remained undeterred by the news. A finance executive said, "The bond was a landmark transaction; it showed that [pandemic] risk can be modeled, it can be quantified, it can be indexed, it can be transferred. It was received very well by the market."[62]

Behind the scenes, leaders at the World Bank and other industries, agencies, and philanthropies continue to think that making pandemic risk investable is a great idea. But we need to debate more robustly what's at stake because the risk of the next pandemic is ever-present. With pandemic response and care, are we at a no-turning-back-to-governments breakpoint? Does what we owe each other in a shared society now *require* complex financial investment devices to raise money for human health suffering? But first, how do pandemic bonds actually *work*?

# 2  WHAT ARE PANDEMIC BONDS?

In a Washington, DC, hotel ballroom in November 2017, two years before COVID-19 activated the pandemic bonds, the then World Bank president Jim Yong Kim and his longtime colleague and best friend, the late Paul Farmer, gave a joint keynote speech to a roomful of anthropologists. At the time, Kim and Farmer were the two highest profile medical anthropologists in the world. About thirty minutes in, from the dais, playing to the crowd of about 700, Kim bragged about the pandemic bonds and that they used the tricky tools of rich people to help sick and poor people. Farmer played wise guy.

> **Jim Yong Kim:** The tools that they have are so tricky, so—
> **Paul Farmer:** The tools are the rich people we don't know [audience laughter].
> **Kim:** The tools are . . . hedges, swaps, leveraged finance—
> **Farmer:** Hedges. I thought you trimmed them [miming cutting a hedgerow with hedging shears] [audience laughter].
> **Kim:** I said, Why don't we insure the poor against pandemics? . . . And it turned out the reinsurance companies were desperate to do it . . . We went to the capital markets and we actually raised US$450 million that everybody knew could completely go away if there's a pandemic. Now it exists. We have pandemic insurance [audience applause].[1]

I knew from studying the bonds, there was some promotional spin on Kim's presentation; the reinsurance companies were willing, but not desperate; the Bank raised US$ 425 million, not US$450. And when I heard the applause, I wondered, Do they know what they are applauding? Unlikely. As Kim must have known, the medical anthropologists in the crowd likely interpreted "pandemic insurance" as "health insurance during pandemics." But the "insurance" Kim touted was not conventional, nor was it health insurance. Pandemic *risk* was what was insured by the bonds, and Kim didn't utter the word "risk" from the dais. Plus, the bonds were structurally complex, with layer upon layer of financial instrumentation. As a former World Bank economist said about the bonds in a radio interview, "There are just so many conditions, exotic terms . . . nobody I know could figure it out. . . . And I'm at Harvard—you know, lots of smart people."[2]

The bonds were an experiment in global health financing. But, like the parable of the elephant and blind men—with each man touching various parts of the pachyderm and thinking they knew the truth about what the beast was (it's a snake, tree, rope, wall, spear!)—the pandemic bonds were different things to different people. They have been described as everything from a save-the-world humanitarian remedy[3] that the Bank promised "will pay out quickly, within days of an outbreak,"[4] to "market medicine"[5] to an "embarrassing mistake"[6] "designed to fail."[7] Were they true bonds? Insurance? Global health aid? A good bet? A gamble?

There is no simple way to explain the bonds. If you glaze over while reading this chapter, it's not you. Investors, academics, and journalists found them convoluted.[8] Even the bonds' World Bank designers didn't agree on what they were. One passionately insisted during an interview: "[It's] perhaps the simplest instrument in the world. I think people just overanalyze things. . . . It's nothing, *nothing* but insurance," their adamance growing noticeably louder with each alternative characterization of the bonds I tried to introduce to the conversation. Another admitted, "I think it's so complicated . . . it's really so complicated," using the word "complicated" to describe the pandemic bonds eleven times in a one-hour interview.

Most of the World Bank folks designing the bonds could explain the mechanics reasonably well. But even among the so-called experts, explanatory depth varied. One of the World Bank designers conspicuously avoided explaining the mechanics of the bonds, not only to me but also when asked pointed questions by journalists at public forums. During conference panels and interviews, this designer deflected direct questions about the bonds' makeup with self-deprecating jokes, charming vignettes, and broad-brush commentaries about the bonds' transformational power, while saying nothing about the bonds' financial mechanisms.

The bonds *are* hard to explain, and not only as financial devices. They also operated as a symbolic empty vessel for people's finance competencies and incompetencies or, as in the case of the World Bank designer, exposed their own insecurities about their lack of Wall Street know-how. For a time, the bonds even served as an ambitious career redemption vehicle[9] for Kim, who championed them as Bank president and even afterward as one of his primary accomplishments during his tenure.

## TALK ABOUT THE BONDS

I began talking and writing about the bonds in late 2015[10] and had my own trouble explaining them to global public health folks. I kept running into a kind of psychological resistance. At a talk I gave at the London School of Economics and Political Science, the moderator, a global health scholar, shocked me and the audience when they abruptly cut the question-and-answer period fifteen minutes short, explaining with real sadness in their voice, "I just can't bear thinking about this anymore." At a big international political economy of global health summit in Norway, a senior Canadian scholar rushed up to me after my talk to tell me that they wanted to know more but just found the investor angle too depressing.

It's no hyperbole to say there was a Mars-Venus difference between how finance folks understood the bonds and how public health folks talked (and resisted talking) about the bonds A finance expert told me they were drawn into working on making the bonds because, they explained, "Pandemics have a potential to start happening more frequently and more severely. It seems like government people are, sort of, asleep at the wheel to a certain extent and what they do is not really working, so there needs to be a bigger rethink on how to approach this from a global perspective. Their way of doing business, so to speak, isn't really working without financing solutions."

The early rhetoric coming out of the World Bank was excited, hopeful, and promising, intentionally raising expectations about the bonds as a silver

## The Pandemic Emergency Financing Facility (FY16)

**CONTRIBUTORS**

GERMANY    IDA    JAPAN

The **Pandemic Emergency Financing Facility (PEF)** breaks new ground by providing the first ever insurance-like mechanism for pandemic risk, offering coverage to all low-income countries eligible for financing under IDA. The World Bank (IBRD) issued Pandemic Bonds and entered into Pandemic Insurance derivative contracts to provide resources from the financial markets to the PEF in the event of a qualified outbreak. Through the provision of public funds to the amount of $117 million, the total amount of risk transferred to the private markets was $425 million.

The PEF is a quick disbursing financing mechanism that provides surge funding to enable a rapid and effective response to a large-scale disease outbreak, thereby preventing its escalation. Eligible countries can receive timely, predictable, and coordinated surge financing if affected by an outbreak that meets predefined activation criteria.

**Figure 2.1**
"Timely, predictable, and coordinated surge financing": how the pandemic bonds were announced in the World Bank's 2017 Trust Fund Annual Report. *Source:* World Bank, 2017 Trust Fund Annual Report, p. 157, https://documents1.worldbank.org/curated/en/428511 521809720471/pdf/124547-REVISED-PUBLIC-17045-TF-Annual-Report-web-Apr17.pdf. Copyright: The World Bank Group. All rights reserved.

bullet for pandemic financing. Interest grew among cat bond investors when they realized it wasn't just the bonds the Bank was selling; they wanted the bonds to catalyze a brand-new pandemic bonds market. The bonds were the future of pandemic risk management, an essential first step for a whole new way of backstopping pandemic response. Depending on who was talking, the bonds were sometimes described as a supplement to government action. But in many World Bank speeches and press releases, the bonds sounded like they were being designed to become the main event.

Rarely do specific World Bank initiatives get as much public attention as the pandemic bonds did. Not everyone at the Bank thought that was a good thing. But from the beginning, they were special that way. From late 2014 to the run-up of the pandemic bonds launch in 2017, the World Bank president Kim reasoned aloud and in public: Instead of going around hat in hand to raise money after a disease started spreading, what if rich people paid? What if rich people's investing tools could pool money before pandemics hit so that the money for a pandemic response was sitting, waiting to be called up if needed? Such a tool would ideally, Kim mused, mean the world would never find itself short of cash to contain a pandemic again. "For the first time we will have a *system* that can move funding and teams of experts to the sites of outbreaks before they spin out of control," Kim said. Yes, the man who had worked for three decades in global health, got his medical and PhD degrees at Harvard, and knew better,[11] called the pandemic bonds pilot project a *system*.[12] No wonder people found the bonds confusing.

There was some frustration among people at the Bank about Kim's loquaciousness, as I learned in my interviews. In speeches, Kim talked—and talked—about the bonds. One retired Bank officer told me, "[Kim] was media savvy, and that's good for the institution." But he was prone to exaggeration and overpromising. From his "money-within-eight-hours" claim to promising the bonds would remedy "a long, collective failure in dealing with pandemics," an approach that would "respond immediately to save lives and . . . protect economic growth,"[13] Kim overpromised when talking about the bonds, which had its consequences. A World Bank official emailed me that "it might be a bit much to claim [the bonds themselves] catalyzed all the interest." There's simply no denying that in the early days, World Bank president Kim did most of the heavy lifting trying to convince the world that bonds for pandemic risk were the way to go.

> **The pandemic bonds were a hybrid financial instrument, a mix of bond, insurance, and global health aid elements.**

### THE PANDEMIC BONDS: AN OVERVIEW

*Fair warning to readers: From here, this chapter is awash in technical details. I geek out on the bonds' mechanics in a way that may only appeal to financiers, scholars, actuarials, and masochists who read every page in order. You may want to skip it for now and come back to it after you've read more of the other parts of the story.*

In 2014, three years before issuing the pandemic bonds, the World Bank launched a new kind of humanitarian aid: its first catastrophe bond to hedge the risk of earthquakes and tropical cyclones in sixteen Caribbean countries. The Bank considered it "an innovation for both our clients and investors [that] marks a further extension of our disaster risk management work."[14] "It's been a journey," one World Bank official told me, "to get investors thinking also in terms of humanitarian solutions." Out of this financial zeitgeist at the Bank, catastrophe bonds for pandemics took root. Their signature mix of insurance mechanisms, investor speculation, and global health aid had never been done before. Their very novelty drew me to study them because this mix raises new questions about capitalist speculation being repurposed as save-the-world innovation.

The pandemic bonds were one component of the World Bank's Pandemic Emergency Financing Facility trust fund[15] (commonly referred to as the "PEF"[16]). In public discussions and media, the PEF and the bonds were often used synonymously, but they are not the same thing. Even Bank officials were sloppy about this. Some publicly played fast and loose with the different response times. The PEF included a cash-on-request component. The bonds part of the PEF required meeting strident time-consuming thresholds that could only be verified by a specialized "third-party calculation agent." Few people in any audience knew the difference.

But I'm getting ahead of myself. The PEF had three components, the bonds being the most dominant, and by far the most talked about. The other two—a cash window[17] and swaps[18]—are not new forms of finance. The cash window was merely a discretionary grant fund by another name, and the PEF cash window gave out US$61.4 million[19] in grants for several different disease outbreaks, not only COVID-19. Swaps were introduced by the World Bank in the early 1980s.[20] PEF swaps raised US$105 million[21] for pandemic response and paid out US$63.34 million.[22] My research is on the bonds.

The three different PEF components are hard to differentiate using World Bank documents. Plus, in contravention of its usual practice, the Bank did not publicly publish a final review of the PEF trust fund, a dereliction repeatedly raised by a former economist at the World Bank, Olga Jonas, as recently as 2023. She called for a full-scale, 360-degree evaluation of the PEF. What the Bank put out was a nine-page PEF Trust Fund accounting of its financials "since its inception to April 30, 2021."[23]

To the non-accountant, the comminglings of PEF account types are confounding. Donations to the cash window are clustered with donations from Germany and Japan for paying investor interest payments on the bonds. Similarly, they batch money raised from the bonds with money earned from the swaps. The most egregious mixing into a single category was that of the US$186.55 million that went to response activities and the US$9.28 million spent on responding agency fees (!) with the US$110.64 million paid as interest to investors. True, these are money-in, money-out accounting notations. But they are *very* different kinds of inputs and outputs in the larger schemes of implementation, purpose, and who received the money.

Artemis, the UK-based insurance-linked securities online information hub, did a much better job than the Bank of transparently parsing PEF numbers. There is good reason to believe their numbers are accurate first and foremost because their veracity can be triangulated. More than that, though, ILS insiders told me there is a well-established backdoor information flow between folks at the Bank and folks at Artemis, unbound by trust fund accounting or Bank media conventions. Artemis reported that the pandemic bonds paid out US$132.5 million for COVID-19 pandemic response (plus US$63.34 million from the swaps),[24] equaling the US$195.84 million payout total, notably quite a bit less than the US$500 million for pandemic response Kim originally touted.

### Who Put the Bonds Together?
The World Bank. Kim (discussed in chapter 5) championed the bonds and tasked three Bank units—Treasury, Health, and Development Finance (discussed in chapter 6)—with making them up. The units, in turn, called up other experts. Treasury enlisted four companies—two corporate reinsurance giants, an ILS broker intermediary company I call TheBrokers, and a data modeling firm I call ModelRisk (discussed in chapter 8). Health consulted primarily with infectious disease specialists at the World Health Organization (WHO) and the US Centers for Disease Control and Prevention

(CDC). Development Finance worked at getting wealthy donor countries such as the United States, the United Kingdom, Norway, and Canada to give money to pay for the bond investors' interest payments. To their dismay, and despite early commitments, only Japan and Germany ultimately paid in.

### Bonds Development Timeline

In the fall of 2014, out of frustration that the West African Ebola outbreak was being starved of funds to contain disease spread, Kim initiated the conceptualization of the bonds, and design work began (figure 2.2). In January 2015, Kim introduced the bonds' design concept at Davos,[25] and he pitched them again at the May 2015 G7 Summit in Germany. A year later, at the G7 Summit in Japan, Kim officially announced the bonds. By the spring of 2017, the Bank had commitments from several big investors, including Sweden's civil pension fund.

### What Diseases Did the Bonds Cover?

The World Bank pandemic bonds were designed to provide funds to fight six viral disease outbreaks: (1) influenza, (2) coronavirus, (3) filovirus (e.g., Ebola), (4) Lassa fever, (5) Rift Valley fever, and (6) Crimean Congo hemorrhagic fever. A bonds designer told me, "We were guided entirely by WHO and CDC and the existing knowledge at that point of time [2016–2017]." During a second interview the designer told me, "[The WHO initially] gave us nine pathogens," and the Bank "covered whatever we could model." The Bank tried modeling Nipah virus, for example, but "we could not quantify the risk of Nipah, so we couldn't bring it to market." (Pandemic disease coverage and its dependence on risk modeling is discussed in chapter 8.)

### Where Could the Bond Money Be Spent?

Payouts could go only to International Development Association (IDA) countries, the world's poorest countries (as determined by World Bank metrics). The IDA is one of the World Bank's five branches, giving grants and, in theory, extending cheap(er) credit to countries that need it most.[26] In the case of a qualifying pandemic, the bonds money could only be released to eligible IDA countries (if they applied) along with agencies pre-vetted by the World Bank (mostly United Nations agencies) operating in IDA countries.

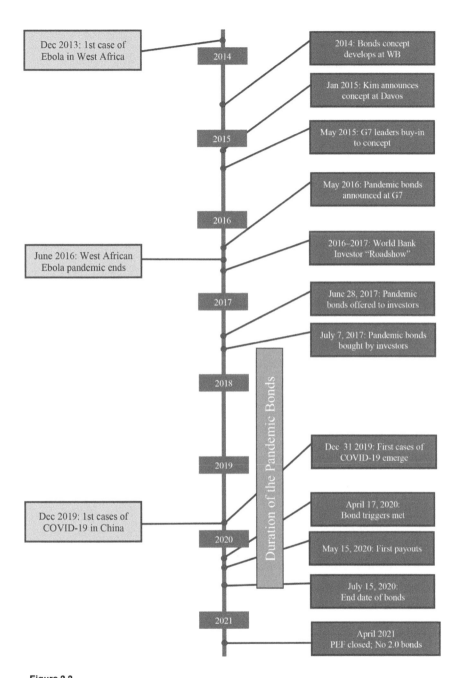

**Figure 2.2**
Timeline of World Bank (WB) pandemic bonds development, from concept to close. *Source:* Author.

Bonds generally work like this: bonds are loans that investors make to governments and businesses for a predetermined duration, like three, five, ten, or twenty years. During that time, the investors earn interest on the money they put down, paid out once or twice a year. In addition to the interest earned, at the end of a bond's duration—the maturity date—investors get back the money they loaned, their "principal."

The pandemic bonds followed that basic formula, but with a twist. When investors purchased the pandemic bonds, they loaned money to the World Bank, which was "held in trust" "in a co-mingled investment portfolio (the "Pool") for all trust funds administered by the World Bank."[27] Here's the twist: For those three years (July 2017–July 2020), if one of the six covered diseases broke out anywhere in the world and met all the preset thresholds—called triggers—the investors could lose some or all of their principal money. That money would then be distributed for pandemic response.

"The bonds" were two bonds, called tranches, officially listed as Class A and Class B. They were alike in their triggering criteria but differed in three ways: diseases covered, interest rates, and the chance that investors would lose their principal. Class A covered only influenza and coronavirus and had a lower interest rate for the investors (6.9%). Class A bonds were considered less risky, meaning they were statistically less likely to cause investors to lose their money. Class B covered filovirus (e.g., Ebola), Lassa fever, Rift Valley fever, Crimean Congo hemorrhagic fever, plus coronavirus. The Class B bond carried a higher base interest rate (11.5%) because Class B bonds had a statistically higher risk of being called in.

Coronavirus was the only virus placed in both Class A and Class B bonds. A bonds designer told me that coronavirus proved especially tricky to model because some coronavirus variants are highly contagious but do not kill people or cause lasting human harm, while other variants aggressively kill and disable, as the world has learned with COVID-19. "We did hundreds and thousands of [modeling] iterations," they said, "but in Corona, in the quantification, we saw weird things happening, which is why you see Corona in both [bonds]. . . . We split up coronavirus into two and we put [the less risky] end of coronavirus in Class A and we put the bulk of it in Class B."

Investors in Class A and Class B bonds understood they could lose some or all of their principal investment if a pandemic qualified, meaning that the preset criteria were met. The bonds were multi-country bonds, for example, which meant that one of the six diseases had to spread to people across a border at a preset growth rate. "We originally targeted single countries and it was just too expensive and nobody was going to buy the bond," a designer said, describing one make-or-break point when decisions had to be made about the bonds pricing. It wasn't the only time investor preferences were deemed more important than conventional public health prerogatives.

Payouts for each of the six covered diseases were capped, which is why, even though the bonds were advertised by the Bank as a US$500 million pandemic financing solution, the payout for COVID-19 was about 40 percent of that. A designer told me, "The corona cap was 195 million; the influenza cap, 275 million. Every disease had a cap," beyond which the bonds wouldn't pay, again, as a way to curb what investors might lose.

### WERE THEY INSURANCE?

Most people know of insurance as the promise of future reimbursement for the loss of business, life, or limb. You pay a premium to transfer your risk of a terrible thing happening; an insurance group or company agrees to accept the risk and pay you if the terrible thing actually happens. But rather than, say, paying for a house to be rebuilt after a fire, the pandemic bonds were designed to pay for ongoing pandemic response.

There was a twist here too. Compared with conventional insurance, the pandemic bonds were insurance with a difference: they were *parametric*. Usually, to calculate payout when a terrible thing happens, insurance companies use a process called *indemnity*, meaning that, for example, if your house burns down, an insurance agent will visit the burn site and assess the loss and the payout *after* the fire. Parametric payouts use triggers set *before* the terrible thing happens; payments are authorized when the predetermined measurement—a "trigger"—is met.

During an interview, a London-based parametric expert gave me this example of a parametric scenario: If, during a hurricane, wind speeds off the

Florida coast hit a predetermined trigger speed—say 175 mph—at a trigger distance of two miles [3.2 kilometers] offshore within a preset longitude and latitude grid, the payout is, in theory, immediate. (I've underlined the data sets and geography triggers used in his example.) This was an actual parametric payout scenario simulated several years ago. In this simulation, the London expert told me, some people were able to get insurance payouts immediately via their phone once the data on speed, distance, and location criteria were verified. Others were slowed by the trouble they had with the phone app. One of the most important differences between indemnity and parametric processes, a parametric analyst told me, is that with parametric triggers, "there doesn't even need to be a loss. If an event happens and the [trigger] is met, there will be a payout." In other words, even if the hurricane verged off and never touched land, investors would get paid just as long as the terms and conditions of the contract were met.

### The Pandemic Bonds' Triggers

Because they used parametric triggers rather than indemnity metrics, the pandemic bonds had some extra twists. For coronavirus, a preset trigger was death. People had to die before a payout was "triggered" (figure 2.3). "We found ourselves counting deaths, which is a terrible thing to do. . . . But frankly, we had no other indicator. With number of cases [as an indicator],

| Coronavirus Maximum Coverage: $195.83m | Payout Percentages Based on: Number of Confirmed Deaths within IBRD/IDA Countries | | |
|---|---|---|---|
| | *At 250* | *At 750* | *At 2,500* |
| Regional (outbreaks affecting 2 to 7 countries) | 29% (US$56.25m) | 57% (US$112.5m) | 100% (US$195.83m) |
| Global (outbreaks affecting 8 or more countries) | 34% (US$65.63m) | 67% (US$131.25m) | 100% (US$195.83m) |

**Figure 2.3**

The number of people required to die from coronavirus before the pandemic bonds paid out. *Source:* World Bank, *Operations Manual: Pandemic Emergency Financing Facility*, 2019, p. 8, https://thedocs.worldbank.org/en/doc/842101571243529089-0090022019/original /PEFOperationsManualapproved10.15.18.pdf, accessed May 4, 2023. See table A.1 in the appendix.

there was so much of noise and that we would never understand whether we had the right number of cases."

In addition to death counts, for the bonds to trigger, other trigger criteria had to be met. As if the death trigger wasn't controversial enough, other triggers drew public ire for the way they delayed payout. They included:

(1) Twelve weeks (three months) needed to pass. Three months in the life of a contagious infectious disease, be it Ebola or COVID-19, is a *long* time. But investors wouldn't have bought the bonds if they were too easily triggered.

(2) Two or more countries needed to be affected. Big, single countries with large infected populations would not trigger the release of funds. Critics took issue with this in 2018 when over 3,000 people died from Ebola *within* the Democratic Republic of the Congo without the bonds money releasing.[28]

(3) The outbreak had to affect at least one World Bank–designated International Bank for Reconstruction and Development (IBRD) or IDA country.[29] In the case of COVID-19, early spread was intense between wealthy countries, conditions not well-imagined by the bonds' designers. The design assumption was that an outbreak would occur in poor countries and spread to wealthy countries, not the other way around. In Sierra Leone, COVID-19 was initially thought of as a European disease because the outbreaks were so big there.

(4) The spread of infection needed to increase at a preset growth rate with a specified statistical confidence level. During the 2018 Ebola outbreak in the Democratic Republic of the Congo, a few cases were found across the border of a second country (Uganda). But the disease "didn't grow fast enough" there, so the bonds' funds were not released.

Data for the pandemic bonds' triggers were provided exclusively by the World Health Organization's Disease Outbreak News (DON) or Situation Reports. One of the bonds' designers told me, "We agreed at the end that we will go with no other data. We will not go with numbers from Johns Hopkins or from Our World in Data [Oxford University], from anywhere else. We'll only look at what WHO is reporting."

Of all the bonds' design elements, setting the trigger criteria took the longest to develop and negotiate. "We set these trigger conditions and we spent a lot of time going back and forth," a designer told me, "with investors and investor representatives, with the WHO and the CDC." Bank units—Treasury, Health, Development Finance, Legal, and Communications—were consulted. Each had their own opinions, influenced by their own areas of practice. Each worked with a different set of principles and hypotheticals. "Bonds are always stressful to model, and there are some bonds that are more stressful than others," a designer said, who then went on say that the pandemic bonds fell at the far end of the continuum as very stressful.

Some of the stress arose because the Bank had to care about which bond terms and conditions the investors would and would not accept before they gave the Bank their money. One investor, who ultimately did not buy the bonds, told me:

> Normally the [reinsurance] structurers and their modelers will spend time with the World Bank and do their own research. That work group comes up with the first prototype, and then they reached out to us investors and say, "Here's what we think the bond could look like; here's what we think the triggers should look like . . . what do you think?" And so we gave a fair amount of feedback and that process almost took a year and a half, as I recall. There were a few instances when it took them a fair amount of time to collate feedback, go back to the World Bank, fine-tune design in some of the issues that we had raised. They came back with version two, so we definitely had at least two iterations of the prototype during this pre-marketing phase. . . . Eventually the question's always, well, how much would you invest?
>
> . . . Given this was a top priority for the executives at the World Bank, they just wanted to make sure that they wouldn't suffer the embarrassment of a failed launch. They took their time to make sure that they had a structure that enough investors liked.

### Terms and Conditions: The Bonds as Legally Binding Contracts

Historically, global health aid has been *allocated*. That means that a wealthy government, international organization, philanthropy, or charity decides what it will give to a project (e.g., clinic), a cause (e.g., polio immunization), or an impoverished government. With foreign aid, legislatures typically debate how much to give. Philanthropies and charities give as much or as little as they want. Aid money can sometimes be pretty fungible, especially in emergencies—I know this from years of on-the-ground experience. I've seen money already approved by the World Bank for an education program redirected for emergency flood response with a single signature.

Not so with the pandemic bonds. The bonds were structured as a contractual agreement between the World Bank and investors, with terms and conditions spelled out in a 386-page prospectus[30] detailing the who, what, where, when, and how of the bonds. The bonds terms and conditions were established up front, and, the small print mattered and was legally binding. Once the contract was signed, the terms and conditions for release of the bonds' money was neither negotiable nor debatable. No legislators were involved; no one was making political hay on how much or how little would be allocated. One World Bank designer grew exasperated as they told me, "Those rules [for disbursement] were cast in stone . . . we got beaten very badly for this." They were especially aggrieved by an article written by a Pulitzer Prize–winning science journalist who condemned the Bank for having the money in the bonds, but not spending it.[31] But the Bank couldn't distribute the funds until the contractual terms and conditions were met.

So, back to the original question: Were the pandemic bonds insurance? Well, the bonds emerged out of a small but growing boutique corner of Wall Street—insurance-linked securities —that got its start by providing speculative financial backup instruments for reinsurance companies that insured insurance companies. Since the mid-1990s, ILS (discussed in chapter 7) built its clout and found its mojo by building increasingly creative speculative instruments. So if your definition of insurance is expansive, is unconventional, and involves rounds of investor feedback, the answer to the original questions is yes, but only in the loosest way, like the way you might say offhandedly to a friend, "You've got some kind of insurance for this, right?"

### WERE THE PANDEMIC BONDS GLOBAL HEALTH AID?

Yes, the pandemic bonds were considered global health, humanitarian, and international development aid, all three historically involving wealthy country donors giving taxpayers' money and technical advice to poor countries. But these bonds had a particular twist on the giving: taxpayers' money from the donor governments of Japan (US$50 million) and Germany (US$17.5 million) funded the bonds' *investor interest payments* with money that likely otherwise would have gone directly to pandemic response in poor countries,[32] as international development executives in Germany pointed out to me.

And in a second twist, a highly unusual move, the World Bank paid itself. An additional US$50 million for investor interest payments was transferred from one of its five branches to another—from its IDA to IBRD where the bonds were "housed"—to cover a shortfall in investor interest when no other wealthy country donors would commit their taxpayers' money going to investor payments. Before the bonds were issued in 2017, the Bank had tried to drum up support for paying investors' interest from the usual wealthy country donors. A designer told me, "We must have spoken with about twenty potential donors, and it was a difficult conversation. . . . We went to many capitals, we knocked on all the doors. It wasn't an easy sell to convince countries." In the end, the donor count went from twenty potential donors to two, so few that the Bank "had to force it by taking a contribution out of IDA to pay the investors," a Bank insider told me. A Bank interviewee rolled their eyes when telling me about one branch giving another branch money to pay the investors' interest. They saw it as an embarrassment for the bonds' designer team that they couldn't get more rich donor countries to commit.

An ironic truth of these "donations" is that the heralded signature accomplishment of the bonds—getting private investors to pay for global health response aid—was dependent on public taxpayers' monies from Japan, Germany, and the IDA to pay private investors' interest payments.

### THE PANDEMIC BOND INVESTORS

Who were these people? Well, if you are a Swedish pension-holder, by extension, it's you. "Sweden operates a public pension system that covers everyone who works and pays tax" and one of the pension companies, AP3, invests

18 percent of the system's funds in global funds and initiatives.[33] In 2017, AP3's investments included the World Bank's pandemic bonds.[34] But I'm likely giving the wrong impression; most of the bonds' investors were not Swedish taxpayers with a defined benefit pension plan. They were a mix of experienced high finance veterans and investors chasing favorable returns in the service of positive social impacts

I met with a diverse set of investors, including some who seriously considered investing in the bonds but who ultimately didn't take the leap. Just to be clear, no individual mom-and-pop retail investors were permitted to invest. Only "institutional investors"—those entities that pool other people's money—were allowed. Pensions are only one type of institutional investor, and the one most likely to have working- and middle-class people in their funds. Most Class A investors (85.6%) and nearly 60 percent of Class B investors were the more classically understood high-wealth folks—that is, dedicated cat bond investors, the people investing endowments, and asset fund managers. Pandemic bonds required a grade of investor[35] that the U.S. Securities and Exchange Commission (SEC) approves of as "sophisticated," meaning that the bonds were limited to accredited investors who are "able to fend for themselves or sustain the risk of loss . . . [and have] sufficient knowledge and experience in financial and business matters to evaluate the merits and risks of the prospective investment."[36]

### WITH A LITTLE (HIRED) HELP FROM FRIENDS

At the end of the first year of the two-year design process, a company I'll call TheBrokers was brought in to plug some of the pandemic bonds' design holes and get the Bank access to big catastrophe bond investors. "The World Bank doesn't have the relationship with the markets that assume insurance risk transfer. So they need to work with service providers that have built those relationships to help place it. . . . [TheBrokers] helped them find the right capital," I was told, meaning the World Bank hired help to find the bonds' investors.

As a corporation, TheBrokers seemed to pride itself on flying mostly below the radar on these bonds. But they knew the smallest details of ILS

IBRD Pandemic Bonds Distribution by Investor Type and Location

| Distribution by Investor Type | Class A | Class B |
|---|---|---|
| Dedicated Catastrophe Bond Investor | 61.7% | 35.3% |
| Endowment | 3.3% | 6.3% |
| Asset Manager | 20.6% | 16.3% |
| Pension Fund | 14.4% | 42.1% |
| **Distribution by Investor Location** | **Class A** | **Class B** |
| US | 27.9% | 15.0% |
| Europe | 71.8% | 82.9% |
| Bermuda | 0.1% | 2.1% |
| Japan | 0.2% | 0.0% |

**Figure 2.4**

World Bank pandemic bonds investors by type and location. *Source:* World Bank Group, "World Bank Launches First-Ever Pandemic Bonds to Support $500 Million Pandemic Emergency Financing Facility," press release, June 28, 2017, https://www.worldbank.org/en/news/press-release/2017/06/28/world-bank-launches-first-ever-pandemic-bonds-to-support-500-million-pandemic-emergency-financing-facility, accessed July 16, 2024. See table A.2 in the appendix.

instruments backward and forward. They were brainy and articulate about the big ideas of catastrophe risk management, explaining to me the meta rationales of risk like no one else. But it wasn't just me they communicated effectively with. They spoke the languages of people with deep pockets, and translated the unspoken logics of insurance-linked securities to people at the Bank. They told me, "What we are doing is connecting parties. Because we have built relationships in this industry for more than 100 years, our role is to bridge and bring the capital markets together [with] whoever wants to lay off that risk. So we work with corporates, public sector clients, sovereign governments, insurers, and reinsurers themselves, anyone who want to lay it off."

Kim initially hoped that another group of friendly investors like endowments and foundations with big funds and socially responsible portfolios, would buy in. But "the bonds were really so complicated" that they didn't understand the investor loss modeling, I was told. Bank officials agreed that most foundations and endowments didn't have the in-house ILS expertise to confidently assess the bonds' financial soundness. Although several were initially interested, only one bought in because it "wanted to support the *idea* of the bonds," I was told by a designer. Country governments also did not invest.

"We met with more than a hundred investors," a World Bank bonds designer told me. "We went to some cities, you know, to London, Zurich, Tokyo, New York, where we explained to people—at that time, they were the potential investors; they wanted to understand the risks. We needed to give them comfort about the product."

On July 15, 2017, the issue date of the bond, there were twenty-six investors. The full list of investors was private and proprietary, as I was told by more than one Bank official. Plus, the bonds were later sold and bought on secondary markets, which means that at any point in the three-year life of the bonds, there could have been five bond holders or a hundred. But there is some intel on the original twenty-six. AP3, one of Sweden's National Pension Funds, already mentioned, publicly announced its investment in the pandemic bonds as a point of pride.[37] Over time, other investors revealed themselves too, including the dedicated catastrophe bond investor Plenum, investment bank Oppenheimer Holdings, investment management firm Baillie Gifford, asset managers Stoneridge and Amundi Pioneer, and financial data company Refinitiv. Other asset managers, including from hedge funds, invested on behalf of millions of people from many countries.[38] In short, the humans who were invested in the pandemic bonds ran the gamut, from middle- and working-class pensioners to already-wealthy folks. When investors lost money on the bonds because of COVID-19, it wasn't just the already-wealthy investors who took the hit.

Most of the investors I met were convivial conversation partners, and some seemed genuinely interested in thinking about new ways of solving the chronic problems of pandemic aid funding, even if they'd never thought much about the how-tos of global health aid before. As a group, they were quick-witted and fun to talk with. Most were intrigued with what I could share with them about on-the-ground health data collection in Sierra Leone (discussed in chapter 9), since the bonds' triggers depended on quality data. There was a tiny sliver of them, though, who were not shy about saying out loud that the people and countries who needed this kind of help from investors are unable to rescue themselves because they are stupid and make bad choices. Conversations with those investors—because of the way they boorishly ignored how humans (including themselves) can be both enabled *and* constrained by political, economic, and social structures far beyond their lines of sight and influence—were rough going.

### 2020 GAINS AND LOSSES

In early 2020, as COVID-19 cases rapidly rose, the bonds' value started to dive. Some investors sold off the bonds to other investors on the secondary market, "over the counter," via regulated broker dealers like Tullett Prebon. "How do the secondary trades happen? I mean, literally?" I asked an ILS expert. The answer: "Someone picks up phone and tells their broker dealer, 'I want to sell this position.' The broker dealer finds somebody who might want to buy it; they negotiate the price on behalf of each side. Then they do the trade. It's very manual. Like you'd see in films about Wall Street where someone's got a phone on one shoulder and a phone on the other. There are literally people doing that today for cat bonds. It's crazy old, but they have to trade through regulated trade desks."

Fearing the bonds would trigger, sellers sold the bonds for less than what they paid, just so that they didn't lose everything.[39] By March 2020, a month before its investors' money was called up for pandemic response, the riskier Class B bonds were advertising on the secondary market at 5 cents on the original dollar.[40] Quite a sell-down.

When the triggering criteria for COVID-19 were met in 2020, investors from Class A and Class B lost, respectively, some or all of their principal investment. Public documents provide some information for me to estimate, with help,[41] the monetary gains and losses of investors who held onto the bonds for their three-year duration. In July 2020, upon maturation of the Class A bonds, investors who bought the bond on its first day and held onto it until the last day got back 83.33 percent of their original principal, meaning a hypothetical US$100 investment returned US$83.33. In addition, they received thirty-four months' interest at the full rate and two months of interest on the reduced principal, at the rate of 6.9 percent plus LIBOR[42] minus 0.4 percent.[43]

In other words, as a group, Class A bond holders started out with a collective US$225 million principal investment. That shrunk to US$187.5 million when COVID-19 triggered a payout of US$37.5 million. Collectively, in the final calculus, when all the gains and losses were tallied, Class A investors had returns of 3.37 percent per year* over the three-year duration of the bond or, as a group, gains of US$19.2 million per year in year one; US$20.88 million in year two; and US$18.02 million in year three, a total gain of US$58.1 million on the US$225 million principal investment.

Class B bond investors who bought the bond on its first day and held onto it until the last day lost all their principal, which collectively totaled US$95 million. But they received thirty-four months of interest payments

---

* I am keen to "show the work" for the calculations of investor returns, even though the World Bank did not run these numbers for the public or make it easy to run independently. A simple back-of-the-envelope calculation, for example, of Class A bond investor return that comes close but doesn't factor in time can be calculated by subtracting the total payout amount ($37.5 million) from the interest total ($58.1 million) that Class A bond investors would have gained. The difference, $20.6 million, is 9.16 percent of the original $225 million; 9.16 percent over 3 years (3.05 percent) gives us the approximate rate of annual return.

More precise estimates—and the ones reflected in the text—are from calculations requiring the use of a thirty-six-degree polynomial, which enables a best estimate of investor loss and gains over time. Using information available from the World Bank prospectus and the publicly available USD LIBOR rates with sixth-month maturity, my colleague Gary Parker ran calculations for both Class A and Class B bonds. Any remaining mistakes in the estimates are mine.

on that principal at a base rate of 11.5 percent plus LIBOR minus 0.4 percent, totaling an average of 14.19 percent interest, which, totaled for the group, came out to US$36.15 million. If you tally up the principal loss plus the interest gain for the Class B bonds, it was a collective net loss of US$58.85 million, a 44.46 percent loss of their initial investment over three years.

For those investors who bought or sold pandemic bonds on the secondary markets within the three-year duration of the bond, there are too many unknown variables to confidently estimate their yield or loss.

I was in touch with several of the World Bank designers after the bonds' money was called in. Most were annoyed that bonds critics—some even within the World Bank itself—were failing to note that investors lost some or all their money in the end. "Critics say, 'Well, the investors are, you know, laughing all the way to the bank," a World Bank bonds designer said. Another added, "What did [critics] hammer each time? That a wicked private sector is making money."

But Class A bond investors did make money. And Class B investors would have, if COVID-19 had emerged in force only three months later, after July 15, 2020. In that case, over the three years' duration of the bond, Class B investors would have made a collective gain of US$38.02 million on a US$95 million investment, a 40 percent gain on their principal investment.

### THE PANDEMIC BONDS AS SYMBOLS OF SOMETHING ELSE

Beyond being a financial device, when the pandemic bonds came up in conversation, they often stood in for "something else."

**Figure 2.5**

Flow diagram of the pandemic bonds processes. *Source:* https://assets.bwbx.io/images/users /iqjWHBFdfxlU/in5jygMnS2.Y/v0/800x-1.png, in Tracy Alloway and Tasos Vossos, "How Pandemic Bonds Became the World's Most Controversial Investment," Bloomberg, December 9, 2020, https://www.bloomberg.com/news/features/2020-12-09/covid-19-finance-how-the -world-bank-s-pandemic-bonds-became-controversial?sref=MvXcvlFy, accessed April 20, 2023. Used with permission of Bloomberg L.P. © 2024.

# What is a pandemic bond?

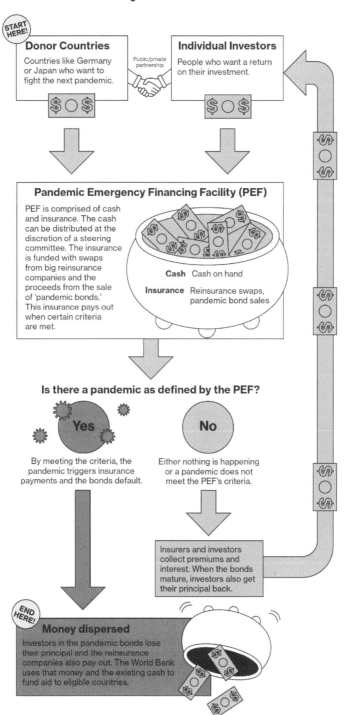

**START HERE!**

**Donor Countries**
Countries like Germany or Japan who want to fight the next pandemic.

*Public/private partnership*

**Individual Investors**
People who want a return on their investment.

**Pandemic Emergency Financing Facility (PEF)**
PEF is comprised of cash and insurance. The cash can be distributed at the discretion of a steering committee. The insurance is funded with swaps from big reinsurance companies and the proceeds from the sale of 'pandemic bonds.' This insurance pays out when certain criteria are met.

**Cash** Cash on hand

**Insurance** Reinsurance swaps, pandemic bond sales

**Is there a pandemic as defined by the PEF?**

**Yes**
By meeting the criteria, the pandemic triggers insurance payments and the bonds default.

**No**
Either nothing is happening or a pandemic does not meet the PEF's criteria.

Insurers and investors collect premiums and interest. When the bonds mature, investors also get their principal back.

**END HERE!**

**Money dispersed**
Investors in the pandemic bonds lose their principal and the reinsurance companies also pay out. The World Bank uses that money and the existing cash to fund aid to eligible countries.

**Bloomberg**

### Pandemic Bonds as a Proof of Concept

"What we're trying to establish is a concept," a World Bank bonds designer told me. "We're trying to show here is that this thing [pandemics] can be insured. . . . We stuck to it because what we wanted to do was to establish the concept, the proof that this is definitely doable."

"It was unclear at the beginning what form of [investor] capital would support this deal because of its newness. . . . It was still in its infancy in terms of breadth and standardizations," an insurance-linked securities specialist told me, continuing,

> On the catastrophe bond side, the process and the structures, and the language and all that stuff, the modeling and all that stuff, it is reasonably well-codified and understood. But on the pandemic bond side, we are not really that close to that point, because there's a mix of motivations in public health, in investing and . . . from the data side, there are improvements happening on a global scale. . . . But it was not pretty in terms of what the WHO was putting out. [The trigger data] was all over the place.

As proof of concept, though, when the bonds did finally trigger, some at the Bank were pleased. A bonds designer told me, "Whenever one of our [ILS] deals triggers, some Bank management gets so happy and [Kim] wants to go out and talk about it. . . . That's not what this is—this is risk management. It is not betting. It's not gambling. We're not hoping to get a trigger. This is risk management. . . . We tell people, don't hope for triggers. But they can't help themselves, they get so excited."

### Pandemic Bonds as Socially Responsible Investing

"Do well by doing good" was a well-worn investment mantra in the decade before the COVID-19 pandemic. "Our job is to generate financial returns, of course, but just making money, that's a pretty meaningless or unspiritual exercise, I can say," an investor told me before COVID-19 hit. "But we can deliver welfare here, and that makes it more interesting. Even if we lose money on this, at least the money goes to good purpose, right?"

Bank interviewees told me it was Kim's dream to be able to sell the pandemic bonds as a socially responsible investment. Likewise, the insurance-linked securities online news and information giant Artemis noted, about the news that a pension fund was buying pandemic bonds, "It's encouraging to see a major pension fund citing the expansion of the ILS asset class into pandemic risks as important enough to mention to its pensioners, clients and partners. It's a sign that ILS and catastrophe bonds can be seen as socially responsible and important investments."[44]

### Pandemic Bonds as Moral Hazard

A moral hazard is a situation where riskier choices are incentivized for you because if the terrible thing happens, you won't have to pay its full costs. It's a term I heard a lot from insurance executives who, as a group, are pretty cynical about human nature. One investor who ultimately decided not to invest in the bonds told me,

> We were mostly nervous about the temptation that those that provided the numbers for calculation might be tempted, might be induced to, I wouldn't say, be less objective, but certainly there was a bit of a moral hazard there. I mean, those providing the reporting numbers would also be directly or indirectly beneficiaries of the pandemic bonds. There seems to be bit of a conflict of interest and not enough independence for how those numbers were collated. . . . Some of the triggers were a bit subjective around counting the number of deaths, and I guess the issue is also, what if the numbers are wrong?

People inside the Bank talked about moral hazard in two ways: "Won't poor countries just stop their own pandemic prevention efforts if they think they can get huge payouts from the bonds?" and "Won't they overreport the data showing high numbers of deaths?" One retired Bank official said, "So if you offer Sierra Leone money if they had an outbreak, why would they invest their dollars today in strengthening their health system? Why don't they build roads instead knowing that money will come if they have an outbreak anyway?"

### Pandemic Bonds Would Transform Poor Countries into Pandemic Bonds Investors

One Bank official who was critical of the bonds told me that early on, there was talk out of the Bank president's office that the pandemic bonds were the path to making poor countries into pandemic bonds investors. "But would they really buy the investment?" they asked. "Like why would they buy insurance and not invest their money into strengthening their own health system?" Smart question. Some of the most impressive current improvements in maternal and infant health outcomes in Sierra Leone, for example, resulted from direct investments made since 2010 by the government in free maternal and under-five healthcare. Insurance is not the focus of that initiative; free healthcare is. The country's investment is in the *care work*, not in buying insurance or becoming bonds investors.

### OUTLOOK

"I hope there isn't a pandemic," a World Bank bonds designer told me in 2018. "But part of me says, 'Well, until that happens, we can't really test [the bonds].'" COVID-19 was that test. Now what? From the beginning, many World Bank folks assumed there would be more bonds in the future, pandemic bonds 2.0, they called it. There are problems, they said, like the size of the payouts, "which is a drop in the bucket because [when there is a pandemic] you probably need billions." But the World Bank's plan was always to do more than one round, learning from each iteration, refining the triggers.

As a point of pride, Kim and others at the Bank liked to point out that the bonds ended up being 200 percent oversubscribed, meaning that there were more investors interested in buying the bonds than the Bank had money to cover their three years of interest payments. "The bonds were an amazing success, showing us that there was tremendous amount of investor interest obviously because of the return," one bonds designer said. The head of an influential Washington, DC, strategic international think tank said, "We can't abandon the concept because the first effort failed. . . . We need to come back to this problem with new ideas on how to do it better."

But in all the design talk, and all the back and forth between the World Bank and investors, and the World Bank and modelers, there was a huge absence. How involved were the leaders of the countries the bonds were supposed to help? Not at all. High-ranking government and private sector officials from Sierra Leone, I found, did not get briefings about the bonds from the World Bank or their intermediaries. "Never heard about anything like this," a Sierra Leonean parliamentarian told me. Same for other African leaders, as I learned in 2016 when I was invited to a closed-door global health security meeting about lessons learned from the West African Ebola outbreak. Three G7 governments hosted the meeting in a castle near London. In a room of ostentatious chandeliers, gilded mirrors, and brocade drapes gracing floor-to-ceiling windows, I presented my research on the pandemic bonds to about fifty high-ranking health and national-security officers from Africa, North America, and Europe. After I explained how the pandemic bonds were supposed to work as a new form of pandemic financing, a high-ranking African officer loudly stated, obviously irritated: "We're not in this. I have never heard of this." Others around the room were also visibly upset. At issue was the complete absence of consultation with African leaders in the making of the bonds. Later, when I joined a lunch table where several African country officers were discussing the bonds, the general tone had shifted to one of resignation. At the end of lunch, I left the table with the impression that during national emergencies like the one posed by the West African Ebola outbreak, it did not matter how the money was made, just that it came. But emotions were strong about two things: that the money must come *in time* to save people from dying and that using death from a dread disease as a trigger for millions of dollars was "despicable."

## 3 SIERRA LEONE, A.K.A. SALONE

In 2014, Sierra Leone, a small West African nation, experienced one of the worst Ebola virus outbreaks in history, ultimately killing almost 4,000 people. When Kim, as president of the World Bank, promoted the pandemic bonds, he was fond of using Sierra Leone in his sales pitches. "The Ebola crisis in Guinea, Liberia and Sierra Leone taught all of us that we must be much more vigilant to outbreaks and respond immediately to save lives and also to protect economic growth," he said.[1]

Because the World Bank made Sierra Leone one touchstone of its bonds, what I know about Sierra Leone and the World Bank bears telling. Sierra Leone was a country, the Bank said, whose Ebola pandemic financing needs would have been met if only the bonds had been available at the time. "If we had [the bonds] during the Ebola outbreak of 2014, it would've paid. We know it would have paid because we set it up so that it would have paid for that event," a bonds designer told me.

My own relationship with Sierra Leone, or Salone, as it is colloquially known, started with the thump of airplane wheels on the tarmac at Lungi airport decades ago. That memory is a bodily feeling: we hit down hard. Stepping out of the plane's cool ecosystem, I remember feeling smacked by Salone's hot, humid air, heavy with the smokey scent of cooking fires.

I cannot get around the fact that my experiences as a twenty-something living in a Sierra Leonean town known for its defiance of British Colonial rule[2] shaped almost everything that came after for me, professionally and personally. Throughout my careers in global affairs and academia, my internal measure of any new program, model, or technology was to ask questions I learned there. What homegrown solutions to the problem already exist? What would local experts think about the proposed remedy? What would they see as anticipatable long-term impacts? What politics appear inscrutable?

For two years, I lived in a town of about 5,000 people in Sierra Leone's eastern province, not far from where the war and Ebola would later break out. There are two main seasons in that town: rainy and dry. During the rainy season, raindrops fall on roofs so hard that people inside houses, schools, and clinics shout to be heard. Rains regularly washed out roadbeds. A day spent on my motorcycle meant traveling muddy and soaked, as much from the rain outside as from sweating inside plastic coats and rain pants. In the dry season, on unpaved roads, vehicles kick up a rust-red dust from laterite clay tracks spewing their high iron content, covering flora, fauna, everything. After riding the roads, I would find the red dust caked in the creases around my eyes, my ears, and, no kidding, more than once, in my bellybutton.

Before the awful eleven-year war, the town bustled with activity. It was a farming, logging, and diamond-brokering community, with a big market and many small industries. Rhythms of rural agricultural town life structured days. Break-of-dawn call to prayer was followed by bossy morning roosters rousing us all out of bed. Walking the mile and back to the market in the morning took about an hour, slowed by rounds of greetings. People worked hard. Townspeople governed themselves well; civic life had an order and predictability. Not all the town's logging and diamond wealth was whisked away; some was reinvested in the community. There were six primary schools, and one secondary school. It was a town known for its healthy moms and babies. Midday, a big meal of rice, a palm oil sauce of leafy greens and fish, chicken, beef, or beans—delicious!—was prepared for me by my neighbors, who took turns cooking for "their" outsider. Relationships were all of a piece in that small town, both precious and petty. People knew each other's business.

Media casts Salone as an always-sickly place, but that's just not accurate. Vibrant health and deadly sickness co-reside. West African microbiomes are among the world's most resilient and diverse. HIV rates in Sierra Leone run very low, despite the country being home to high-risk epidemiological indicators, for reasons not medically understood.[3] But malaria is ubiquitous, and I got it four times in my first year. During the worst bout, just before losing consciousness, I was carried from my house by neighbors posted around me like pallbearers and gently laid in the back of a truck on top of thousands of oranges, freshly picked and smelling divine. My neighbors had hailed the first vehicle they saw, and the driver kindly agreed to drive me to the local hospital. I got better, and started thinking of malaria like the common cold, like everyone else.

### SALONE AND THE WORLD BANK: EARLY YEARS

At the time of creation, it is said, God created a tiny country rich in mineral wealth, with diamonds, gold, bauxite, rutile, iron ore, chromite and platinum; an abundance of off-shore fish; relatively fertile land; and plenty of rainfall. People from the neighboring territories became furious and demanded equal treatment. God however, cautioned them with the caveat that they should first wait and see what kind of government would rule over Sierra Leone.
—A. B. Zack-Williams[4]

Salone is a study in the difference good governance can make, and how the lack of it increases human suffering. In 1961, Sir Milton Margai, who had been working diplomatically with British colonizers for a smooth transition to Sierra Leonean independence for the previous decade, came to power as Sierra Leone's first prime minister. Widely admired domestically and internationally as a genius of good governance, he unfortunately died in 1964. His much less politically-competent brother took his place briefly before Siaka Stevens[5] rose to power.

Stevens, who came to power in 1968, started out as a populist and ended up a tyrant. He failed to manage Salone's abundant arable land and natural resources in a way that provided even basic food and fuel for its citizens. In the 1960s, the Sierra Leonean economy had been growing at a steady 7 percent per year.[6] By the mid-1970s, economic growth slowed and political tensions heightened. Stevens began executing political challengers and murdered the governor of the central bank after a public confrontation.

The World Bank knew about Stevens's tyranny but turned a blind eye. The Bank prided itself with making loans "without regard to political or other non-economic influences or considerations."[7] The World Bank pumped more than US$125 million in loans during Stevens's reign,[8] which is over US$310 million today. In a poor country in the 1960s, 1970s, and 1980s, those millions bought favor as well as political intimidation. Too little was spent on health, education, and infrastructure.

Sometimes the Bank stood up to Stevens. A World Bank political economist remembered[9] withholding approval for a project that would have bulldozed a poor neighborhood to improve the view of the ocean from the president's mansion. The morning of their departure back to Washington, the official and their boss were called to Stevens's presidential suite; they assumed they would be jailed. Seated in Steven's office, positioned across from two taxidermized lions whose glass eyes glared at them, they were only allowed to leave Sierra Leone after vowing to remind their Bank bosses back in Washington of earlier quid pro quo arrangements the Bank had made with Stevens.

I saw Stevens a few times. He was old by then, and he would leave office a couple of years later, dying soon after. Once, alerted by people cheering and pointing, I saw Stevens as I walked a street in Makeni, a northern city. His entourage drove slowly by, while he waved out a half-opened window, en route to visit his Limba relatives. People called him "Pa," for the folksy way he spoke to them and the way he favored the northern district, dealing out jobs and money to his political base. Another time in Freetown's soccer stadium, I saw him, by then puffy-faced and big-bellied. He was surrounded by a phalanx of bodyguards, who kept people at bay by swinging heavy metal chains at shoulder height, the centrifugal force multiplying the harm as the chains whacked the heads and chests of the daring or oblivious. And I missed seeing Stevens by a day when I visited the Tongo diamond fields, his visit the next day brought to my attention when I asked why men were painting only the road-facing sides of buildings. He was not expected to get out of his car, and they had only so much paint. By that time, he had already made Salone a one-party state and, with the same stroke of his pen, adjusted the constitution to put an end to multi-party elections.

Of course, Sierra Leone's contemporary weaknesses in health care cannot be blamed exclusively on Stevens or the Bank. Salone's misfortunes after independence are not singular; similar adversities occurred in many postcolonial countries, an unfortunate amalgam of political pressures from outside and within. Global political and economic priorities simply do not align with the best health interests of Sierra Leoneans. But it's fair to say this: the World Bank did not help the young country of Sierra Leone grow stronger or more democratic.

### THE WORLD BANK IN SIERRA LEONE: TERMS AND CONDITIONS

At independence, Sierra Leone invited assistance from the international community. "We want our door to be open to anyone who wants to come and help us with capital, mobility, and technical knowledge," said the Minister of External Affairs.[10] In 1964, Sierra Leone government representatives signed a first World Bank loan, US$3.8 million to build a Freetown electricity power plant. At the time, the Sierra Leone currency was worth 2 leones to 1 British pound.[11] (In 2024, the exchange rate hovered around 30,000 leones to 1 British pound.[12])

When I dug into the 1964 loan agreement between Sierra Leone and the World Bank, I found loan terms and conditions that are similar to—in a meta kind of way—the pandemic bonds terms and conditions: they met the criteria of international banking at the time, just as the pandemic bonds contracts comply with contemporary international investor law. But the terms and conditions do not meet what medical anthropologist Jim Yong Kim (yes, the same Jim Yong Kim who became a World Bank president) once claimed as his life philosophy, "a preferential option for the poor,"[13] which is a philosophy for taking the side of poverty justice and recompense when making a difficult decision. Historically, Sierra Leone has not seen favor from the global economic system.

The early (1960s) World Bank loan terms for Sierra Leone were not crafted with any particular consideration for newly independent nations, or recently postcolonial ones. The terms and conditions for Sierra Leone were boilerplate, like those used with European countries for postwar reconstruction. "After vigorous debate within the Bank, it was decided to use the same rate for all loans granted at any given time because; it would be difficult to have different basic conditions for different countries and even more difficult to have different interest rates for different countries."[14]

Yet compare the terms and conditions of 1964 Sierra Leone loan with the very first World Bank loan made in 1947 to France. In 1947, France was an imperial power with over fifty colonies. The Bank offered the French loan at a 3.25 percent interest rate. France had famously sent a one-page request asking for US$500 million for general reconstruction costs for post–World War II building and repair. The Bank approved a loan for US$250 million, the equivalent of over US$3 billion today. At the time, it was a full third of the Bank's total loanable resources. Seventeen years later it offered Sierra Leone, a former British colony only three years independent, a fledgling nation-state, a loan for a power plant at 5.5 percent interest (table 3.1). The Bank has long said it offers favorable concessionary loan terms for the poorest

**Table 3.1**

Comparison of first World Bank loans to Sierra Leone and France

|  | France | Sierra Leone |
| --- | --- | --- |
| **Year** | 1947 | 1964 |
| **Loan amount** | US$250 million (US$3.07 billion today*) | US$3.8 million (US$33.1 million today*) |
| **Total loan cost to borrower** | 5.75% | 6.375% |
| **Commitment charge** | 1.5% | 0.375% |
| **Commission** | 1% | 0.5% |
| **Interest** | 3.25% | 5.5% |
| **Grace period before payback begins** | 5 years | 3 years |
| **Payback schedule** | 23 years | 18 years |

* US Bureau of Labor Statistics, "CPI Inflation Calculator," https://www.bls.gov/data/inflation_calculator.htm, accessed July 23, 2023.

countries in the world. History tells a different story. Today, Sierra Leone is one of the world's most indebted countries.[15]

In the 1960s and 1970s at the World Bank, the economic violence of colonialism remained ostensibly irrelevant to its lending. Colonialism was not something that the world's preeminent development bank chose to consider, accommodate, or make reparations for. And the World Bank carried their blind eye forward. The laws and customary practices of international banking did not acknowledge with the actual postcolonial hardships of Sierra Leone. Neither were the loans shaped by the economic experts who live there. It is no wonder that by the 1980s, Sierra Leone was heavily indebted and missing payments, just as a new idea—structural adjustment—was taking hold at the Bank.

### USES OF SIERRA LEONE

"The first thing we do to a Sierra Leone," the chief of the World Bank's West Africa Projects unit is on record saying, "is give them a structural adjustment program. . . . Free cash! . . . We literally would go into Sierra Leone, and we'd see a guy, you know, this general has just made a coup. You know, he doesn't know anything about economic reform. And [the Bank director] says, 'Mr. President, do you want to be a respectable presence in this world? You need a structural adjustment . . . and he says, 'Sure. Where do I have to sign?'"[16]

For Sierra Leoneans, it was the worst luck: the twinning of a corrupt dictator president and an international bank betting on a high-stakes structural adjustment initiative designed, in theory, to stabilize and improve economies. "Only now the Bank is realizing . . . what we were brought into. We were brought in to make the life a little bit [better] for the people we were trying to get rid of," the unit chief said retrospectively.[17] In other words, people at the Bank knew they were giving money to bad governors.

About the same time the World Bank began its structural adjustment program in Sierra Leone, my twenty-two-year-old self was learning about the World Bank for the first time. Over cups of palm wine and bottles of Star Beer in provincial bars far from the capital city, Freetown, where the

Bank was headquartered, I heard people openly disparage the World Bank. Impressions were not favorable. The few rural country visits Bank officials made outside the capital, were short, choreographed performances, rushed from start to finish, like the visit to Tongo, the diamond field, as Sierra Leoneans sweated to show what they had done with the miserly trickle of Bank money doled out to them by Stevens's government. Bank folks were known for staying in neat, well-staffed, air-conditioned enclaves, moving from hotels to car to office, rarely building up any kind of sweat themselves in the equatorial heat of the day.

In retrospect, it is easy to see how big international lending institutions made the situation in Sierra Leone worse. As a postcolonial country, Sierra Leone legitimately needed money on credit to nation-build. Bank officials encouraged programs and policies in Sierra Leone that made their bosses in Washington happy, but did not necessarily solve problems in Salone. World Bank archives reveal that Bank officials were rewarded with raises and promotions when they could say, "'I signed a SAL [structural adjustment loan] with this impossible country,'" a West African Project chief reported. "If you don't have programs in every country, then you're not a good director. . . . That's a problem because you have a natural incentive to show action . . . that's very dangerous because you start linking SALs to career success. . . . [You hear,] 'You do your SALs or I'll cut your budget.'"[18]

Structural adjustment loans compounded Salone's governance problems, but the World Bank (and the IMF) kept lending. Loaning money served the double purpose of showing that there was cash flow to poor countries, but also that neoliberal macroeconomic policy conditionalities were being implemented.[19] Under structural adjustment, Sierra Leone was required to do several things in exchange for cash. Shrink government (fire people). Stop subsidizing fuel and food (charge more for basic necessities). Privatize critical infrastructures (add profit margins to basic utility costs). Weaken the currency. In 1986, the leone, Salone's currency, was "floated," meaning its value fluctuated according to world currency exchange rates. Enjoined by World Bank and IMF, the leone lost massive value in a short period of time. In June 1986, the exchange rate was six leones to one US dollar. By April 1987, it was 700 percent less valuable, fifty-three leones to one US dollar; by May 1990, 160 leones to one US dollar.[20] (In 2024, the exchange rate hovers around 22,000 leones to one US dollar.[21])

About the same time Sierra Leone's currency was being floated, the World Bank was found messing with the food supply, meaning they started toying with the price of rice. It would be hard to overestimate the real and symbolic importance of rice in Salone. In Lower Bambara, when my neighbors asked me if I'd eaten, they meant: Had I eaten rice that day? Rice is the staple food, and no matter what else I might have eaten, I hadn't had food until I'd eaten rice.

For decades, Sierra Leone was self-sufficient in rice production. But after independence, the World Bank forced Salone to change the rules about rice storing and marketing, which made rice unprofitable for farmers to grow one grain more than their families could eat. In the Bank's campaign to privatize the world—the neoliberal theology promoted by the Bank in the 1980s and into the 1990s—it urged the Sierra Leonean government to get out of the rice business. It wanted private businesses to import Salone's rice supply.

A British economist who worked for the World Bank as a consultant at the time reported that he was directed by the Bank to destroy the Sierra Leonean government department that kept the price and supply of rice steady.[22] At the risk of losing his job, he nevertheless ran calculations that revealed a harsh reality: privatizing rice would cause a famine. The few private businesses in Sierra Leone with enough capital to bring rice into the country knew the leone was worth too little, and its continued devaluation meant they would have cash problems if they tried to import rice from the world market. They would get stuck with leones that nobody would take in exchange for a harder currency like the pound or dollar. The British economist figured that not only would the reluctance to import rice for the country have meant a countrywide rice shortage, but whatever rice became available in the markets would also cost more. There were other problems too: shipping times for Asian rice, timed to Asian growing seasons, meant there would be times of the year when the private suppliers would have too much rice to ship and store cheaply. For private sector importers, it wasn't profitable to keep the rice supply stable enough to feed people year-round. The likelihood of famine loomed. At the cost of not being hired again by the

World Bank, the consultant shared his calculations with the Sierra Leonean officials who were set to sign the documents that would have turned over Salone's staple food supply to private sector operatives who weren't much interested in bringing rice into the country. Government officials did not sign.

The World Bank was not the only organization undermining Sierra Leonean farmers from growing enough rice for the whole country. In the open-air markets of Lower Bambara, I saw stacks of fifty-pound bags of rice stamped with US flags and the message: "A gift from the American people." Rice-producing US states received subsidies from the US Department of Agriculture to overproduce rice, thus flooding the US market with surplus. The solution? Send the rice to poor countries as food aid. In Lower Bambara, Arkansas rice was sold—yes, sold—just a penny or so per cup cheaper than the local rice. For families buying ten cups per day and looking to save money, they bought the cheaper rice, even though they missed the flavor of the local rice, they said. (The robust, nutty flavor of Mende rice is delicious— the best I've ever had.)

By 1990, classic precursors to war—food insecurity, a series of corrupt government, a weak economy—were simmering in Sierra Leone. They combined with an intensification of diamonds, drugs, and weapons trading in eastern Sierra Leone, where war would break out in 1991. Global media wrote of the war as a civil war, but, in truth, the violence was between multiple regional warlords, not two-party strife. Some of the violence was perpetrated by government forces. During the war years (1991–2002), the World Bank loaned Sierra Leone over US$300 million. Little is known about how that money was actually spent.

### THE CASE OF THE MISSING HEALTHCARE SYSTEM

Economic recovery after the war was slow, but a dozen years passed, and peace was sustained. The year before Ebola hit, 2013, *Forbes* named Sierra Leone the second-best country for new foreign investment in the world. People were hopeful. In the Freetown neighborhood where I stayed, I noticed people were less fatalistic. The adage "It's left to God" was replaced by "It is not easy." When I returned in January 2014, the economy looked so promising that I was hearing, "Sierra Leone will be a middle-income country by 2035." And then Ebola hit.

"The problem Sierra Leone had with Ebola was not even that they needed money quickly; it was that they had destroyed their health systems years before," a World Bank official told me rather offhandedly. *They* had destroyed their health systems years before. Really? *They* did that? But, wait, Salone never got a fair chance to build a health system in the first place. The country had been burdened by the small print of the Bank's loan agreements since 1964 that required that whatever money the country accumulated— from taxes, mining permits, mineral export fees, and bonds—first had to be used to pay back the international banks.[23] By long-standing legal agreement, building a healthcare system for the Sierra Leonean people has been contractually second to World Bank debt repayment.

When Bank officials blame Sierra Leoneans—and behind closed doors, they often do—they ignore the ways that international institutions hobbled the building of functioning government health systems in poor countries. During the last decades of the twentieth century, international actors— banks, aid and trade organizations, foundations, and governments—worked hard to move the responsibility for meeting human needs *out* of government, weakening government systems around the world.[24] They actively portrayed the for-profit sector as always better, faster, and smarter. Privatize everything! Make government small! Impose austerity measures! Cap salaries for doctors and nurses, teachers too! The long-term commitments and the investments required to build a healthcare *system* from the bottom up were, in fact, discouraged by the international banks' terms and conditions.[25]

Think about the ecosystem that the World Bank helped create in Sierra Leone. Building a national healthcare *system*, which is what Sierra Leoneans said they wanted in the 1960s and continue to say they want now, requires an accumulation of money to buy facilities and equipment and build workforce expertise—the staff, stuff, and space of health systems.[26] It requires intensely sustained, decades-long, concentrated, and wide-ranging effort.

But in the year before Ebola hit, 2013, the government was paying for less than 10 percent of their citizens' health expenditures. Miscellaneous donors contributed almost 25 percent. Over 60 percent of money spent on health care[27] was coming directly out of the pockets of Sierra Leoneans.[28] That's what underinvestment in government-directed healthcare[29] looks like: most health services are paid for out of poor people's pockets. Or, worse, not at all.

## EBOLA, 2014–2016

On February 27, 2014, I was in Freetown with several graduate students conducting research on health data and was reading through morning news feeds on my tablet when I saw a report of a hemorrhagic fever "like Ebola" in Guinea, Sierra Leone's neighbor to the north and east. At the time, Ebola wasn't known to be in West Africa. It had been virulent in Central Africa, 2,500 miles (over 4,000 kilometers) away. But two weeks later, the Guinean government confirmed with lab results that its hemorrhagic fever was indeed Ebola.

As I and members of the research team began asking Sierra Leoneans working in the government health ministry about Ebola, we found that they of course knew about it. Some ministry officials were working quietly to close the borders with Guinea and Liberia. But they found they had a fight on their hands with Sierra Leonean finance ministry officials, who were taking the position that the government was stable, and the future looked bright. Why mess that up? the finance folks were saying. Any news of Ebola in Sierra Leone would spook foreign investors. Private companies would close or leave. That classic tension between health and economy reared. The borders stayed open. Ominously, during that same period, our graduate student team member working in Freetown's WHO office said that *no one* was talking about Ebola.

At least 3,956 people died from Ebola in Salone from 2014 to 2016. Borders did eventually close. The few major industries shut down; some left the country for good. Wealthy diaspora Sierra Leoneans, who had returned after the war, again dispatched themselves and their families to Europe and North America. Economic and social losses to the three small West African nations from Ebola are estimated at over US$53 billion.[30] Ebola cost Salone a lot.

## HOW MUCH MONEY DID SIERRA LEONE RECEIVE WHEN THE PANDEMIC BONDS PAID OUT FOR COVID-19?

When the World Bank was first selling the pandemic bonds, it promised $500 million for pandemic response. Kim talked a lot about Ebola and how bond payouts would cover events like the West African outbreak. I heard from multiple World Bank officials that the bonds' triggers were specifically designed to release funds as if the 2014 West Africa Ebola conditions happened again.

In 2020, though, the world did not get Ebola; it got COVID-19, a disease the bonds also covered. In May 2020, six months after the first case of COVID-19 in China, the World Bank pandemic bonds paid out US$195.84 million to sixty-four countries. The government of Sierra Leone received exactly US$0 from the pandemic bonds (figure 3.1). On the World Bank ledgers, though, "Sierra Leone" received US$1 million.[31] That million was given to UNICEF and disappeared into its general account. It's notable that the World Bank and the IMF did give the Sierra Leonean government, a country that makes their Highly Indebted Poor Country list, over US$230 million in loans for COVID-19 that it will have to pay back, plus interest and origination fees. Oh, the uses of Sierra Leone.

**Pandemic Emergency Financing Facility (PEF)**
**Country Allocations**

**Updated February 2021**

| Country | PEF Funds (US$) | Fund Recipient |
|---|---|---|
| Afghanistan | 8,869,070.67 | UNICEF; WHO |
| Bangladesh | 14,872,047.79 | UNFPA; WFP |
| Benin | 1,000,000.00 | Government |
| Bhutan | 1,000,000.00 | Government |
| Bolivia* | 1,500,000.00 | UNICEF; WFP; WHO |
| Burkina Faso | 4,715,073.93 | UNICEF |
| Burundi | 1,632,612.21 | UNICEF |
| Cabo Verde | 1,000,000.00 | Government |
| Cambodia | 1,213,332.35 | Government |
| Cameroon | 7,392,057.22 | UNFPA; UNICEF; WFP; WHO |
| Central African Republic | 1,000,000.00 | IFRC |
| Chad | 2,322,283.54 | UNFPA; UNICEF |
| Congo, Dem Rep of | 13,181,549.40 | UNFPA; UNICEF; WHO |
| Congo, Rep of | 1,286,905.17 | UNFPA; UNICEF; WHO |
| Cote d'Ivoire | 2,818,731.45 | IFRC; WHO |
| Djibouti | 1,000,000.00 | Government |
| Dominica | 1,000,000.00 | WHO |
| Ethiopia | 7,236,953.41 | UNICEF |
| Fiji | 1,000,000.00 | Government |
| Gambia, The | 1,000,000.00 | Government |
| Ghana | 3,287,552.45 | FAO; IFRC; UNFPA; UNICEF: WFP; WHO; |
| Grenada | 1,000,000.00 | Government |

| Sierra Leone | 1,000,000.00 | UNICEF |
|---|---|---|

| Papua New Guinea | 1,252,504.28 | Government |
|---|---|---|
| Rwanda | 1,000,000.00 | Government |
| Sao Tome & Principe | 1,000,000.00 | Government |
| Senegal | 1,564,968.47 | UNICEF; WHO |
| Sierra Leone | 1,000,000.00 | UNICEF |
| Somalia | 3,076,207.76 | UNICEF; WHO |
| South Sudan | 1,581,306.85 | WHO |
| Sri Lanka* | 1,809,695.98 | Government |
| St Lucia | 1,000,000.00 | Government |
| St. Vincent & the Grenadines | 1,000,000.00 | WHO |
| Tanzania | 3,986,804.71 | Government |
| Timor-Leste | 1,000,000.00 | Government |
| Togo | 1,000,000.00 | WHO |
| Uganda | 2,845,574.63 | Government |

**Figure 3.1**

Pandemic bond payout for COVID-19. Original World Bank document is three pages; abridged here by author to show the official amount of payout to UNICEF in Sierra Leone. *Source:* World Bank, "Pandemic Emergency Financing Facility (PEF), Updated February 2021," https:// pubdocs.worldbank.org/en/140481591710249514/pdf/PEF-country-allocations-table.pdf. See table A.3 in the appendix.

## FRONT STAGE

Risk is so amorphous. What kind of conjury was it for the World Bank to package up pandemic risk and sell it to the world? The Bank, its president, and its designer units formed a trilogy of tales worth telling.

# 4 THE BANK THAT TOOK PANDEMICS TO WALL STREET

The pandemic bonds' natal home, the World Bank,[1] is a wily behemoth, an international financial institution beloved by some,[2] despised by others.[3] Seen as Altruistic. Innovative. Necessary. Loathsome. Evil. Some want to shut it down.[4] Still others think it just needs a good reform.[5] *Urban Dictionary* calls it "[a] conspiracy designed by neoliberal capitalists to rob developing countries of their resources and ensure unequal distribution of wealth."[6] An economist credits (and blames) it for bringing postcolonial nations into the world economic system.[7] A humanities professor links its US corporatism with old-style European imperialism.[8] A sociologist claims it was central to "Northern wealth accumulation."[9] Almost every country government in the world is a dues-paying Bank member. It loans out billions of dollars every year. In short, the World Bank is a lot of things to a lot of people.

When the Bank got its start in 1944, there wasn't a lot of cash in the world system. World War II wasn't quite over, but the Allied powers, led by the United States and England, knew that European cities would need cash to rebuild. And they were keen to fashion a new global postwar economy that gave them an edge. At a glam-rustic conference center in Bretton Woods, New Hampshire, in the United States, 730 representatives from forty-four countries met to hammer out new monetary rules. The United States had an upper hand—the war hadn't been fought on its soil; it went to war comparatively late (1941); it hadn't spent as much as its Allied partners fighting; and it was a rich country to begin with. The deal, what became known as the Bretton Woods Agreement, established the US dollar as the world's reserve currency and set up two new international financial institutions, the World Bank and the International Monetary Fund,[10] whose new home would be in Washington, DC (they originally shared a building). The Bank started off with about seventy employees; it now has over 15,000 working in Washington and around the world.

In 2018, I visited the World Bank DC headquarters for rounds of interviews. After making my way through its security labyrinth, I was trooped through a hallway lined with historical placards declaring that the Bank's first purpose, to my surprise, was *peace*. "Ours is a mission of peace—not just lip service to the ideals of peace—but action, concrete action, designed to establish the economic foundations of peace on the bed rock of genuine international cooperation."[11] European countries were exhausted and impoverished after two twentieth-century wars. Peace, it was theorized, would be achieved through economic growth and prosperity.

In 1946, in the immediate aftermath of World War II, the World Bank started out with about US$750 million to loan. Two years later, the Bank's mandate was overshadowed by the Marshall Plan, a huge US aid-to-Europe program. The Bank was a bank, but the Marshall Plan gave away its money as grants, about US$13 billion, with no interest and few strings attached, and much more attractive terms and conditions. Nevertheless, the Bank endured.

In a self-preserving move, the Bank turned to new customers, that is, to poor and colonized countries. By the mid-1950s, the Bank was conducting trainings to build country capacity" by providing training for local officials "from developing countries" who oversaw World Bank–funded programs and projects.[12] Sounds innocent enough. Made sense from the Bank's point of view. Bank loans needed repayment and it wanted Eurocentric accounting and accountability. But its approach ended up to something akin to me taking out a car loan and being forced to adhere to coercive personal financing imperatives—"Don't spend so much on housing. Reduce your food budget. Your health insurance plan is too expensive. Stop going out on Saturday nights. Prioritize your loan payments. Or else." Or else what? Your credit rating will be trash and you'll be indebted to us forever and a day.[13]

By the 1970s and 1980s, the Bank's infamous structural adjustment loan programs emerged and proved devastating to fledgling postcolonial economies and their populations' health.[14] The Bank's neoliberal scheme required Sierra Leone and other poor countries make huge concessions to their sovereign decision-making to get loans. The Bank was not the only player promoting US-styled capitalism in newly independent countries, but it was a major one.

## FIRST IMPRESSIONS

At this point in the narrative, my twenty-two-year-old self would have said, "But wait, isn't the World Bank an international development assistance organization? Doesn't it work in poor countries, loaning money and technical expertise to fix big existential problems—like broken democracies—as well as smaller practical ones—like broken water wells?" For a long time, I thought that was the extent of it. Herein lies the Bank's multiple personality problem. Bank? Development agency? Databank? Knowledge bank? All these monikers have been used by the Bank to describe itself. Will the World Bank that took pandemics to Wall Street please stand up?

The very first time I met World Bank folks, I was in Sierra Leone at a US Embassy reception in Freetown. I can still see in my mind's eye a phalanx of World Bank officials striding into the room. They wore the confident superiority of smart people who give money away for a living. Aloof. Conversation at arm's length. And their shoes. Their shoes signaled their approach to Sierra Leone. New. Polished. Not worn. Not soiled. They didn't walk the streets of Freetown much, and, compared with my own dusty dogs, they definitely weren't trekking daily or riding motorcycles on the red clay upcountry roads either. As a group, they were not a with-the-people, "nothing-about-them-without-them" kind of folk.

The World Bank I came to know in Sierra Leone operated not like a bank, but rather as a particular kind of big, deep-pocketed development assistance agency: highly interventionist and hugely prescriptive. The Bank officials I met in Sierra Leone were fly-in-fly-out types. They understood very little about the village-level life that 80 percent of Sierra Leoneans lived at the time. The Bank made mistakes common to other drive-by development[15] agencies—holding too little regard for what already works in communities and often delivering impractical advice for meeting local human needs. It focused on what communities lack, not what is already working, sometimes destroying what functioned well through whatever innovative problem-solving fad was trending out of Washington. Most egregiously, they regularly failed to recognize or capitalize on the problem-solving smarts of people they said they wanted to help.

Bank ideas spread like a fever across the international development industry. When I began working in Washington, for a US humanitarian aid agency, the week-long orientation featured a World Bank economist who pitched theories about "development" and the "free market." He talked excitedly of economic growth trickling down to the masses. When he finished and I realized that his talk was also the agency's development principle, I raised my hand and asked, "Is this the extent of the agency's economic doctrine of development?" Yes, it was. "What about an approach that would meet basic human needs first and foremost and grow economies from there?" I asked. Oh, no, the economist assured, meeting basic needs would trickle down from economic growth. That seemed backwards to me. Supporting human needs first—health, education, and social protections—would strengthen communities and countries better and faster, wasn't that obvious? No, I would learn, mine was an altogether different philosophy.[16]

What I hadn't understood at the time was that the Bank was midstream in its grand neoliberal makeover of poor postcolonial countries, restructuring their economies and imposing austerity programs "for their own good," indebting them for decades to come. Kim learned this early in his career. Many years before becoming the World Bank president, Kim said about his time in Peru working for Partners in Health, "We saw people unable to feed themselves. We saw health care services being cut back. We attributed a lot of those things to the World Bank."[17] By requiring poor and fledgling governments to privatize critical infrastructures, deregulate labor, and weaken their currencies, the Bank was a major player in a global ideological economic overhaul. This was a perversion of the World Bank's original Bretton Woods inspiration, which was to bring peace by *balancing* the global economy and strengthening its weakest member governments. Pooling wealth and extending credit was its original mandate, not masterminding economic transmogrifications. The Bank had gone off course and there was no one to stop it.

## BEDFELLOWS: THE WORLD BANK AND WALL STREET INVESTORS

There was something else I'd missed in the din of its development activities: the Bank's connections with Wall Street are deep. Hidden, but profound. Over 90 percent of the Bank's funding comes from private investors. The Bank hooked up with Wall Street before the ink was dry on the Bretton Woods Agreement. "The language used to draft the [agreement] kept Wall Street in mind,"[18] recalled a deputy to the American team lead negotiating the Bank's first charter documents. Wall Street was considered essential to the young Bank. After the war, it needed New York investors because that's where the money was. London had been the world's major financial capital for over a century, but ten years of war in just thirty years' time had emptied England of much of its cash.[19] Into that void, the New York City capital market rose in stature, unseating London as the center of global finance. Links between the Bank and the Street were evident enough at its start, prompting the Soviet Union in 1947 to decry the World Bank as a branch of Wall Street, subordinate to the political interests of "one great owner" (the United States).[20] The USSR refused to ratify the Bank's founding governance terms on those grounds, sitting out World Bank membership for four decades (Russia joined the Bank in 1992).

The economists crafting the Bretton Woods Agreement knew the Bank could build its own credit and credibility by selling bonds on Wall Street. It worked—and still does—like this: when an investor buys a World Bank bond, investors are, in effect, loaning the Bank money for a term. The Bank, in turn, uses that money during the bond's term, much of it for loans to its borrowers, like Sierra Leone. It's the classic buy-low, sell-high strategy. The Bank went on to build its coffers by borrowing at a low interest rate, lending at a higher interest rate, and pocketing the difference.

"The Bank is by now so well established . . . that it is difficult to recall what a novelty it was, or with what condescending skepticism it was treated by the financial community, when it started operations," said one of the Bank's chroniclers.[21] "[The Bank] was thought of as a do-good institution, as a wild idea, without any respectable support," he said.[22] In 1946, the first Bank president, Eugene Meyer, a former Wall Street investment banker, traveled from Washington, DC, to New York to visit old friends and meet potential new investors. Meyer's advisor remembered, "The [New York] bankers with whom we met could not have been pleasanter—or less interested." They "wanted nothing further to do with international lending—and certainly not with a novel international agency."[23] They worried the Bank would encourage unsound financial practices both within the Bank and among its borrowers. One New York bank economist worried that, because the Bank would work with different currencies and exchanges, it would become a site for currency manipulation and money laundering.[24] Of course, the Bank didn't emerge from the New Hampshire conference eight decades ago as a fully formed powerhouse. In its early years it was just a bank standing in front of the world seeking acceptance. Like the pandemic bonds but on a much grander scale, the Bank itself had to be made up laboriously. The first World Bank president's advisor recalled: "[N]obody knew where to begin. We were inexperienced. We didn't know what kinds of questions to ask, what kind of investigation to make. We hadn't developed the kind of project approach that worked out later. Just like any other new institution in a new field, at that time we were trying to struggle along finding our way, and we had all these pressures to operate very quickly and make a lot of loans very quickly."[25]

### THE FIRST BONDS

Sales did not look promising in the weeks leading up to the World Bank offering its first bonds. But the Bank's 1947 bonds debut was a success,[26] by no small measure because it was managed by Wall Street stalwart Morgan Stanley. "The link to Morgan Stanley meant access to a deep reservoir of institutional knowledge and expertise in the capital markets and myriad connections in international finance."[27] Fearing there would be too little interest

**The New York Times**    WEDNESDAY, JULY 16, 1947.    **FINAN**

IN CEREMONIES AT STOCK EXCHANGE YESTERDAY

## WORLD BANK BONDS QUICKLY MARKETED

First Offerings Made on Floor
of Stock Exchange Here
and Bring Premiums

---

PRICES LEVEL OFF LATER

---

Oversubscription Announced
at Noon—1,600 Dealers to
Receive Allotments

---

Bonds of the International Bank
for Reconstruction and Development changed hands yesterday for
the first time. The first dealings
took place on the New York Stock
Exchange's public market immediately after the Exchange opened
for trading, and while the bank
was still being pressed for allotments from dealers all over the
nation.

In the presence of Emil Schram,
president of the Exchange, and an

Emil Schram, center, president of the New York Stock Exchange, was host to bank officials at first
offering to the public of bonds of the International Bank for Reconstruction and Development. John J.
McCloy, president of the World Bank, is at right, and Kyriacos Varvaressos, an executive director, at left.

**Figure 4.1**

Financial section page of the *New York Times*, July 16, 1947: the first World Bank bonds sale.

in bonds, "Morgan Stanley—together with First Boston (a predecessor of Credit Suisse)— . . . put on road shows in 18 cities to attract interest from investors."[28] When the bonds were offered, the Bank had more buyers than bonds and raised US$250 million.

For the Bank's first twenty-two years, it was led in turn by four white American men with strong ties to New York investment banking—among them, former presidents and a vice president of Chase Manhattan and First Boston. At the time, the primary job of World Bank presidents was to make it into a financial institution worthy of investor confidence. "The first year of the Bank's existence was marked by a vigorous, if unacknowledged, tug-of-war. . . . [Its leadership] combined vision with wisdom and diplomacy with the sterner stuff of financial discipline," wrote a deputy with a front-row seat.[29] They wanted to build an institution with such a solid financial reputation that New York City capital investors would give the Bank the benefit of the doubt. Build they did, with a lot of help from their Wall Street friends.

## ISN'T THAT SPECIAL? THE BANK'S EXEMPTIONS, EXCEPTIONS, AND EXCEPTIONALISM

**Author:** When the Bank is making up something like the pandemic bonds, is there anybody telling the Bank that it can't do such and such?

**World Bank Official (WBO):** No.

**Author:** No . . . no? Are there legal teeth anywhere?

**WBO:** The Bank operates completely outside of any national laws. It's completely autonomous in that regard. It's not subject to any national laws.

**Author:** How can that be?

**WBO:** So, it's a good question. . . . The [Bank's founding] Articles of Agreement give it autonomy.

**Author:** So, what keeps the Bank in check?

**WBO:** Oh, you wouldn't push something outrageous that would jeopardize your credit rating, right?

"We are actually exempt. The World Bank is exempt from SEC rules," another World Bank interviewee told me in a crowded hotel restaurant, lowering their voice to almost a whisper. The World Bank is exempt from the usual US Securities and Exchange Commission (SEC) registration and reporting requirements in place to "protect investors, maintain fair, orderly, and efficient markets, and facilitate capital formation."[30] To sell its first bonds in 1946, the Bank received a special exemption from the SEC, a condition that was later made into law by US congressional legislation in 1949,[31] with the intention of making the US market bigger for the Bank to invest in.[32]

And about that credit rating. Again and again in my interviews, Bank officials brought up the Bank's AAA credit rating, which the World Bank has had—in an unbroken run—since 1959. "The credit rating is what makes the Bank. Having a AAA credit rating allows it to borrow money cheaply and relend it. That is like the Holy Grail inside the institution. Don't mess with that," a Bank official told me.

Standard & Poor's and Moody's—two major Wall Street credit rating agencies—are not infallible raters of creditworthiness, as Michael Lewis shows in *The Big Short*.[33] Bond issuers must pay for the ratings. Without customers like the World Bank, the rating agencies would have no business. There's plenty of cynicism about the integrity credit ratings in the financial world, but bond sales wouldn't happen the same way without them. To potential investors, a AAA rating from Standard & Poor's and Moody's signals that the World Bank has been deemed unlikely to default on its bonds.

The World Bank Group describes itself as unique. It is, but not for the reasons it advertises, like its global partnerships or potential to build shared prosperity. Its curbs are few, shaped loosely by the interests of its more powerful government members. It's unlikely to do anything crazy that would disrupt its relationships with Wall Street, people told me. What makes it most unique is the Bank's largely unfettered freedom to make up financial products, an absence of meaningful oversight regulation or an oversight body, and lots and lots of cash. Worry about a credit rating is hardly a check equal to regulatory rule of law and active oversight. The Bank has an uncommon amount of freedom to do whatever its leadership thinks is best—even when they're dead wrong about how to catalyze global prosperity, as they were in the decades when they imposed trickle-down and austerity schemes on poor countries.

### A BANK OF ITS TIME, IN AN OLD-TIMEY, RACIST WAY

Although its founding charter expressly positioned the Bank as an apolitical institution, day-to-day interactions were anything but. In the mid-twentieth-century, when European countries took out World Bank loans, they were still colonizing powers. Even though there was "a certain distaste for colonialism on the part of some in the Bank,"[34] the Bank favored colonizer nations in the early years because they were considered more creditworthy. It loaned money in 1954 to France, for example, for railways in colonized Senegal, Mali, Niger, Burkina Faso, and Cote d'Ivoire, rather than to the countries themselves.[35] Hardly an apolitical move.

Behind the scenes, there was something else that ran unchecked: unconcealed stereotyping and experimentation. A transcript[36] from a meeting about a 1951 loan made to Belgium for the Congo[37] quotes a Bank economist describing the Congolese as "a people that, before the Europeans came, didn't have the plow or wheel, didn't know the art of writing, and still does not have a draft animal."[38] The economist was apparently ignorant of the Kingdom of Kongo, which by the early fifteenth century was the major hub of an extensive central African trade network and had ambassadors in Portugal and the Vatican.[39] The economist continued, "It is impossible for the Congo to progress unless the native population is brought along in the advance of civilization."[40] Belgium, which terrorized Congolese by raiding villages and amputating limbs in its colonizing land-grab, had extracted rubber, diamonds, and uranium from the Congo for more than fifty years, a rule by terror. Belgium, though, for World Bank purposes, had the better credit record. An executive director concluded, "I hope that we in the Bank look on [the Congo] as a kind of guinea pig. . . . There are going to be problems of which we here are as yet hardly aware. . . . Certainly the native problem is one . It is allied with health problems, which will clearly come up, and the movement of populations to areas where they will be confronted with new limitations, new vices, new diseases. But all that can be very interesting. That is why I would like to treat it as a guinea pig and from time to time have full and detailed reports on how it is working."[41]

In its first two decades, the Bank operated as if hundreds of years of colonialism and the trans-Atlantic human enslavement and trafficking systems had not happened. Turning a blind eye to international political and human rights issues became World Bank policy,[42] glossed over with an "all members are equal"[43] approach. Colonial reparations be damned. The Bank accommodated neither the resource extractions and human enslavement that weakened country regions nor the heinous crimes against humanity that strengthened other country economies, enabling accumulations of wealth that undergird wealthy countries to this day.

In the 1960s, when over fifty colonized countries became independent (like Sierra Leone from Britain in 1961), the Bank was often the first and sometimes the only bank to offer loans for critical infrastructures like roads, electricity, and agriculture. It was known as "lender of last resort" because it loaned to fledging nation-states with few options for borrowing and who did not yet have their own credit lines or ratings recognized by the international monetary system. The Bank's all-members-are-equal approach proved inherently unequal, perpetuating into the present roughly the same division of wealth today as those of the pre-independence movements of the 1950s (see table 3.1 comparing first-time loan terms for both Sierra Leone and postwar France).

### BECOMING AN INTERNATIONAL "DEVELOPMENT" DYNAMO

So when did the Bank start behaving like an international development do-gooder? A sharp turn toward development is often credited to Robert McNamara, the Bank's fifth president, who in 1968 became the Bank's first without an investment banking background. He wanted a poverty-alleviation Bank, pushing employees "to deal with poverty and aid rather than with direct and visible forms of wealth creation and investment."[44] Under McNamara, the Bank began its education, health, and agriculture programming in earnest. He also expanded the Bank's capital market reach, adding Frankfurt and Tokyo capital markets to the primary and original source of the Bank's borrowing, New York City.

James Wolfensohn, an investment banker and the Bank's ninth president from 1995 to 2005, similarly prioritized fighting global poverty. But he and the next two World Bank presidents, Paul Wolfowitz and Robert Zoellick, maintained the Bank's ideological commitments to neoliberalism as *the* guiding ideological framework for the global economy. They attempted "to renew the legitimacy of [the Bank's] developmental mindset, while maintaining a market-centric mentality."[45] World Bank presidents since have been obliged to promote both international development and markets, ignoring the contradictions, making the ability to talk out of both sides of one's mouth—the banker side and the international "development" side—a job requirement.

In 2012, US president Barack Obama nominated Jim Yong Kim—a physician, anthropologist, and global health and development professional with no banking or finance experience—as World Bank president. Tensions in the Bank between the banking and international development arms have festered for decades, but Obama justified his choice this way: "Despite its name," he said, "the World Bank is more than just a bank. It's one of the most powerful tools we have to reduce poverty and raise the standards of living in some of the poorest countries on the planet. . . . It's time for a development professional to lead the world's largest development agency."[46]

## MAXIMIZING FINANCE FOR DEVELOPMENT: "THE PRIVATE SECTOR CAN PLAY A MUCH BIGGER ROLE"

Under Kim, the World Bank became a finance innovator, "a multiplier and accelerator."[47] It advocated not just for more money, but for smarter money.[48] "Leveraging" became a key word in the Bank's publications, appearing in one online World Bank publication repository fifty-three times more often (483 instances) between 2010 and 2019 than between 1990 and 1999, when it appeared only nine times in ten years.[49]

The Bank under Kim publicly and aggressively championed maximizing finance for development,[50] and making billions into trillions,[51] arguing that its "business model is well suited to help move the international community from billions of dollars in [public sector funding] to trillions in finance for development." In 2018, the Bank offered a twenty-three-part training video about how public funds should "be used to mobilize and leverage the large and growing pools of private finance."[52] In short, taxpayers' monies should be put in play to catalyze return on investment for private investors and provide cut-loss guarantees if private investors put their money into public goods, meaning any market losses would be minimized or reduced to zero.

Kim speeches and the Bank's promotional material cited a US$2.5 trillion gap[53] standing in the way of ending poverty by 2030 (e.g., figure 4.2). He used "The Gap" to justify a turn to more financialized solutions. According to Kim, "[m]aximizing finance for development mean[t] finding win-win solutions, where investors get a good return and countries utilize these resources to meet their development goals."[54] Mobilize private investors. De-risk their potential losses. Leverage investor advantage. The pandemic bonds fit right in to these sensibilities.

As the Bank began "solving" The Gap with new financialized schemes, it suffered brain fog about the lessons learned from P3s—an earlier ideology of

---

**Figure 4.2**

*Source:* World Bank, "Maximizing Finance for Development," April 10, 2018, https://www.world bank.org/en/news/infographic/2018/04/10/maximizing-finance-for-development, accessed August 5, 2021. Red oval around The Gap added by author. Copyright: The World Bank Group. All rights reserved.

# MAXIMIZING FINANCE FOR DEVELOPMENT

We cannot achieve the World Bank Group's goals – ending extreme poverty and boosting shared prosperity – without much more funding for efforts that help the poor. And to meet the Sustainable Development Goals by 2030, countries need to scale up financing from billions to trillions of dollars.

Private finance is the largest resource to help fill this gap.

**Cost of meeting SUSTAINABLE DEVELOPMENT GOALS**
## $4.5 TRILLION
A YEAR

## $2.5 TRILLION GAP

**DEVELOPMENT AID**
## $135 BILLION
A YEAR

+

**REMITTANCES, FOREIGN DIRECT INVESTMENT, PHILANTHROPY**
## $1 TRILLION
A YEAR

**Developing countries are doing their part**

Raising more resources domestically, combating illicit flows, becoming less aid dependent

▼

## THE PRIVATE SECTOR CAN PLAY A MUCH BIGGER ROLE

**PRIVATE FINANCE, INNOVATION & EXPERTISE**  OFFER SOLUTIONS TO REACHING DEVELOPMENT GOALS

Achieving the SDGs could open up $12 trillion of market opportunities

◄

▼

**Developing countries see the opportunity and are seeking help**

For private investors, embracing new and expanded markets not only makes good business sense, it creates jobs and opportunities for people in the world's poorest countries

◄

The World Bank Group can bring together the public and private sector

◄  ►

Together we can fill the financing gap for countries and the poor public-private partnerships promoted by the Bank beginning in the 1990s.[55] P3s combined private sector capital with public money backstopping losses, with governments typically forgoing any profit sharing.[56] Over time, P3s were shown to have serious performance problems, which were especially acute in the health sector where human suffering is the cost of not getting it right.[57] When the going got tough, private sector investors and philanthropies walked away, abandoning failing projects when there wasn't *enough* profit, and leaving governments to deal with problems.[58] In health sectors in places like Sierra Leone, P3s exacerbated a dysfunctional fragmentation of health care.[59] Communities were left in the lurch.

Still today, in bouts of continuing institutional amnesia, the World Bank willfully ignores its role in creating The Gap. It overlooks its own decades-long drumbeat for small government and transferring public lands, resources, and utilities into private individuals' hands, and its wholehearted embrace of neoliberal conditionalities that gutted poor governments' ability to provide health, education, and social protections, including food security, for their citizens. Its mandates to downsize literally left governments too small to orchestrate essential services. The Bank appears to have forgotten its long history of enabling vested private interests and its abject failure to use its power and influence to catalyze fair redistributions of public goods. The Bank created the weather and then started loudly complaining about the drought.

### FINANCIALIZING PANDEMICS

When Kim started thinking seriously about a way to finance pandemic response, "blended finance"[60]—the mixing of public and private funds— was trending in elite global finance circles as *the* way to solve the world's greatest problems. Governments and philanthropic foundations needed to entice the private sector, the thinking went, to invest more in socially essential goods like education, health, roads, and food security, by guaranteeing (by paying back) some or all investor losses (which has become known as "derisking"). A *Financial Times* journalist put it this way: "The idea is to encourage mainstream private investors to finance projects they would otherwise shun because the risks were unmeasurable, long term or too idiosyncratic to hedge."[61] In other words, rather than supporting alternatives to raising funds for the common good, deep-pocketed institutions like the World Bank and foundations like Rockefeller, Bloomberg, and Gates (as well as the United States Agency for International Development) coddle private investors afraid to invest in social sectors because they fret they will not get enough return on their investment, a.k.a. make enough money.

Of course, it's not the private sector's job to take care of people the way good governments do. But that's the problem when turning public services over to the private sector. Friedman's business-of-business-is-business sensibility,[62] twinned with deregulation and antitaxation policies,[63] meant governments also don't have the money they need to help people.

The World Bank and other development banks have wielding privatizing investment schemes since the 1980s,[64] but their latest versions of financialization solutions are next-level. Of course, the huge expansion in the last decades of the role of finance in the global and national economies was much bigger than Bank operations. Financialization is a global phenomenon. But there's no denying that the Bank has led the way in the international development industry as "a broker for private investment"[65]and, more recently, financialization.

"We are the incubator, the pandemic bonds live here," a World Bank official told me. The Bank brokered the financialization of pandemics by making the risk of a pandemic—something previously unfinancialized— into a financial device that could be sold by the Bank. The Bank pulled the bonds-makers together. "There's just nobody else that can do that. They made it easier for a country to cede [pandemic] risk to the private sector," an ILS designer told me.

By the time the pandemic bonds were issued in July 2017, the "Maximizing Finance for Development" and "Billions to Trillions" campaigns were in full swing at the World Bank.[66] The new bonds were on brand. And they had something in common with the Bank's founding Bretton Woods documents: they were designed to meet Wall Street investors' needs and eccentricities. Investors were their target audience; they set the conditions. The bonds were designed to Wall Street specifications, not to Sierra Leonean governors and their government counterparts who would ultimately be held responsible for their citizens' well-being.

\* \* \*

My early confusion about the Bank's truer purpose? Conducting research on the pandemic bonds has cleared that up for me. It's a bank. There's no refuting its vast power and influence *as a bank*. Conversely, its record as an international development agency is not impressive. When I lived in Sierra Leone, expectations ran high that Sierra Leone would become a sovereign and self-determining nation, indebted to no one. There are a lot of reasons why the more than US$4 billion of World Bank loans and grants to Sierra Leone over fifty years' time[67] was insufficient for meeting that challenge, not all of which fall to the Bank. But it's fair to expect that the World Bank's four billion would have bought Sierra Leone more shared prosperity, to use the Bank's slogan. Something did not work out well enough. Blame it on Salone, as the Bank is wont to do behind closed doors. Or maybe the world's foremost development bank just isn't very good at "development" in some of the world's poorest countries.

# 5 PERSONALITY MATTERS: JIM YONG KIM

During my research I asked three Bank officials, "Would the pandemic bonds have existed without Jim Kim?" They said, respectively:

> No. No. No way.

> I doubt it. I think at the time, he was keen to show that he was the smartest, most innovative guy in the room.

> No . . . he's a political animal. He saw himself as the principal from the very beginning. . . . He pursued the pandemic bonds to improve his brand, one thing among many.

I need to say this: I don't like writing about fellow anthropologists. We are a motley crew of strange and special people, a scholarly cohort mostly ignored by policy and project folks whose outcomes we could help improve, if they let us. We quietly conduct our research and—surprise!—we uncover nuance and get a good handle on why things work and why they don't.[1] But most politicians and project and policy folks want simple recommendations. It can get awkward. A Gates Foundation project officer once bullied a colleague, accusing them of "boiling the ocean." "Why can't you just accept simple explanations for things?" they asked. Yeah, but that's not what we do. We're splitters, not lumpers. We tease out deeper meanings for a living. Governors come to us when they can no longer ignore that the easy fixes aren't working, like during the West African Ebola outbreak in 2014.[2] As a group, we're not well understood, and I am usually protective of us.

Only one of us has risen to the rank of World Bank president. Only one oversaw development of the pandemic bonds. I have no choice but to write about Kim. His personal ambition is indispensable to the creation of the bonds. And here's where it gets even messier for me: his turn toward investor finance as *the* solution to global poverty was tangled up in a deep and persistent need to prove himself as up to the task of leading the world's premier international financial institution.

Twelve years before becoming president, Kim coauthored one of the most forceful and incisive condemnations of the World Bank, a nearly 600-page book that attributes over fifty policy-related health disasters to the World Bank and the IMF.[3] Financier David Rubenstein stated pointedly during an interview with Kim, "You led a protest against the World Bank [in the mid-1990s]. In fact, you said that the World Bank, maybe, should be shut down."[4] Yes, "twenty years ago, I was part of a movement that tried to close the World Bank," Kim said in another interview.[5] After he became Bank president, though, he talked about the Bank differently. "Over the last twenty years, I've never seen an institution that changed as much as the World Bank has changed. People who don't deal with us on a daily basis don't realize how much we have changed,"[6] Kim said.

Indeed, by 2015, three years into his seven-year tenure at the Bank, he was promoting Wall Street–World Bank fusion as a brand-new solution for poverty eradication. Bank folks had been driving private investment in poor countries for decades, but Kim said the quiet part out loud, often to the dismay of some subordinates. Kim pushed hard for "private investors— sovereign wealth funds, private equity firms and insurance companies—to pony up trillions of dollars for projects. . . . [Investors] can reap rich returns by putting their money to work alongside the World Bank."[7] Kim traveled the world selling the World Bank's "power to catalyze and ['crowd source'] trillions of public and private sector dollars."[8]

\* \* \*

I've used Kim's own words here and relied on interviews with current and former employees of the World Bank, as well as on information from global affairs experts, journalists, and others. They've helped me sort out how and why Kim's personality mattered in the run-up to the July 2017 launch of the bonds. I did not interview Kim; in the early stages of the research, I requested an interview, which he declined (he was out of town when I was in Washington). But he directed Bank team members overseeing the pandemic bonds to meet with me. Some did, although one rather insecure fellow avoided me like, well, the plague.

### NEED FOR SPEED

Kim knew pandemics' containment has a need for speed. Contagion rates, especially of airborne diseases, rise exponentially by the day. Historically, pandemic aid was "late, inadequate, and slow" when "speed is of the essence," he said.[9] "Passing the hat around once a pandemic strikes is too costly, both in human lives and in economic terms."[10] "A speedy response can save thousands of lives and potentially trillions of dollars," he said.[11]

In early 2015 at Davos—a Swiss resort town and home of the World Economic Forum where global political and economic leaders meet annually— Kim aired the idea of coupling pandemic aid with Wall Street investment. For speedy pandemic response, he advocated, let's combine donor contributions with capital market solutions. Davos attendees gave Kim's idea a warm reception, and he returned to Washington excited and emboldened to pursue it full-tilt. In the kind of synergistic development assumed to be more common to Silicon Valley than the World Bank, Kim marshaled interest among G20 leaders for fast-dispersing pandemic aid into a plan for the pandemic bonds.

By late 2015, the pandemic bonds began to take shape within the Bank, combining donor funds with bond and derivative elements. "He went around asking staff, 'What's an instrument we could create?' He was fascinated by the different financial instruments," a World Bank official told me. "This was his baby," one of the bond designers said, describing Kim's mien in the early days of the pandemic bonds development.

In speeches, Kim outlined several ambitions for the bonds. The bonds would introduce a new investor-centric structure that would catalyze money from a new source—private investors—for pandemic preparedness and response. Loftier still, Kim envisioned the bonds in perpetuity, catalyzing a stable market for pandemic bonds, and moving the world forever away from what he called "cycles of panic and neglect"[12]—the public fear and frenzy when pandemics hit, followed by years of inattention as deaths wane, followed again by fear and frenzy when the next pandemic threat emerges. "Find win-win outcomes—where owners of capital get a reasonable return, and developing countries maximize sustainable investments," Kim encouraged, as he aggressively campaigned for a new way to create money to pay for pandemics.[13]

Smart as he was, Kim had to have known that the bonds would not disperse "with the first case" or that "with the first case, we [would] have a bunch of cash that will go right out to try to stop it."[14] The criteria were a known deceleration feature. Criteria for releasing the money were intentionally stringent, designed to compel investors to invest, not to release the money with the first case. Yet, less than a year before the bonds went on sale, Kim told a reporter that "millions of dollars are *instantly* released to fight similar disease outbreaks in the future."[15]

Finance was not a field Kim was eminently qualified for.[16] But he was a charismatic and an often-compelling salesman. He was not shy about actively courting rich investors to do good and make money at the same time. His 2017 TED talk was a clarion call: "Eight trillion [dollars] is literally sitting in the hands of rich people under their very large mattresses. What we are trying to do is now use [the tools] that rich people use every single day to make themselves richer, but [that] we haven't used aggressively enough on behalf of the poor. . . . All of you who are sitting on trillions of dollars of cash, come to us!"[17]

## PRECOCIOUS BRILLIANCE AND SOME BLATANT RULE BREAKING

Kim's personal story is remarkable, one of great ambition and many talents. Born in Seoul, South Korea, he grew up in a family that moved to the United States when he was five. He became valedictorian and president of his small

Iowa high school class, as well as captain and quarterback of the football team and point guard for his basketball team. At a science camp before his first year at the University of Iowa, he learned that there was a class of universities called the "Ivy League."[18] A year later, he transferred to Brown University, intent on studying political science and philosophy. But he was soon persuaded by his father to "get a skill," so after graduating magna cum laude, he went on to Harvard Medical School. Indulging his passion for the humanities, he also applied to the then-new joint MD/PhD program in medical anthropology at Harvard. "In my year, nobody else applied, so I got in," he told an interviewer.[19] There Kim met Paul Farmer.

Kim has described Farmer as "one of my heroes and my closest friend in the world."[20] In the years just before their meeting, Farmer had been working in Haitian health clinics alongside the humanitarian activist Ophelia Dahl. Farmer and Dahl, along with two others, would start a small health charity—called Partners in Health (PIH)—in 1987 with US$1 million in seed money from an American benefactor. That small charity would grow into what is now a world-renowned medical justice organization working in eleven countries with over 18,000 employees, 99 percent of whom are from the countries served.[21] Farmer invited Kim to join the fledgling charity a few months after its official start.[22]

Kim seems fond of telling stories about the high-minded gab fests he, Farmer, and Dahl had in those early start-up years. Late into the night they talked about what they were going to do with what Farmer called "their ridiculously elaborate educations"[23] and privilege, debating questions like: What was the nature of their responsibility to the world? They committed themselves to working for "the poorest, most marginalized, most outcast people and then [to] do everything we can to provide them with the best possible healthcare, education, and social protection. . . . We're going to stay and work on the losing side,"[24] said Kim.

The young Kim "wanted to make Farmer's preferential option for the poor [the duty to provide the best available health care treatments for poor people] his own life's work,"[25] wrote author Tracy Kidder, who made Farmer and Kim about as famous as anthropologists can be by writing about them in his 2003 book, *Mountains beyond Mountains*. Kidder characterized Kim as a kind of Robin to Farmer's Batman in a fight against the crime of health care inequity.

In the early days of PIH, there was a righteous verve to Farmer and Kim's crime fighting. They were can-do cowboys, bending rules in their pursuit of global health equity, a noble pursuit. Kim, Farmer, and the local PIH teams worked hard to save lives. No question. And they saved lives, because, in their view, no one else would. They stepped up, intervened, applied their considerable smarts and creativity to solving health problems in countries not their own. To this day, they have admirers all over the world.

It bears repeating that during PIH's start-up days, coincidentally, countries like Haiti, Peru, and Sierra Leone, to get loans from the World Bank and the International Monetary Fund to build infrastructure—roads, power plants, water reservoirs—had to agree to let their national economies be redesigned. Structural adjustment programs had many requirements. One of the most detrimental required that poor countries spend any monies they had in the federal treasury on paying back World Bank or IMF loans *first*. The countries were not *allowed* to spend money on health, education, or social protections first. Because poor country governments ran short on funds for basic human needs, the broadscale effect was a gap in services, including health care.

Into that gap walked nongovernmental organizations (NGOs) of all kinds—small medical charities like PIH and big ones like World Vision. Some knew what they were doing, some didn't. PIH, in my view, has done some of the best NGO work in the world. But the point is that many poor country governments' inability to provide basic human services in health, education, and social protection in poor countries *was imposed*. The World Bank (and the IMF) had a monetary *theory*—neoliberalism—about what would work best for poor country economic development, including healthcare. Forty years later the evidence is in: structural adjustment didn't work as advertised.[26] Most of those countries are still poor and healthcare *systems* have yet to be built.

So PIH arose at a time in world history when there were gaping holes in the social fabric of many poor countries and little to no healthcare infrastructure. Global leaders and lenders were encouraging governments to cobble together NGO and private sector health providers instead of meeting their health care needs with healthcare *systems*. Two very different approaches.

Farmer, Kim, and PIH responded to health crises when others did not. But their approach was often by-any-means-necessary. Some people find this commendable. But for those who hold that health sovereignty—self-determination—belongs to local governments,[27] their antics were problematic. Peruvians called them *médicos adventureros* ("adventuring doctors"),[28] and it was not exclusively meant as a compliment.

In the early years of PIH, "[n]either Paul nor Jim had a license to practice [medicine]."[29] When Peruvian authorities wouldn't let PIH doctors treat tuberculosis (TB) patients and one died, Farmer wrote an angry letter in protest. "Inappropriate behavior in a foreign doctor," Peruvian public health officials replied.[30] Kim's version of the story is that PIH was treating drug-resistant TB when the government wouldn't. A Peruvian official "threatened to kick us out of the country"[31]—as if countries have no right to regulate foreign doctors who set up shop within their borders. Farmer and Kim persisted, fighting for their right to treat people and conduct research. In Peru, they conducted unapproved research on Peruvians who they believed might have multidrug-resistant tuberculosis.[32]

At one point, Farmer and Kim owed a Boston hospital US$92,000 for TB drugs that they had "borrowed" from the hospital. "They would stop at the [hospital] pharmacy before they left for Peru and fill their briefcases with [TB] drugs. They had sweettalked various people into letting them walk away with the drugs. . . . That's their Robin Hood attitude."[33] In a film about their work, Kim packs his suitcase with dry ice to keep the drugs cool and makes a joke about customs officials assuming he was a tourist to Peru because he was Asian.[34] From their point of view, Kim and Farmer saw themselves as making good on their youthful promises of improving health disparities by using their privilege to help poor people.

But, of course, there are other, less flattering words for what Farmer and Kim did. I am far from the first to note the liberties they took during the start-up stages of PIH, the apostolic influence they cultivated, and the blind admiration they have enjoyed.[35] For Kim, tag-teaming with Farmer fortified a growing sense of personal exceptionalism. He could—and should—do things that other people literally could not.

### AN IDEA MAN WHO GETS A JOB DONE

Those early years of PIH nurtured personal characteristics in Kim that were to become professional trademarks. Kim has shown an uncommon, even ingenious ability to take lofty ideas and operationalize them. This was such a pervasive personality trait that one of Kim's strategic advisors who worked with him at Dartmouth College shared a standing joke: Kim is allowed "[o]nly one new idea per day."[36] Kim's "fondness for the new and better idea might be his salient weakness, but it sometimes served him well," Kidder wrote. "He didn't care where an idea came from."[37]

In the 1990s, it was an audacious idea to provide the best available health care treatments to the poorest people. It wasn't being done. "There are a lot of door-closers, the people who say: 'No, I don't think we can do that.' 'No, there's no funding.' 'No, that's not how we do things here,'" said Dahl, the PIH cofounder. "Jim asks the right questions and knows how to advocate and make the case."[38] Kim explained in an interview, "I just felt like, okay, that's the contribution that I usually try to make, you know, the contribution of convincing people that something that they say is impossible is, in fact, possible."[39] Kim was still at PIH when he borrowed an idea about how to get pharmaceutical companies to lower their TB drug prices, an idea that succeeded. "I really see [Kim] as the one who really did this. He just pushed and pushed and pushed. Eighty-five percent of it was [Kim]," a Dutch nonprofit lobbyist told Kidder.[40] "[Kim] really has a rigor for thinking through problems and finding pathways to solutions that no one else sees," said Dahl.[41]

Kim was only a couple of months into his three-year medical residency in infectious disease when he quit. He told Farmer he wanted to recalibrate his considerable skills to work on international policy. Operationalizing ideas—that is, selling concepts, gaining support, and convincing people to try a particular approach—is work that Kim found more satisfying than medicine. "Political work is interesting to me . . . I prefer it to taking care of patients."[42] He began shifting gears during his PIH stint in Peru. He doctored for a while but then turned to training, administration, fund-raising, and politics.

Kim seemed to love the sport of global health politics and relished networking and kingmaking. This included helping Lee Jong-wook become the director-general of the World Health Organization (2003–2006). As Kim tells it,

> One of the luckiest things that happened was my good buddy, Dr. Lee Jong-wook—he was like the only other Korean doing any global health stuff, right?—And he happened to become the head of the tuberculosis department at WHO. And so, he and I met, we became very, very good friends.
>
> And then I helped him run his campaign to be director-general of WHO. He had zero chance, by everyone's account of winning the election, but we just went crazy and did all these tricky things. We didn't cheat, we didn't cheat, but he understood the system and we made the most out of the system.
>
> You know, there was only thirty-two countries voting. Haiti was one of them and, of course, the president of Haiti was our good friend [because of Partners in Health]. Grenada, the country of Grenada was voting, and one of our good friends was the relative of the prime minister of Grenada. . . . So we put all these things together and [Lee Jong-wook] became director-general of the World Health Organization.[43]

In 2003, Kim left PIH in Peru to work for the WHO in Geneva, where he made good on another big idea—treating poor people with HIV with the best available drugs. The program he directed, "3 by 5," was the all-in-one catchphrase and goal: treat three million people for HIV by 2005. "The consensus at the time," Kim said, "was [that] it's impossible to treat those people with the drugs that we had. . . . I would say things like, okay folks, if our generation lets twenty-five million people die in Africa, even though we have the medicines, just because we think it's too complicated [and] difficult, we will forever be remembered as the generation that let Africa and African young people die, right. We will be known for that just as much as the Nazis are known for the Holocaust."[44] Kidder wrote, "[Kim] wasn't above hyperbole or dramatics" to achieve his goals, [45] an observation with a throughline to the pandemic bonds.

Convincing people that it was righteous to treat people with HIV was exhilarating for Kim. "At that moment I was never more alive. I felt like my head was on fire because there were just so many things coming at us. Over a three-year period, we really did change the world. We changed the world from a place where they were saying it's impossible, to one where we had a million people on treatment,"[46] Kim said during an interview.

But the regular day-to-day program implementation bored him. Once he felt that the 3-by-5 program was on its way, he was ready to leave. "At that moment, I thought, now I've got to go on and do something else. I mean it sounds crazy. I should have taken some victory laps. I should have taken time to enjoy that. But once I've, once we've, shown that it's possible, once everyone's convinced, that's when I sort of lose energy."[47]

The WHO gig earned Kim recognition and esteem. Kim received a MacArthur Foundation "Genius Grant" (2003); *US News and World Report* listed him as one of America's Best 25 Leaders (2005); and *Time* magazine cited him among the 100 Most Influential People in the World (2006). He left the WHO in 2006 to return to Harvard where he became the head of three departments: global health, health equity, and human rights. Fifteen years after Kim won the MacArthur grant, a former World Bank official who had worked closely with him would tell me during an interview in a quiet Washington coffee shop that it was the worst thing that could have happened to him because it confirmed what Kim had long believed: he was the smartest man in the room.

## TEETERING ON HIS PEDESTAL

Kim's early successes in global health seem to have set him thinking that he could work uncommon miracles in any field he set his sights on. Beneath Kim's impeccably polite exterior and practiced humility was a man who thought he could do anything. In 2009 while at Harvard, he was contacted about becoming the president of Dartmouth College, one of the eight elite Ivy League colleges, known for academic excellence and selective admissions.

Think of the draw for Kim: at eighteen, he hadn't even known what the "Ivy League" was, and he was being recruited to become the president of one. Kim told interviewers:

> Everything I've done is so improbable and so lucky, right. So, the guy who was the headhunter for Dartmouth interviewed me for about three hours. And after the interview he said, "Look, you have no chance at all. I think you're an interesting guy, but you have no chance of becoming president of Dartmouth. But you know, I have to go through the steps and so I'll present you."
>
> He presented me [to the Dartmouth search committee] and a banker at Morgan Stanley said, "No, no, don't throw him out. I want to meet him." They said, "Why? He's got none of the experience that you need to be president of a university." But the banker said, "He's competitive, he's got it, he takes on big problems. He's competitive and I think we need someone like that."
>
> After that, I just read everything I could find about Dartmouth. I found the most interesting things about its history, things that the search committee didn't know, right.[48]

> I said to them, "My work for my entire life has been focusing on the lives of the poorest. I don't think I can do this [job] because it feels to me like you're asking me to turn my back on the poor." And someone on the committee, in what was a brilliant recruitment technique, said, "No, no, no. We're not asking you to turn your back on the poor. We're asking you to turn the faces of Dartmouth students to the poor." And I thought, "That sounds great!" Turns out that's not really the job of the president of a university.[49]

Kim's tenure at Dartmouth was brief and tumultuous. A storied Ivy League college founded before the US Revolutionary War (1769), Dartmouth is a place where its sixteen previous presidents had stayed on average for fourteen years. Kim was there less than three. He left several initiatives unfinished. Some folks in the Dartmouth community were bitter that he left so early, accusing him of disingenuity,[50] slick talk,[51] and me-first leadership.[52] At Dartmouth, his anthropological ear-to-the-ground grew tone deaf. Concerned with the health effects of binge drinking, for example—including alcohol poisoning and sexual assault—Kim attempted to study the problem like a communicable disease. But he refused to take on the social hubs of the problem, the fraternities and sororities. The man who built his reputation on medical intervention used his anthropological background as a reason *not* to intervene. "One of the things you learn as an anthropologist," he said, "you don't come in and change the culture."[53] The Peruvian government officials who had wanted Kim out of the country would likely agree. No matter. Kim was primed for the world stage, and he soon left Dartmouth for the World Bank.

### AN INTRIGUE: KIM AT THE WORLD BANK

Kim was a controversial choice for World Bank president. A Harvard professor who worked at the Bank for seventeen years called his nomination "like picking the shortstop for the New York Yankees out of the scrub leagues."[54] Kim was widely recognized as an expert in international health, but not in international finance or development economics. A former vice president of the World Bank said, "I don't think he understands the World Bank is not a very large NGO. The work of the World Bank is to create a system so that he doesn't need to come and create a clinic in Haiti."[55]

At the time, other potential nominees were considered eminently more qualified, like Ngozi Okonjo-Iweala, a former Nigerian finance minister and World Bank official (and who currently serves as director-general of the World Trade Organization). Okonjo-Iweala had experience on both the giving and receiving end of the Bank's aid. "There is no way you can say with a straight face that this man is more qualified to head the World Bank than Ngozi," a former Bank economist said, who made a distinction between what he called Kim's charity work and the job of managing the multi-jurisdictional tasks of the World Bank. "Development is about countries becoming prosperous, democratic and capable," the economist said. "Charity work is helping people cope with the fact that they live in places where they don't have those things. . . . There's no question that Kim has done terrific things, but I wouldn't nominate Mother Teresa to head the World Bank if she were still alive."[56] The economist's comments appeared in *Forbes*, the high finance magazine, in 2012. Three years later, *Forbes* named Kim the forty-fifth most powerful person in the world.

Kim's first years at the Bank were about trying to change it. "He saw himself as a change agent at the Bank and he felt like he was bringing in ideas from the outside, which were grassroots oriented and making sure people thought about those impacts," a former World Bank official told me. Health, Kim argued, needed to be World Bank business. He brought in acolytes who said the same thing: Instead of saying, "'We don't do those things,' Jim is saying that if poor people's lives are at risk . . . then it is our business," said the Bank's health practice lead.[57]

"He had a lot of good will in the beginning," a retired World Bank official told me. But inside the Bank, the good will quickly soured. Since his days as Dartmouth College's president, he had worked with a management guru.[58] At the Bank, he enlisted several more, including Harvard Business School professor Michael Porter, and McKinsey, the global management consulting firm.[59] In the fall of 2012 McKinsey surveyed staff and provided Kim with an "organizational health index,"[60] which Kim used to chart a restructuring of the Bank. In 2013, ORC International, a marketing research company, conducted an employee engagement survey. Completed by over 12,000 of the Bank's roughly 15,000 employees, the survey revealed a 17 percent drop from 2009 in clarity about "the direction in which the WBG [World Bank Group] Senior Management is leading the institution."[61] A year later, it dropped a further 9 percent. Two years into his tenure, only 33 percent of Kim's employees thought he and his administrative team were leading them well.[62]

Kim's biggest source of internal strife was that he wanted to reform the World Bank.[63] The Bank had long been organized by geographic regions. But Kim wanted an organizational structure that moved power and money away from regional vice presidents to fourteen new "global practice" units, which included health as a newly prestigious organizational unit.[64] He wanted the Bank structured for what he and his coaches considered cross-cutting synergistic solutions. Entrenched bureaucracy, he argued, "had turned our six regional units into silos, with each one reluctant to share its technical expertise with the others."[65] Some employees were not happy with the reforms[66] and protested.[67] Others stayed quiet, worried about losing their jobs and status. Some left the Bank. "The wrong changes have been done badly," a former World Bank economist told the *Guardian*.[68]

Kim excelled at articulating the big, purposeful ideas about what the Bank should be doing, coining terms like "maximizing finance for development" and "billions to trillions."[69] But he became known within the Bank for brooking few challenges to his vision. "We're still working with mental models that hinder us from having higher aspirations," Kim said during an interview.[70] A former Bank manager told me, "What people tell me is there is a fear of speaking out and disagreeing, because there is a tone of retaliation and payback that emanates from the 12th floor [the President's office] since Dr. Kim arrived."[71] More to the point, the *Guardian* concluded that "Kim's habit of enunciating grandiose aspirations comes with a tendency toward autocracy."[72] Internal strife ran rampant. "He didn't like managing people, and day-to-day management was a big weakness. He wasn't like Wolfensohn [the ninth World Bank president] who loved getting around the Bank and talking to people," a recently retired Bank official told me, continuing, "I know he was an anthropologist, but Jim didn't really listen a whole lot at the Bank. After a while, he had his small cabinet of people internally and externally and they shut out a lot of others." Within the Bank it was understood that Kim played favorites and had a temper. Early on, he fired a bunch of upper-management folks. "It was always on people's minds that he would fire people for whatever reasons," I was told.

Kim especially had trouble with World Bank staff who accused him of behaving "like the 1%."[73] "Jim loved the Hollywood-Davos part of the job in a way that other presidents didn't," a former longtime Bank official told me, adding that Kim is a studied and polished communicator who performs well in the limelight. "He was a very mixed bag. He could be really persuasive at times, and he could be really petty at times," said Bank interviewees. "Kim created this kind of arbitrary decision making and culture of fear by firing people. So they just gave him what he wanted." "[Kim] was extraordinarily arrogant," one World Bank official told me. "When he was upset or he hadn't had enough coffee, or had a few beers, he was very frank about how he thought people were stupid or other institutions were getting in his way."

Like previous Bank presidents, Kim faced the steady drum of public calls to close the Bank, which has been ongoing for decades. But, in Kim's case, the ever-present threat of the World Bank's obsolescence seemed to galvanize him. "We could become less than the sum of our parts," Kim bemoaned.[74] At least as early as 2014, Kim admitted he knew[75] that the "World Bank risk[ed] sliding into irrelevance."[76] He recalled being at a meeting "with some of the most powerful figures in the global economy. . . . I sat there and thought, '[The Bank is] completely irrelevant to the majority of these countries. . . . [W]e are seen as just a bunch of do-gooders.'"[77]

Throughout his tenure at the Bank, Kim endured a great deal of criticism, a lot of it quite personal. Kim would spend much of his tenure at the World Bank working hard to prove that he was up to the task of leading the economic behemoth. "Finance and macroeconomics are complicated, but you can actually learn them," he was fond of asserting.[78] Still, pundits and insiders continued to question the relevance of his credentials and doubted his capacity to run the World Bank bureaucracy, which is bigger than that of some small nation-states. "Dr Kim is personable, Dr Kim is articulate, Dr Kim looks very moved by what he has to say," a former Bank manager said.[79] As his speeches and public interviews became infused with the nuances of finance, a reporter cheekily noted that Kim "used the phrase 'deals on the table' seven times in an eight-minute speech."[80] A former Bank official summed it up: "Jim moved on, he wasn't a Robin Hood character anymore."

### THROUGHLINE

With the pandemic bonds, Kim saw a throughline. He needed an exemplar—like the bonds—to show the world what a World Bank–led era of Wall Street–facing "development financing" could look like (figure 5.1). "Fast dispersing." "Rapid response." "Quick financial flow." These are the terms Kim used to sell the pandemic bonds. "The bonds were very much built around the timing of the West African Ebola outbreak. It took so long to pass the hat to get the money," one of the bonds' designers told me. "Our assignment was to get the money at a point where if we had it for Ebola, we would have had it the day President Kim wanted the money to flow, which was like August [2014] or whenever."

ANDREW MANGUM FOR THE NEW YORK TIMES

# In Wall Street's Image

Jim Yong Kim is trying to revitalize the hidebound
World Bank. By Landon Thomas Jr., Page 3.

**Figure 5.1**
Jim Yong Kim, photo by Andrew Mangum in a *New York Times* article. Photo used with permission. *Source:* Landon Thomas, "The World Bank Is Remaking Itself as a Creature of Wall Street," *New York Times*, January 25, 2018, https://www.nytimes.com/2018/01/25/business/world-bank-jim-yong-kim.html.

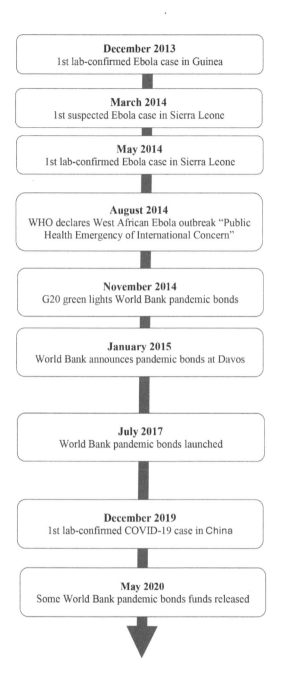

**Figure 5.2**

Timeline of the pandemic bonds relative to the Ebola 2014 and COVID-19 outbreaks. *Source:* Author.

For all his career, Kim had taken impossible ideas and pushed them through to implementation. In a speech he said, "[With] pandemic insurance, I was told fifteen times it could not happen."[81] Kim was undeterred. But, unfortunately, by 2015 he had established a management style at the Bank that inhibited his employees from even offering up sound advice. One senior official told me, "I was asked to prepare comments [about the bonds]—and I concluded things like the fact that the triggers were really complicated. And, like, why would countries buy insurance for pandemic response instead of putting that money directly to response? I sent my comments up, but my boss told me, 'You're absolutely right, this is a lemon. But it's a done deal, [Kim] wants it. That's it. Case closed. I'm not forwarding these comments to him.'"

After two years of design and about one million dollars in support costs later, Kim had himself a bond (figure 5.2). When the bond issuance officially closed, Kim, surrounded by supporters and designers of the bond, pumped his fist. Relief flashed across his face (figure 5.3). He had done it.[82]

**Figure 5.3**
Screenshot sequence of the relief on Kim's face when the pandemic bonds successfully sold from World Bank Treasury video, "Milestones in World Bank Bonds History: 1947–2017," YouTube video, October 16, 2017, https://www.youtube.com/watch?v=TAJOZEaPJoA. Copyright: The World Bank Group. All rights reserved.

## A COMPLICATED CAREER LEGACY

One thing is clear: Behind a cool and usually diplomatic exterior, Kim is a complicated man. Despite his youth-to-middle-age commitments to improve on-the-ground health outcomes, when he became World Bank president, he fought hard to save the Bank and stave off questions of its enduring anachronisms. During his tenure, he did succeed at bringing much more attention to human health at the Bank. Surprising everyone, though, he unexpectedly resigned in February 2019,[83] about a year before the COVID-19 pandemic, a historical moment that he may have been uniquely well suited for, had he roused the physician-anthropologist within.

Soon after he resigned, Kim told a *Nature* reporter, "I spent seven years at the World Bank. So I'm a finance guy."[84] Kim considered the pandemic bonds one of his three top accomplishments. In a public interview five days after his departure from the Bank, Kim said, "The question I kept asking was, 'Why do we have to wait until some country decides to be generous before responding to pandemics?' There should be something like an automatic mechanism. So we actually created pandemic insurance, and it still exists . . . and so we'll never have to sit around and wait again."[85] He was proud of the bonds.

Then, a year later, when it mattered most, the world waited—and waited—and waited—for the World Bank's pandemic bonds to trigger and pay for COVID-19 response in poor countries.

\* \* \*

As a medical anthropologist, I am not alone among my peers in having watched Kim's transformation from a global health expert to "finance guy" with more than passing interest. It's fair to say that Kim knew—as a Partners in Health lifer; a director of Harvard's global health, health equity, and human rights programs; a WHO department head; and the author of a book on the political economy of health disparities—that well-run, well-funded healthcare *systems* are fundamental to human health, especially during pandemics. As Bank president, Kim could have used his prodigious talents to incentivize, cajole, and manipulate all players to establish a worldwide network of primary healthcare systems as a first line of defense against pandemics and, in fact, all sickness and disability. He could have worked to rid the world of the "pay the Bank first" loan repayment rule to make exceptions for poor countries building healthcare systems. As president of the World Bank, Kim was in one of the top five most powerful positions in the world to figure out what configuration of public and private sector investment would reliably deliver the healthcare services that give *all* people a fighting chance to survive the next pandemic and thrive. Instead, as a signature accomplishment, the physician-anthropologist-finance guy championed a new way to make pandemic risk investable.

# 6 THE DESIGNERS: TREASURY, HEALTH, AND DEVELOPMENT FINANCE

The visitor's entrance to the World Bank's H Street headquarters in Washington, DC, is not designed to feel friendly. It's a post-9/11 "visitor management system," which funnels visitors into narrow spaces as we pass through single file, making us easier to control. Visitors must show passports and get a picture taken. In exchange, we're handed a magnetic-strip access card, good for only a few hours. A guard points us down a narrow passageway emblazoned with huge, wall-covering emerald timeline placards regaling World Bank milestones: "1947 World Bank Enters Bond Market," "1980 World Bank Group Approves First Structural Adjustment Loan," "2003 Master Derivatives Agreement Results in First Swap Transaction." Reaching turnstiles, we run our ID card through and walk into the light-filled Wolfensohn Atrium, named after a popular Bank president.

Having successfully run the twenty-minute security gauntlet, I searched for a stranger I'd never met, one of the Bank's pandemic bonds designers. Although the bonds' design involved about a hundred people from multiple industries in the United States and the world, its beating heart was in-house at three Bank units headquartered in Washington: Treasury; Health, Nutrition, and Population (which I shorten here to Health); and Development Finance. The units spoke very different languages, figuratively speaking, and didn't understand each other's expertise much. But they were team players who successfully delivered the product they were tasked to make up.[1]

## MAKING UP PANDEMIC BONDS

If you're like most people, you probably don't think much about how financial instruments get made up. But here's the thing: they must be made up. Often laboriously. The successful launch of the Bank's new pandemic bond device depended on the three units working successfully with each other, plus hundreds of hours of work by other folks from the insurance-linked security industry (discussed in chapter 7), a risk data analysis company (discussed in chapter 8), and the World Health Organization.

From the late 2014 conceptualization of the pandemic bonds to their eventual launch in mid-2017, World Bank employees from the three units held together loosely as a central designer group. Their stories are a collection of partial stories, in the way that Claire Wendland uses the word "partial":[2] each one is incomplete; each one reflects preferences; and when taken as a whole, each contributes to a fuller-ness, an abundance of information from which to gauge what happened and why.

At the top of the pandemic bonds design apparatus was Kim. "He wanted to merge financial instruments and disease response," an official told me. It was not a secret that Kim had a lot riding on them. Making up the bonds served Kim in three ways: First, the bonds could be seen as an original World Bank innovation addressing an urgent need. Second, their design would show doubters inside and outside the Bank how his organizational reform of the Bank worked. Last, the bonds—those confoundedly complicated devices—would convey to the world that Kim was truly a finance guy.

## THE DESIGN UNITS

By tasking the three units to come up with the pandemic bonds design, Kim activated the synergistic solution-making reform he was trying to implement throughout the Bank. Kim needed to show that he could, in fact, mix and match experts from different units into bespoke work pods to get important jobs done.

While Kim promoted the bonds in international financial circles, he left the bonds' design details to people in Treasury, Health, and Development

Finance, requiring them to make the thousands of decisions that brought the bonds to life. Health and Treasury had not worked together before on a catastrophe bond-type device. But Treasury had worked before with reinsurance companies and investment brokers on catastrophe bonds, and there were many ways Kim's new priority project was familiar ground. The Treasury designers knew a successful launch would depend on the device's design and pricing details. In other words, the bonds' bespoke design elements would have to entice the investors to invest.

### Treasury

The World Bank Treasury has achieved a global reputation as a prudent and innovative borrower, investor and risk manager.
—World Bank Treasury unit website[3]

In an unassuming glass building a ten-minute walk from the World Bank's Washington headquarters, over 200 World Bank Treasury employees quietly make hundreds of decisions every day that shape the global economy. From the sidewalk, a passerby would have no way of knowing World Bank Treasury business went on inside. Unmarked and outwardly unremarkable at street level, I couldn't find it at first. No one working at the deli and retail offices next door could tell me where it was either. As if it didn't exist.

I did find it, and, inside, there was none of the kettling security of the H Street headquarters. Just two guards sitting at a desk in a spacious, wood-paneled lobby, one who retrieved a day pass for me, the other who joked with me as I passed through the metal detector on my way to the elevators.

Several floors up, the Market Solutions and Structured Finance unit of the World Bank Treasury—their answer to poverty embedded in their name—makes its home in an open-plan design. Most employees had cubicle workspaces at the room's center. There were only a handful of individual offices. There was little personal privacy. Meeting rooms were glass-walled; transparency built into the floor plan, the whole suite looking like a stage set for a quintessential Wall Street film It was a workspace floor plan I saw repeated across the finance industry.

The World Bank Treasury competes with New York City Wall Street firms for employees. Recruitment videos, like one with a percussive background

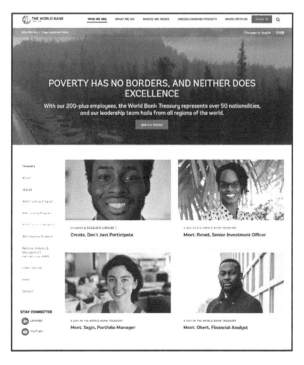

**Figure 6.1**
Screenshot from World Bank Treasury, "Create, Don't Just Participate: The World Bank Student Careers," YouTube video, August 25, 2020, https://www.youtube.com/watch?v=RdLvR0mf MPk&t=4s, accessed April 11, 2024. Used with permission.

beat and an edgy voiceover (figure 6.1), aims to appeal to young business school graduates with Ivy League educations:

> The World Bank Treasury is one of the few places where you can be on the leading edge of finance.
>
> The first currency swap? Yeah, that was us. It's now a $500 trillion market.
>
> The first green bond? We issued the world's first. Since then, over $800 billion have been done.
>
> The first blockchain bond? That was us too. And it's revolutionizing the way financial markets operate.
>
> We don't sit around and watch. We push hard to create new markets, while making existing markets more sustainable and transparent. Sounds cool, right?[4]

"Treasury was on top because nothing will move without them," one of the pandemic bonds designers told me. "Treasury led the market placement of the bonds, and they were the main interlocuters with the investors." A retired Bank employee said, "Health needed Treasury's stamp to say [the pandemic bonds] are not going to jeopardize the financial integrity of the Bank. . . . The Health people trusted that if Treasury put its seal of approval on it, then it was okay."

In Treasury, I found an unexpected humility in the people I interviewed. Some were US Ivy League–educated; all had worked for capital market firms in New York, Europe, or Asia in some capacity. As a group, they were great at multidimensional thinking. Very fun to talk with. They had a deep understanding of the bonds' mechanics. They expressed genuine compassion about on-the-ground challenges of health service delivery and data collection; they just didn't make either of those implementation concerns a priority. Developing the bonds was a long process, they said. "Extremely 'complicated' maybe makes it sound too intellectual, but it was definitely a long process of going back-and-forth trying to come up with the right balance." The "balance" was a direct reference to the challenge of building bonds that investors would buy and that also looked to Health folks like it could solve shortfalls in pandemic funding.

### Health

Building human capital starts with health.
—World Bank blog[5]


Back at the H Street headquarters, designers from the Health unit had to work hard to keep up with the basic finance elements of the pandemic bonds. Not all were successful. Even a year after the issuance of the bonds, at a World Health summit meeting, when an Oxford University economist asked one of designers for details about the bonds, they were unable to answer the questions asked, and seemed unable to make meaningful distinctions between insurance for people contracting infectious diseases and the financing of disease risk. This was in keeping with Health unit folks playing down the complexities of the bonds' design and playing up simpler analogies, like that the pandemic bonds are, as one said, "insurance against pandemics. That's all. The same way as you probably have auto insurance, house insurance, or life insurance." Well, no. Not actually."

But another Health unit designer went to great lengths to learn and understand what the Treasury folks cared about, an approach that helped the units adhere as a design group. They said, "Treasury cares about making sure that there is a right volume of investors, there is stability in investment processes, and there is a price that is attractive to investors. They're balancing three things: volume, stability, price. . . . And I'm happy that they're part of my team."

During Kim's tenure, "his personal interest in health gave Health a little more bargaining power," a retired Bank official told me. After the West African Ebola outbreak, Health wanted a pool of money standing at the ready for any future pandemic response. So did Kim. One designer told me, with a storyteller's flair for rhetorical questions and third-person narrative:

> Health wanted money early. They looked around everywhere. Who could give [them] money early?
>
> Could Health get a trust fund that they can hang onto for five hundred million dollars, or a billion dollars? No.
>
> Could Health get contingency financing? No . . .
>
> Can they get the insurance thing done? That's when Health went to Treasury. [Treasury] is a wing at the World Bank that . . . specialize[s] in matters to do with money and instruments. . . . "Can Treasury put together something for Health?"
>
> [Treasury] said, "It's never been done before."
>
> [Health] said, "Yes, it's never been done before. That doesn't mean that it *can't* be done."

One of the biggest roles the Health unit played was as the contact point between the World Bank and the World Health Organization (WHO). "All the data that we have used [for the pandemic bond triggers] come from WHO," a World Bank official said. One of the designers magnified the role of the WHO in the bonds design by analogizing, "We were living with WHO the entire time because they are the repositories of the data. I don't have the data, I get the numbers. I'm a third-party receiver of the numbers. I don't know whether it is a suspected case or a probable case or a confirmed case. I don't track that. That's not my job. It is WHO's job, so we entrusted them with that responsibility." Another designer said, "The WHO helped us work through the viruses. . . . We took all of our calculations back to WHO experts, many, many, many times and we said, "Look, this is what we are finding, we don't know what to do with it." And they said that, you know, the strong recommendation was to go with the whole family of coronavirus and same thing for Ebola. . . . So that was the guidance and understanding."

Despite our shared backgrounds in global health, my experiences with World Bank folks in the Health unit were hit and miss. On the whole, they were a pricklier bunch than Treasury, more defensive when answering questions, more uncertain about their answers, and often more evasive. One seemed especially aware of every critical pundit publicly writing or speaking about the pandemic bonds, down to the spelling of last names and gossipy things about them. One commentator had asked them for a job but didn't get it. Did I know that? they asked.

### Development Finance

Development Finance is at the vanguard of pursuing innovative approaches to tap private resources, including through the issuance of bonds on the capital markets.

—World Bank Development Finance unit website[6]

"Development Finance are the primary storytellers, always trying to raise more money," a retired Bank official told me. "They don't actually have any day-to-day responsibilities. They don't lend money to build clinics, like Health, or oversee currency benchmarks, like Treasury." Another recently retired official said, "Development Finance knows they need to go out and market the Bank. They need to say, 'We're this institution on the cutting edge. We're so innovative. We're nimble because they were connected to the market, to Wall Street.' That's the spirit they would have walked into it with. These are the results we're getting. These are the needs of the countries we're serving. [And the pandemic bonds were] kind of a unique instrument that did try to draw on the private sector," they said. "But there's no capacity in Development Finance to judge the technical design [of the pandemic bonds], there's no capacity at all. They're just in charge of having good relations with the major donors to the Bank."

In short, for the World Bank's pandemic bonds, the Development Finance unit was their spin doctor. Their job: schmooze and sell the bonds in the most favorable light. Development Finance was responsible for getting donor money lined up for the bonds—a job assignment that didn't work out as well as expected. They were also tasked with assuring that investors, donors, other bankers, and the public interpreted the bonds favorably. Again, mixed results. The bonds were clearly a tough sell. It bears repeating that at the beginning of the process to make up the bonds, around twenty wealthy country donors expressed interest in supporting them. Development Finance ginned up that interest. Donors backed out, though, as details emerged about how their money—which is typically taxpayers' money from country governments—would be used to pay private investors. In the end, the pandemic bonds ran short of the fundraising goal to raise US$ 500,000. When detailing this part of the story to me, a former World Bank official said, "The bonds are a great story about the wrong way to do this."

The Development Finance folks I met were accustomed to controlling narratives, and, during interviews, they quickly turned cagey on me. They appeared unsure about how to best respond to an anthropologist's questions, some of which, admittedly, were a bit pointed. To the person, each one had a tell (usually the eyes) as they internally processed which version of the truth they should share. In sum, my interviews with them were notable for two reasons, unusual ones in my experience. I've rarely seen interviewees spin and retract so quickly—or nimbly—when faced with counterfactuals. And despite having personally interviewed well over a thousand people for research projects, I've never had my time with interviewees shaved down so quickly when it became clear to them that my counterfactuals were likely to keep on coming. "I really must look at this text" or "take this phone call" or "pick up my children early from daycare" had never before been converted to dismissal as smoothly and efficiently as it was with World Bank Development Finance folks.

For more than two years, the pandemic bond designers convened with each other face-to-face, on the phone, and by email, hundreds of times to make up the bonds. "We went through a very large number of iterations and back-and-forth and back-and-forth because there were many, many, many moving parts," a designer said. No single unit was expert in all parts of the bond. Treasury understood the finance. Health understood health data and modeling. Development Finance focused on the wealthy country donors supporting the bond—Japan and Germany—and worked to keep them feeling generous. "[The three units] didn't understand each other's business very well, and they just kind of stuck in their lanes," said a World Bank official who reviewed the early bond design documents.

"We were all learning. It was new, unchartered territory," a bonds designer asserted, minimizing Treasury's established expertise making up earlier Bank catastrophe bonds. Still, another designer insisted, "We did it very much together, we're on every call together. We were just focused on different issues." A Bank official sketched it out this way:

> The Health guys had to tell the Treasury folks what they want to insure, because Treasury had no idea what viruses to cover, you know? Health got the WHO involved in saying how much money will be needed and at what point in an outbreak. Do we cover the flu? Do we cover corona? Do we cover Nipah? Treasury had no idea what level of cases, at what level of deaths the money should be released. Is it 250 filovirus [e.g., Ebola] deaths? How much money is needed at what point? You know, is 5 million enough? Is 10 million enough? Do you need 100 million? Health says what it wants and Treasury gives options. . . . They can say, "It's not worth it" or "Yes, we can do it, but it will be so expensive." Like when I'm building a house and I say I want to have a bathroom here and the architect says, "Sure, I can do it, but it will look awful and cost you a million dollars."

Each time they changed a design element, the investor payout probabilities changed. "Then Health had to check in again with the WHO and ask, 'Does it still make sense for you?'" said a designer. "We had to keep adding things to the bonds, like the multicountry [trigger criteria]. We originally targeted single countries and the bonds were just too expensive and nobody was going to buy them," said another designer, adding, "We would add bells and whistles to make it cheaper and then they would have to ask if it was still useful from a public health perspective. And so with that tension, it just took forever to come up with the right balance."

One of the designer units was quite modest about their role in the pandemic bonds, choosing to emphasize the teamwork involved. When I asked about leadership during the bonds' design phase, members of the other units literally said, respectively, "I am heading it up," "I parented it," and "I am the director." They obviously weren't all in charge. A retired Bank official laughed when I mentioned this and said, "It's not unusual at the Bank, like when there's something that's got a big spotlight on it, that's being hyped, that people want to take credit for it. Everyone wants to claim it as *their* innovative novelty instrument."

When one of the least conversant designers left the Bank for a new job, they initially credited themselves in their new workplace bio with "inaugurating the first-ever insurance for pandemics," solo. Other designers who left the Bank also, at first, touted the pandemic bonds as one of their career triumphs. Now, since COVID-19 broke and the bonds failed to release funds as promised, quickly and efficiently, responsibility for developing the world's first pandemic bonds has disappeared from designers' current workplace bios.

### DEATH TRIGGERS AND PUBLIC COMMUNICATIONS

"Death sounds bad," a World Bank bonds designer told me. "A lot of people told us, that's crazy, how could you ever do your insurance based on death? That's so horrible. We had to admit that we were confusing everybody with our early communication about the bonds because we couldn't say 'death,' and we couldn't say 'trigger.'" Another designer added, "We would write in all the details for the press releases . . . and our communications people would say, 'That's way too complicated. Who could understand this?'"

Early on, the World Bank communications unit circulated press releases saying the bonds' money would be released when certain thresholds were met. When a critic of the bonds argued that the Bank hadn't divulged that a potential pandemic disease had to cross borders to trigger the bonds, one of the designers thought, "That can't be true. And I went back and looked at the press release and it just says 'certain parameters,' so they were kind of right. We didn't say it had to be multicountry and we didn't say it had to be a death." "Our official response," another designer said, "was [to argue] that life insurance is one of the biggest insurance markets in the world and it triggers on death. They have good marketing, though. They call it life insurance." Another designer admitted, "We were partly to blame. A lot of people that told us, 'That's crazy, how could you ever do the instrument based on death?' And, yeah, that sounds bad, right? But, come on, we're only insuring bad things."

"Our [World Bank] communications people [also] said trigger sounds like a gun, so that's not good," said a designer, adding, "So we had to come up with a new word: 'activation criteria.' And then the insurance [ILS] people looked at it and said, 'What is this, like this is something before the trigger that has to be met?' That confused the reinsurance people and investors because in their market you always have a trigger. Triggers in that business are what prompt payouts when investors lose money."

World Bank Communications officers told the designers it was best not to even name the diseases covered—coronavirus, filovirus, flu, Crimean Congo hemorrhagic fever, Rift Valley fever, or Lassa fever. They were directed to say "certain pathogens." One of the designers complained, "I went back and read the press release and it was so sterilized. . . . By trying to be so PC [politically correct], not saying 'trigger' or not to shock people by saying 'deaths,' you know, or not to confuse people by talking about coronavirus. I think that was just silly," they mused, reflecting on all the unfortunate communication missteps, adding, "Coronavirus! Ha! We all know what that is now."


## IN THE END, A FINANCIAL DEVICE

What the people in the three Bank units pulled together—conceptualizing the bonds' mechanics, coordinating hundreds of people's efforts, and coaxing investors to buy a new device—was, by the sheer dint of the labor and smarts involved, remarkable. They got the bonds' mechanics to *function*.

In many ways, though, the design process was conventional, old school World Bank. Sierra Leoneans, Liberians, and Guineans were projected only as the intended recipients of a pandemic payout, never as bond investors. West Africans were not consulted in the making of the bonds at all. The making up of the bonds even sidestepped the Bank's own regional expertise in West Africa. A Bank official with decades of experience there told me that they were asked late in the process to do a read-through of the design, and they knew that data for the triggers would be an issue, "I didn't see the data systems in place." "Never mind" was the response.

Having worked professionally in several global affairs agencies, I can say that when I'm walking the halls, the World Bank feels different from all of them. The Bank has a deep bench of talented staff. Lots of money, making for lots of prestige. It feels jazzier, certainly, than government agencies. And jazz is a useful analogy for the pandemic bonds' collaboration within and between the three units and with the other designer folks they brought in. The bonds' creation was improvised, iterative, reactive. Lots of beats going at the same time. No one knew where those beats would land. The threat of a bad set loomed, just like in a jazz riff when the pianist can't keep up with the percussion, or the saxophonist pinches the reed, or the bassist is too drunk to make it through a chord progression. A World Bank designer told me they were thrilled when the bonds drew the "right" kind of attention from the "right" people. They had worked hard to make pandemic risk investable. In July 2017 at the bonds' launch, it appeared to them that they had gotten the pandemic bonds right.

# BACK STAGE

What kind of magic trick is it to take this thing—risk—which is real but also an idea, an anticipation, a danger—and quantify it? How does the fear of a terrible future thing happening get translated for a financial device? What transforms bodily infectious disease risk into something that can be enumerated? Priced? Sold? How do the hacking and fatigue symptoms of COVID-19, the messy leaky-body effects of Ebola, and the sheet-drenching fevers of other Marburg viruses become a number, tidied up and datafied into neat analyzable bits, suitable for investors to use to decide if they wanted to risk losing their money?

The insurance-linked securities industry and a catastrophe modeling group performed this metamorphosis for the World Bank's pandemic bonds. And the data—those bits that determined the fates of millions? That's a different kind of behind-the-scenes storytelling, with no shortage of mud, sweat, and tears.

# 7 RISK BUSINESS: INSURANCE-LINKED SECURITIES

As the puzzle pieces of my research on the pandemic bonds began falling into place, the role of insurance-linked securities (ILS) emerged as an element I could not ignore. (I tried.) The problem was that I had no idea what ILS was. Hadn't known the industry existed. Knew no one in the industry. Zilch. How would I even study it? Googling around in the summer of 2017, I learned of an international reinsurer's conference in Baden-Baden, Germany. By that point, I had learned enough to know that ILS grew out of the reinsurance industry in the mid-1990s, as insurers tried to deepen and diversify their portfolios so they wouldn't run out of money when big weather events hit. I know Germany well, did my PhD research there, and speak some German. Off I went.

Every autumn, for about fifty years now, 2,000-odd reinsurers take over the German town known for its curative hot spring spas, and a picturesque stone canal graced with impeccably pruned ivy, with white swans so big I wondered about steroids in the water. In the town typically thick with tourists, for four days each year, serious-faced, mostly white businessmen (5 to 1, men to women) rush around in dark suits and Oxford brogues, conferencing in buildings along the canal. By night, it's a Bavarian junket where the boldest among them join in stays-in-Vegas frivolities. In a local café, I overheard a group from a Toronto company bragging about staying out until 5:00 a.m. but triumphantly making it to their 9:00 a.m. meeting. They reminded me of my high school friends who were model students 360 days a year but lived to let loose for that one week at band camp.

**Figure 7.1**

The first hours at the conference venue, I had no idea what was going on. There was no conference schedule, no expert panels, and no nametags. It felt like being in a village that doesn't have street signs because everyone there already knows where everything is. Official conference registration proved useful for only one thing: getting an online directory of other attendees' contact information. The conference was just a series of appointments. Who knew? Obviously, all the other attendees.

In the big, boxy, glass Kongresshaus (convention hall), on four huge, cavernous levels with floor-to-ceiling windows, hundreds of reinsurers met each other at numbered tables three to eight feet apart, two to six people per table. As they settled into their chairs, they placed their business cards in front of them like totemic offerings. The "conference" was these thirty-minute meetings, like a variation of speed dating, pre-scheduled by the conference-goers themselves, one right after the other. There was a class structure to the conference: the corporate presidents and vice presidents weren't in the Kongresshaus. In bespoke Italian silk suits, they conduct their deal-making in the posh five-star hotels along the swan-filled canal, entertaining each other with top-shelf liquor and caviar.

Everyone was there to either enliven business relationships that already worked well or to sort prospective collegial kernel from undesirable chaff. They vetted each other unapologetically. "It's all about trust," two reinsurers from Tbilisi, Georgia, told me as we traveled together on the public bus from our hotel to the Kongresshaus. "We need to trust people to do insurance. We want to look across the table and see what's in someone's face." "The industry is mired in legacy," a thirty-something reinsurer told me, "which a lot of people put down to using relationships instead of technology. People are still trying to do business in the same way they have for 100 years."

Not knowing any of this, I had scheduled only two appointments. But my luck turned late in the first day when I met an insurance executive (described in my "Author's Note") who introduced me to some folks, who introduced me to others, one of whom was a reinsurance executive who had worked with the World Bank on the pandemic bonds design. I was in the right place.

### MAKING RISK INVESTABLE

*(If you skipped chapter 2's detailed explanation of the bonds' mechanics, now may be a good time to go back and read about them. With more pieces in place, the details will likely make more sense.)*

For millennia, humans have tried to come up with ways to ensure that life's tragedies don't devastate them for the rest of their lives. Insurance has been around in recognizable form for over 4,000 years. *Re*insurance—providing insurance for insurance companies concerned their businesses could be wiped out by a major claims event—has been around since the 1800s. Alternative risk transfer (ART)—the category of the global insurance industry that ILS falls into—emerged in the 1970s as a way for investors to provide an extra layer of financial protection—through additional diversification—for extreme weather and mortality events that threatened to bring down whole companies. ART instruments are designed to pool financial assets from investment vehicles like hedge funds and pensions, getting their money managers to gamble on securitized risks.[1] ILS, which started up in the mid-1990s, gassed up short-term, high-yield risk investment as a response to what pioneer ILS-ers considered the slow, stodgy way insurance was done. "We were looking at how the insurance industry was made and where the capital came from, seeing if we could identify opportunities to make transactions work more effectively and efficiently," a prominent ILS expert told me. What do you mean by efficiency? I asked. Lower operating costs, cheaper borrowing. A loan might cost 3 or 4 percent, "but I might be able to pay investors less than that depending on the risk they're covering," they said. "We didn't start out thinking that ILS was going to help governments or do humanitarian aid, like it does now. At first, it was really just a case of the insurance industry finding more efficient ways to source the costs of doing business."

New "efficiency features" regularly get introduced in ILS and written into contracts. Parametrics, like the death trigger measure in the pandemic bonds, were hugely popular in the early aughts, years when indemnity-based triggers declined.[2] "I'm really big on pushing the tech, like using satellites," one ILS consultant told me. "We've seen crop insurance in Ethiopia that pays out based on how green the earth is because it's moisture related. [People] are looking at wildfire and burn scars, so payout would be based on that." Another told me, "A CEO might want these new sensor sticks that attach to a factory wall. They get a payout when flood waters hit a certain level." Right now, indemnity is more popular again because "people in the industry have figured out that parametrics are really good when a company needs fast cash but not so good at matching with, like, property loss. A chief financial officer is going to be very aware that when a big hurricane happens, they're going to take a massive hit and need capital quite quickly to pay claims and things, and ILS will be a $100 million layer that pays out."

Early on, my biggest mental stumbling block was in assuming that the pandemic bonds were for some *thing*. Hospital facilities? An economy? Sick human bodies? No. Insurance-linked securities investors speculate on risk itself. ILS doesn't trade in things or commodities; its investors buy risk. It bears repeating that the pandemic bonds covered the *risk* that a pandemic would happen. The draw for investors is the quid pro quo: if ILS investors are willing to hold the risk of something terrible happening for a period of time, they have the chance to make significant returns. Like with the World Bank's Class B pandemic bond: if COVID-19 hadn't triggered the bond, those investors would have earned a 40 percent return on their principal investment over the three-year life of the bond (see chapter 2 for details).

ILS is a small but booming market industry, a US$170 billion offshoot[3] of the US$5 trillion global insurance industry. Its products have grown in popularity because their contractual details are tied to modeled probabilities, like those of the pandemic bonds, rather than large-scale "exposures" where monetary gain lies in the profit margins between what people paid in premiums before their houses *did* burn down and all the other people who also paid for coverage just in case. ILS gives investors a different set of conditions for making money (and losing it), an attractive diversification feature. ILS gains and losses are very specific: investors make (or lose) money by speculating on specific variables of a specific catastrophe, like where and when and at what intensity a catastrophe will happen in the future. "Underlying it all are contracts, just like in regular insurance," an ILS expert said. Long before the pandemic bonds, ILS was busy standardizing the investability of risk.

### FINDING ILS

*February 2020, New York City, midtown Manhattan*: In a part of the city where some addresses take up entire blocks, I, again, cannot find the venue to save my life. The hour I'd planned to hang out before the ILS conference started whittles to forty-five minutes, then thirty. I hurry past so many huge, empty, big-windowed lobbies that I wonder if wasting space is a design feature meant to convey that building owners are so rich they can afford to use prime real estate for nothing. Unhoused people sleep against their parapets.

Then, tucked off Sixth Avenue, on a side street that looked more like an alley, I notice several men dressed like *Matrix* movie extras—identical to the Bavarian spa town conference-goers—converging on a single door entrance between a wobbling tower of construction scaffolding and a rolldown metal garage door. Forget my phone and Google Maps. I followed the people.

With its skinny little lobby and narrow hallway leading to an up escalator, the conference site entrance was spot-on staging for an understated industry. I made my way to registration. Exhibitors rimmed the hall periphery, with fine faux leather notebooks, pen sets, and other swag on offer in exchange for conversation, which was research access made in heaven. FinTech, the acronym for the twenty-first-century technology companies supporting the finance industry, was well represented. I heard a few product spiels and started my conference listening tour.

Nerd that I am, I found the small, boutiquey Wall Street industry kind of enthralling, in a gotta-say-that's-very-clever way. And I liked the insurance-linked security folks I met, a mix of dedicated cat bond investors, pension plan executives, asset fund managers, brokers, and data modelers. Only a few were bombastic. Most seemed like me, quietly nerdy about the thing at the center of our work lives—for me, health, and for them, risk. To them, risk is a vibrant, dynamic, alive thing that needs to be tamed, channeled, and priced for sale.

Before studying the pandemic bonds, I spent years working in government thinking a lot about public management of the terrible big-ticket events that happen to humans. But I had not thought much about how the private sector manages the risk and the uncertainties of life behind the scenes. So I had a lot to learn. Over the last twenty-five years, ILS has created opportunities for private investor money to cover all kinds of risks on the assumption that if investors are willing to pay the premium, insurance contracts can be made up for just about everything. A World Bank designer told me, "In our discussions with the insurance industry, folks at every step of the way told us one thing: Everything can be insured," although the price may be high. This isn't entirely correct because, as I show in chapters 8 and 9, insurance needs data. But it is true that *a lot* different kinds of things *can* be insured, everything from body parts to mustaches.

ILS is the next gear you didn't know your car engine had. Where else do "terrorism," and the "World Cup" get brought together under an SPV (special purpose financial vehicle), as they were in 2006 when FIFA (Fédération Internationale de Football Association), the world soccer-governing body, got US$260 million worth of coverage against the risk of a terrorist event causing game cancellation in Germany?[4]

## THE WORLD BANK NEEDED ILS EXPERTISE

In the fall of 2014, when Kim started his hunt for a financial tool that might provide pre-pooled funds for future pandemics, the World Bank Treasury folks entered those conversations with some recent ILS experiences top of mind. A few months earlier, the Bank's Treasury had issued its first catastrophe bond, the Caribbean Catastrophe Risk Insurance Facility (CCRIF), which covered tropical cyclone and earthquake risks in sixteen Caribbean countries.[5] For almost a decade before that, the Bank's Treasury unit had been a behind-the-scenes promotor, though not issuer, of cat bonds, bringing people together, to make bonds shaped to particular needs.

Jim Yong Kim was eager to change the way money for pandemics had been pledged and pooled for decades. Usually, after an outbreak begins, lots of countries and organizations pledge aid; fewer than half follow through.[6] Insurance-linked securities folks like to say that ILS instruments shorten the distance between risk and money, which was what Kim was looking for. His grand ambitions for the pandemic bonds were not a secret. An insurance-linked securities expert told me, "As I understand, the pandemic bonds were a passion project for the head of the World Bank who really wanted to develop them."

"All we were trying to do is expand the pool capital for them," an ILS expert said. "Our job was to help the World Bank, and all the constituency that was involved, and do what is executable. In ILS, when you're not careful, you can spend years developing something that nobody will buy. Or you could buy something that the markets love, but it is not useful."

Behind Kim's public speeches about the bonds, in 2015 and 2016, details about the bonds' structure began to emerge in dribs and drabs to the broader ILS community and other industries via off-the-record quotes (and leaks) to journalists. The structure seemed likely to be able to tap the never-before-used source of private investor funding for pandemic response, and included the news that two major reinsurance companies had helped design and structure the bonds. One of the World Bank designers told me, with no shortage of self-congratulatory bravado, that "What the World Bank did was invite some of the largest [reinsurance] companies in the world: Swiss

Re, Munich Re, Gen Re, many others, and [two] showed interest. We said, 'Okay.' And then we worked out a deal with them, that this is how we shall develop this, and this is how you come into play." (When the bonds were launched and investors began lining up to buy them, both designer reinsurance companies queued up to invest. It's unclear from public documents if their investments were made in the bonds or in the swaps. One company reneged as the prices tightened, but the other did indeed become an investor. Conflict of interest flags were never formally raised, but in my interviews, I heard whisper campaigns about the inappropriateness of the reinsurer investing in a public health device with triggers they helped design.)

### PRICING THE FUTURE

Pricing ILS instruments depends on the technology available to do the work. In the 1990s, as more data became more available across the globe, insurance risk assessment—understanding the odds of losing money—grew less stochastic and more complex and consummate, requiring highly specialized computer data expertise. Risk modeling firms rose (like one I call ModelRisk in the next chapter), developing computer-based modeling to organize and crunch data specifically for the reinsurance industry. FinTech (financial technology) was born, and has become an essential element of the ILS industry, which prides itself on that fact.

Reinsurance companies and ILS use FinTech for forecast modeling and pricing, which is why the World Bank needed to hire a modeling firm when they started making up the pandemic bonds. They needed *future* probabilities. "For us to get the right insurance thing, we needed a lot more than just a number . . . we cannot be simply modeling the disease that has already happened," a Bank official told me, which is what the WHO generally does. Without the futures modeling, the Bank wouldn't have been able to the establish the threshold triggers or price and sell the bonds or. "It's a chicken-egg problem. If you don't have a model somewhere, you don't know what the [future] risk is, you cannot really put a price tag on it," a designer told me. ILS FinTech enabled the Bank to "put a price tag on [future] infectious disease risk," a reinsurance specialist reiterated.

Regular public health epidemiological modeling wasn't good enough. "I'm not at all plugged into the public health world," an ILS expert told me. "But I haven't gotten the perception that there's a lot of ex ante [before the event] modeling of risk going on. No one seems to be modeling the frequency of [infectious disease] events actually occurring in a given country, in a given year, and what's the probability of actually getting into an event that has five thousand cases or whatever." "[Pandemic] risk transfer clearly encourages ex-ante response plans. If anything, COVID-19 reveals that the world could use such plans," a reinsurance specialist argued.[7]

More than that, though, FinTech in ILS gave investors a high enough level of trust in the Bank's bonds to put their money in on them. Before the bonds went on sale, the investors told me they vetted the Bank. They needed to know if the Bank knew what it was doing in the ILS space. Was it able to properly price pandemic risk? Was it using sophisticated enough tools? The World Bank bonds' designers saw this too: "[Investors] are not interested in the probability of a payout only. They are also interested that there's a probability that they will lose everything. All of those things had been taken into account, in designing how we calibrate when the data is reported, how we calculate the moving averages, how we calculate the growth rate," said one designer.

"The World Bank has been instrumental in helping countries tap our market," an ILS executive said. "But we've helped them too. ILS effectively converts the global bond market into the largest de facto insurance company ever seen, . . . significantly reduc[ing] the burden of catastrophe costs on taxpayers [which] helps accelerate resilient recovery in times of disaster."

### AGAIN, RISK CARVED OFF FROM RESPONSIBILITY

While I found the machinations of the ILS industry intellectually fascinating and its people great fun to talk with, I cannot get beyond a fundamental conundrum of their involvement with pandemic response problem-solving. When it comes to pandemic response, something important is missing. A data analyst told me, "You can have something mundane in the real world and somehow, if it were to meet all the contract terms, you can set up a payout. Alternatively, something could be severely bad in the real world, but it just doesn't make it into the contract," meaning that investors just won't agree to the terms, *no matter how severe the threat to humans*. And there it is: Some severe human health threats cannot be made investable. We will face catastrophes anyway, but the private sector is not obliged to plan for, provide, or organize or to implement our survival.

In this small, specialized industry, with its exceptionally good mathematics and clever tools, the industry's end point is about generating money; ILS doesn't *do* response or global health implementation. It's simply not what the ILS industry does. Neither its people nor its investors need to care about creating and sustaining health systems as frontline deterrents to pandemic contagion. They're risk experts who are, as a group, exceptionally deft at packaging and selling risk. ILS has no interest—or obligation—to implement Paul Farmer's clinical care mantra of "staff, stuff, space, and systems" when health risk meets reality. Responsibility for improved health outcomes? The actual hard work of pandemic disease care? Of building care systems? For all its strengths and food-for-thought provocations about transferring risk, ILS doesn't hold the hardest risk portfolios; the public sector does, no matter the severity.

# 8   MODELING RISKS

In the pub of a five-star hotel in that bucolic Bavarian town with the giant swans, I met a three-man team from a firm I'm calling ModelRisk,[1] which had been hired by the World Bank to do the data modeling and investor analytics for the pandemic bonds. ModelRisk had been modeling catastrophes since its founding in 1987, using historical data to predict the chances and timing of future catastrophic events. Early on, ModelRisk used government weather data to model the likelihoods of hurricanes. Then they began modeling earthquakes. Around 2009, one of ModelRisk's Yale-trained senior epidemiologists took a serious interest in modeling infectious disease. In the financial scheme of things, ModelRisk's timing was excellent. By 2012, ModelRisk was advertising the strength of their new model's ability to estimate "excess mortality," that is, the difference between the number of people who usually die in a given place in a year and the additional number who would die from a seasonal disease. They wanted to sell their analytics to insurance and reinsurance companies who were creating new devices to hedge their risks of bankruptcy-threatening payouts.

With mouth-watering Bavarian *Flammkuchen* served to tables around us, the three risk modelers from ModelRisk tag-teamed their thirty-minute presentation for me, all the while not quite sure what an anthropologist was or why I was doing research on their industry. I tried explaining until one of them interrupted: "Basically you're trying to find out what different types of approaches there are to modeling those infections and how they can, in the end, potentially be used to foster pandemic bonds . . . did I get it right?"

**Figure 8.1**

Yeah, pretty much. They made clear that they had not personally modeled the World Bank pandemic bonds, but they knew the folks in Boston who did. Did I want to meet them?

## OFF TO BOSTON

It was spring and Boston was resplendent in full, fragrant flower. I found ModelRisk's brownstone headquarters within walking distance of the Boston Commons, the Boston Public Library, and where I stayed on Newbury Street. ModelRisk leased office space in one of Boston's priciest zip codes and had neighbors like Bain & Company, the private equity firm. The building was Class A rated, real estate lingo for newer construction in a "good" part of town, with friendly concierge service in the ground-floor lobby, and gated underground parking. It was that kind of neighborhood.

ModelRisk's reception area was vast and empty but not in the way that other companies use space to communicate that they can afford to waste real estate. It was bare like they were boxing up and about to move shop (which, as it turned out, they were). A handful of plaques and statuary remained on two windowsills, which, on closer look, included some participation awards and three of the same trophy monumentalizing when *Forbes* named

ModelRisk to its top twenty "World's Most Innovative Companies" list. I wondered if there were hundreds more in a closet somewhere. Flipping through ModelRisk's annual report lying on the coffee table, I found a full-page spread with the *Forbes* honorific again, noting that they won it the same year that Tesla, Netflix, and Amazon did.

## MODELING THE ODDS

Two ModelRisk modelers glided into the waiting room to collect me. They were thirty-somethings, casually dressed, and friendly. They made an impressive team, one seriously competent epidemiological scientist, the other a gifted actuary-cum-salesperson, a Great Explainer, who handled hardball questions with impressive diplomacy. From the outset, playful back-and-forth animated our conversation, which lasted all morning and into the afternoon. They were fun to talk with, and impossible for me not to like. They saw themselves as a part of a company that built its reputation by predicting average and potential losses from catastrophes, applying old data to new problems, creatively fitting modeling technique to problem, usually for clients who needed risk models for catastrophe bonds.

The three of us made our way through a huge room full of cubicle workspaces bursting with employees. ModelRisk holds the largest share of catastrophe risk modeling business in the insurance-linked securities industry. A World Bank designer told me that in 2015, "we went far and wide looking for somebody who could help us do the calculations. We spent three months hiring. [ModelRisk] bid, as did many, many, many others. There were three companies that made it to the last round. [ModelRisk] won our contract."

Long before the World Bank hired them, they had a huge customer base. Still, the ModelRisk modelers were demonstratively thrilled that the World Bank accepted their bid. They spoke about their hopes for getting future high-profile humanitarian aid contract work as well. "It takes a lot of resources to develop a model," they said. The expertise they'd gained developing the pandemic risk model, they knew, had applications for other potential customers. Much later, as our meeting stretched into the afternoon, when

I asked them why they agreed to meet with me, they said they were always looking for new clients. Perhaps my book would bring them new customers, one said, laughing, "Always on the lookout."

The modelers made a point of telling me about their impartiality. "If you have both parties—the Bank trying to give investor money away and the investors trying to maximize theirs—upset with you over the model, that's at least some validation that you're doing something right," one of the modelers joked. Small print in that 386-page World Bank bonds' prospectus spelled out their impartiality in more legalistic terms: "[ModelRisk] does not represent investors or their interests in any way . . . [it] does not sponsor, endorse, offer, sell or promote the [bonds], nor does it make any representation or warranty express or implied, to any person regarding the advisability of investing in the [bonds]."[2] This, along with twenty-eight other disclaimers.

> **ModelRisk Boston (MRBo):** From a modeling standpoint, what I can say is that we really do our best to build our models based on the evidence and science, [with no] favor of any party.
>
> **Author:** That's the reputation that you have.
>
> **MRBo:** Yeah, we try to get as much data as there is out there, as much data as we can extract and then build models based on that, not anything else. We don't wake up and then come up with some numbers. We just try to find the best values that are representative of the real world.
>
> I can definitely say [that] a lot of our clients say neither yay or nay about what's going on. They're hyper-focused on us building the best model possible. They'll ask questions but it's not asking necessarily about right or wrong. . . . They just want more detail on X or they want more expansion on Y, okay, [so then our team] works in that avenue [and] tries to do the best we can.

A whopping sixty-three pages of the World Bank's prospectus for the bonds are devoted to explaining ModelRisk's modeling,[3] amid all the other legal, financial, and defining terms of the bonds. The Bank hired ModelRisk to build mathematical models that would give private investors two very important pieces of information: What were the chances (1) that a pandemic would occur that (2) would cause them to lose their money. For the first, it modeled the likelihood of the six infectious diseases covered by the bonds becoming pandemics using simple yes-no-how-many variables, such as: Had the people affected experienced the disease before? Did the country have primary healthcare? How many doctors? Hospital beds? Did it have diagnostic, treatment, and disease mitigation technologies? Once a disease started to spread, did the country have the capacity to contain it? Or would it spread in a way that would meet the triggers?

ModelRisk was also the bonds' "third-party Event Calculation Agent," to use the World Bank's term. The Bank needed the optics that an external arbiter would determine the fate of millions of dollars. Someone outside the Bank needed to run the WHO health data and calculate if and exactly when each of the bonds' trigger criteria was fairly met. In short, by running the numbers, ModelRisk determined whether the pandemic bonds money got triggered for pandemic aid, or if the investors would get their principal back. A pivotal role, once COVID-19 broke.

### WHO'S ROLE

The World Bank needed the WHO brand. Investors who knew little about global health or on-the-ground health data collection learned from the Bank that there is an international health organization, a part of the United Nations, responsible for the world's health data. They told me they were reassured: WHO checked all their boxes as a legitimate, trustworthy, official global health data agency. "An investor looks at an organization like the World Health Organization and says, 'Okay, that's a credible institution, I can go by their data,'" one said.

Although I can think of one Bank designer who would surely argue the point with me, the World Health Organization's biggest contribution to the bonds was as a brand name provider of data, not a day-to-day operations or design partner. Most Bank folks didn't seem to mind the confusing optics; a few even nurtured it. Bonds' sales benefited from the appearance of two global institutional behemoths joined together, legitimizing the bonds as a mega-institution-backed innovation that would backstop major pandemic financing challenges.

Besides the branding, the WHO helped in three other ways: as a consultant, as a provider of old epidemiological data, and as a provider of new pandemic disease incidence data. There were face-to-face consultations between the World Bank's Health unit and the WHO, one designer joking they should have bought an apartment in Geneva, for all the time they spent there during the bonds' design. But when it came time to do the heavy lifting to model the risk that investors would lose their money, the WHO doesn't do that kind of work. ModelRisk does. And for the future risk modeling, they didn't use WHO data exclusively (see table 8.1). "The WHO is one of a large parcel of groups of data that are super trusted. . . . They provide tons of data, they provide outbreak information, they provide how many cases, how many deaths, just assessments of what's going on. . . . But I just want to say for the modeling, when we're building risk parameters, the WHO, CDC, university epidemiologists, HealthMap, Pro-Med, our modeling used

**Table 8.1**

Major data sources for modeling the World Bank pandemic bonds

| Source | Description |
| --- | --- |
| OAG Aviation Worldwide | Passenger origin and destination statistics |
| UN Population Division | Trends in international migrants by destination and origin |
| US Census | Daily commuter rate statistics and demographic information for the United States |
| UN Food and Agriculture Organization | Global gridded density of domestic poultry and pig populations (~5 km) |
| LandScan | Global human gridded population (~1 km) |
| World Bank | Geographic distribution of age/sex cohorts and GDP |
| World Health Organization | Geographic distribution of hospital beds and physicians per capita |
| Global Register of Migration Species | Migratory waterfowl population data |
| Global Cover | Land use/land cover data |
| UN FAO Emergency Prevention System for Animal Health | Reported cases of influenza in wild birds, domestic birds, and swine |
| Scientific literature | Epidemiological and biological research on the dynamics, disease spread, and governing parameters (e.g., transmissibility, virulence), historical impact, mitigation impact, temporal data sets, and other characteristics of the relevant pathogens |

*Source:* World Bank, *Prospectus Supplement*, June 28, 2017, I-4, https://thedocs.worldbank.org/en/doc/f355aa56988e258a350942240872e3c5-0240012017/original/PEF-Final-Prospectus-PEF.pdf. See figure A.1 in the appendix.

data sets from all of them." In short, the WHO was one of many sources of health data ModelRisk used to model the risk that investors would lose their money. That said, it was the only data source used at the later stages, during the pandemic when ModelRisk, as the World Bank's third-party calculation agent, checked WHO data against the bonds' triggers to see if they were met and the bonds' money would be released.

It's the modeling that reveals how the WHO's role in the pandemic bonds was circumscribed. As almost any public health professional can tell you, there is some futures modeling done in public health, but here's the difference: public health usually looks back; ILS models look forward. Public health usually models past disease incidence and prevalence; ILS uses past data to model future risk many years out. When epidemiologists have tried to do more forecasting, there have been some very public failures. When public health epidemiologists at the CDC attempted to predict how quickly Ebola would escalate in West Africa in 2014, their 1.4 million death estimate was off by over 1.3 million deaths,[4] subjecting them to public derision.[5] Studies have shown that epidemiological forecasts for "less than 2 months into the future tended to be more accurate than those made for more than 10 weeks into the future."[6] In other words, typical public health modeling was inadequate for projecting the likelihood of infectious disease outbreaks throughout the three-year duration of the bonds, and certainly not to the satisfaction of investors.

But the WHO was out of its depths with the pandemic bonds' mechanics for another reason: the granular focus of the World Bank pandemic bonds was not on the future health risks to humans in the case of a pandemic, but on the future financial risk that investors would lose their money.

## A MODEL OF MODELS

*(If you skipped chapter 2's explanation of the bonds' mechanics, now may be an especially good time to go back.)*

What did ModelRisk *do* with data? As a friend characterized the process to me once, "Data go into a supercomputer, and while in there, the computer does a magic thing using a secret sauce that some people call an algorithm, and, change-o-presto, risk gets priced!" Yeah, pretty much.

ModelRisk's pandemic risk Model was a model of models, meaning that smaller sets of equations were run in a particular order and later combined. (I'll use Model with an uppercase "M" to denote ModelRisk's master Model and a lower case "m" for the submodels.) ModelRisk's proprietary algorithmic equations shape each model, and then use others to mathematically tie the sub-models together. For example, for each of the bonds' six covered viruses, the Model included sub-models of virulence, transmissibility, countermeasures, and contagiousness over space and time specific to the individual disease. ModelRisk simulated the beginning of an outbreak for each of the six viruses covered by the bonds. They also had short- and long-range models meant to represent both viral containments and spreads over time. They developed models to show where people in over 200 countries were expected to die, become disabled, or survive. "[ModelRisk] subsegmented the risk of the individual pathogens to a much more granular geographic profile than the old epidemiological models," a reinsurer told me.

In both Bavaria and Boston, ModelRisk folks told me that modeling pandemics before they happen is just plain hard.

> **ModelRisk Bavaria (MRBa):** It's not that easy, right? Transmission rates should be a factor, right? And human to human transmission. Case fatality rates link to travel patterns, so is the country where it spread connected to other countries? How are they connected with flights? How frequently do they fly? Is it transmitted by ship? And so on. So we have all this aviation and shipping data for a lot of countries. Also, when it comes to the US, we also have the inland flights within the US, so we can take this into account. The time until active containment, the transmission rate, and vaccination production. Hospital beds and also how the doctors are protected against it in the hospital, so that's also an important factor. I think Sierra Leone would not be the best, they would not get the best rating. We have the aviation data, population division, from US Census [and] we get a lot of data regarding commuter rate, so the daily basis and also seasonality are important to take into account.
>
> **Author:** Is this exhaustive? It's not exhaustive . . .
>
> **MRBa:** I think it's not.

One ModelRisk modeler in Boston described how ModelRisk worked to give the Bank what it wanted:

> We had to give [the World Bank] quantifiable risk against a lot of different assessments. When they asked a question, we might provide just that one: "Oh, you asked about A, here's the risk." Or we might do a few different things and say, "Here's a few options based on what you said." Or they might sometimes just say, "Before we do A and B, have at it and figure something out for us," and then we'll come up with an option, and then they'll look at it and then be like, "We wanted to do some more around this stuff," then you do that kind of stuff. It was a back-and-forth process.

### Running the Numbers

With the data ModelRisk had, one of the first things they did was run a Monte Carlo simulation, named after the well-known European casino town because "the element of chance is core to the modeling approach, similar to a game of roulette."[7] It's a mathematical technique run on a computer that generates the possible outcomes of an uncertain event, using the law of large numbers (a theorem of the average of many trials becoming more accurate as more trials are run). ModelRisk generated over one million simulations of the six diseases covered by the bonds from reportedly over 175 sources in total, as one of the modelers told me. "We do 500,000 years [of probabilistic modeling] because we want to consider all the feasibilities [for a] whole calendar year. . . . It's the same thing as if I roll the die 500,000 times. You'd have lots of outcomes of that. You can run the probabilities many, many, many times until you see convergence [patterns in the results]. That's why we selected 500,000 times to be able to figure out what might happen, based on the historical data."

### What's Left Out

Despite the massive volume of enumerative data ModelRisk's Model aggregated, there was a serious data omission that the modelers could not figure out how to include: narrative, qualitative data, like the kind I collect as an anthropologist. In Bavaria, the ModelRisk team briefly showed me the PowerPoint slide (figure 8.2) they were using to explain to Bank folks what they were doing.

# Major Variables Included in the [ModelRisk] Pandemic Model

| | |
|---|---|
| Start Location | The location of the first case whose model assumptions were based on past experience and exposure to zoonotic reservoirs. |
| Transmission Rate | Expected rate of new cases per case at time t=0. Modeled using binominal distribution and varies based on seasonality and country latitude. Effective rate of transmission is impacted by the number of susceptible people in the population. |
| Case Fatality Rate (CFR) | Provides the estimated rate of death per case. CFR is event and country specific (ex. Industrialized vs. non industrialized). |
| Travel Patterns | Modeled using the travel patterns between cities. Includes international air travel data, border crossing data (non-air), commuter flow data (where available), and gravity flow model (where commuter flow is not available). |
| Time until Active Containment | Represents modeling of the number of days it takes for active containment by national and international health organizations to take affect. Not applicable to Influenza. |
| Transmission Rate following Active Containment | Expected rate of new cases per case following active containment. Not applicable to Influenza. |
| Vaccine Production | Represents modeling of the number of days it takes for vaccine production to begin. Applicable to Influenza only. |
| Country Specific Variables | Consideration of country specific factors such as economic development (ex. GDP per capita), health metrics (ex. hospital beds per capita), and cultural practices. |

**Figure 8.2**

Major variables included in the [ModelRisk] pandemic model. This is a copy of a publicly available online slide, modified to maintain the anonymity of the pandemic bond modeler. The words "cultural practices" highlighted by author. Permission received from source. Source shared on request. See table A.4 in the appendix.

The slide is public now, but in 2017 it wasn't. In that Bavarian pub, the team didn't allow me to study it or take a picture when I asked. But they put it in front of me to scan for about ten seconds and, being an anthropologist, the last two words, "cultural practices," popped off the page at me. I knew that funerals and home health care were two cultural practices that significantly influenced the early case and death rates of Ebola during the West African outbreak. Anthropology—as a narrative science and method—enabled anthropologists to be the first to locate where and how people were getting sick.[8]

> Author: On the slide at the bottom, you listed "cultural factors" . . . but where would you, for example, find quantitative data for elements like cultural factors?
>
> ModelRisk Bavaria (MRBa): We have to combine a couple of data sets because no one is looking for that.
>
> Author: Because in the case of 2014 Ebola, it was the modifying of funeral and homecare practices that ultimately made the greatest impact, pre-vaccine, to contain Ebola.
>
> MRBa: They're hard to model.
>
> Author: Very hard to model, aren't they . . .
>
> MRBa: The funeral thing would be a thing we would have to accommodate afterwards, because we can't just model it in the scratch.

There's a reason modelers avoid using data like "the funeral thing." Funeral "things" can't be enumerated. If it can't be enumerated, it won't work[9] in the Model, even when it's the biggest factor in disease containment.

The modelers know there are these cracks in the model. "It's an unfortunate thing, but, you know . . . [modeler laughs, with a shrug], it's an unfortunate thing!" The shortcomings of models are nothing new. All modelers know there are flaws and that models are sometimes incapable of incorporating the most essential data points in the spread of disease. One modeler said: "The whole purpose of this thing is getting data, available data, and trying to show some ways to solve the problem and that's the whole purpose of the model. The model is not supposed to give you the 100 percent accurate answer because it's not capable of it. I've thought about it a lot for these years, and I think, yeah, as everyone says, all the models are wrong but some of them are useful!"

## ALL MODELS ARE WRONG, BUT SOME ARE USEFUL: A BRIEF HISTORY

The ModelRisk folks took pleasure in doing the work in what they saw as the best possible way to hit the mark effectively. When ModelRisk modelers estimated rates of disease transmission during a pandemic, they reduced complex human-disease interaction to numbers so that they could enter them into mathematical equations required to work the models. To an anthropologist, this can look like an erasure of human suffering. To a modeler, it's how to get the job done.

> **ModelRisk Boston (MRBo):** So if all these things get quantified, then we will consider them in the model.
> **Author:** So you give all data a numeric value in order to plug it into the model?
> **MRBo:** In essence, we try to come up with an equation that represents a numeric version of them.

Health risk modeling was not always so dependent on enumeration. In a now-classic 1916 epidemiological article on modeling how malaria spread, the Nobel Prize–winning British physician Robert Ross theorized how to merge math and social life. His "Theory of Happenings" (figure 8.3) integrated "demography, public health, the theory of evolution, and even commerce, politics, and statesmanship"[10] with mathematical equations. His early versions of what became the popular public health SIR (susceptible-infectious-removed) model grouped nonlinear differential equations into meaningful relationship with each other to predict the course of an epidemic over time, laying the groundwork for today's models.

Over the twentieth century, as the disconnect between enumeration and cultural factors grew in epidemiological studies, narrative observations of human health suffering were effectively stripped out of modeling. Contemporary epidemiological analyses rely almost exclusively on enumerative

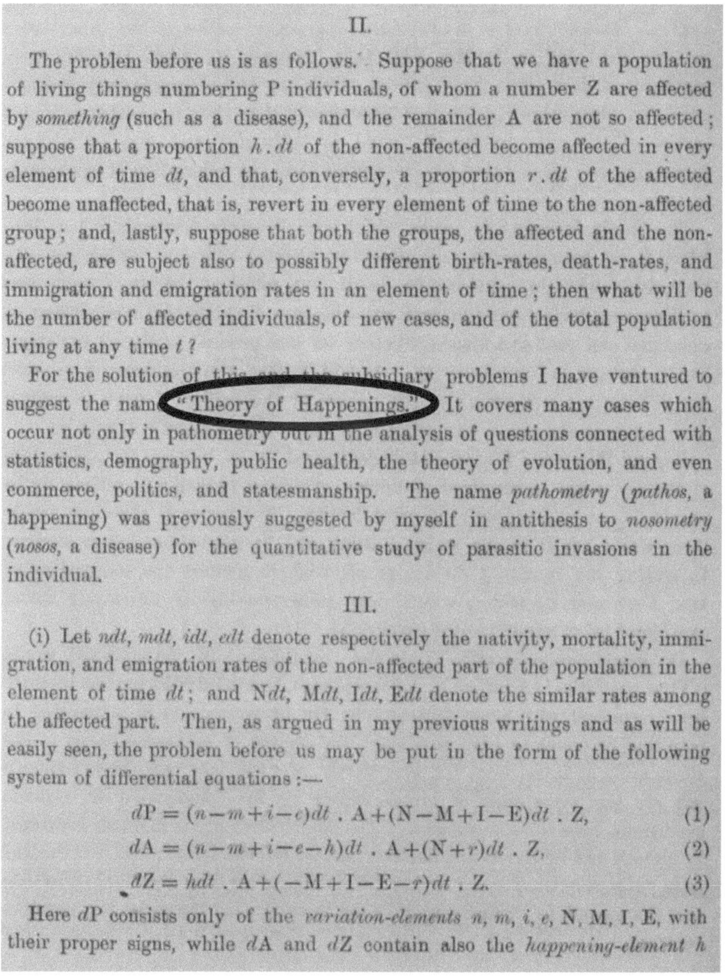

## II.

The problem before us is as follows. Suppose that we have a population of living things numbering P individuals, of whom a number Z are affected by *something* (such as a disease), and the remainder A are not so affected; suppose that a proportion $h \, . \, dt$ of the non-affected become affected in every element of time $dt$, and that, conversely, a proportion $r \, . \, dt$ of the affected become unaffected, that is, revert in every element of time to the non-affected group; and, lastly, suppose that both the groups, the affected and the non-affected, are subject also to possibly different birth-rates, death-rates, and immigration and emigration rates in an element of time ; then what will be the number of affected individuals, of new cases, and of the total population living at any time $t$ ?

For the solution of this and the subsidiary problems I have ventured to suggest the name "Theory of Happenings." It covers many cases which occur not only in pathometry but in the analysis of questions connected with statistics, demography, public health, the theory of evolution, and even commerce, politics, and statesmanship. The name *pathometry* (*pathos*, a happening) was previously suggested by myself in antithesis to *nosometry* (*nosos*, a disease) for the quantitative study of parasitic invasions in the individual.

## III.

(i) Let $n\,dt, m\,dt, i\,dt, e\,dt$ denote respectively the nativity, mortality, immigration, and emigration rates of the non-affected part of the population in the element of time $dt$; and $N\,dt, M\,dt, I\,dt, E\,dt$ denote the similar rates among the affected part. Then, as argued in my previous writings and as will be easily seen, the problem before us may be put in the form of the following system of differential equations :—

$$dP = (n-m+i-e)dt \, . \, A + (N-M+I-E)dt \, . \, Z, \qquad (1)$$

$$dA = (n-m+i-e-h)dt \, . \, A + (N+r)dt \, . \, Z, \qquad (2)$$

$$dZ = h\,dt \, . \, A + (-M+I-E-r)dt \, . \, Z. \qquad (3)$$

Here $dP$ consists only of the *variation-elements* $n, m, i, e, N, M, I, E$, with their proper signs, while $dA$ and $dZ$ contain also the *happening-element* $h$

**Figure 8.3**

Ross's 1916 "Theory of Happenings" (on p. 208, circled by author) laid the early foundation for pandemic modeling of today, though without the "demography, public health, the theory of evolution, and even commerce, politics, and statesmanship" elements he included. *Source:* Ronald Ross, "An Application of the Theory of Probabilities to the Study of A Priori Pathometry— Part I," *Proceedings of the Royal Society A* 92, no. 638 (February 1916): 204–230, https://doi.org/10.1098/rspa.1916.0007.

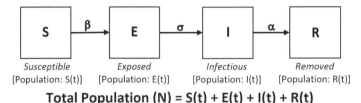

**Total Population (N) = S(t) + E(t) + I(t) + R(t)**

**Figure 8.4**

Basic outline of a SEIR model. *Source:* Matt J. Keeling, Matt J. and Pejman Rohani, *Modeling Infectious Diseases in Humans and Animals* (Princeton: Princeton University Press, 2008). https://doi.org/10.1515/9781400841035.

**Table 8.2**

ModelRisk's modeled probability of start country for coronavirus

| Country | Modeled probability (rounded) |
|---------|-------------------------------|
| China | 17% |
| India | 17% |
| Pakistan | 4% |
| Iran | 3% |
| Nigeria | 3% |
| Other | 55% |

*Source:* World Bank, *Prospectus Supplement*, June 28, 2017, I-23, https://thedocs.worldbank.org/en/doc/f355aa56988e258a350942240872e3c5-0240012017/original/PEF-Final-Prospectus-PEF.pdf. See figure A.2 in the appendix.

representations of viral and human activity. ModelRisk models are no exemption to this. One of their pandemic bonds sub-models, for example, anticipated how the six covered viruses would move from person to person. ModelRisk started with a widely used, contemporary SIR progeny—SEIR (figure 8.4)—and modified it, "yielding a total of 112 [enumerative] categories in their complete SEIR model."[11]

Some ModelRisk modeling was spot on (table 8.2 and figure 8.5). Three years before COVID-19 broke out in December 2019 in Wuhan, China, ModelRisk's modeling identified that China and India had the highest probability—17 percent each—as the site for a first case of pandemic-level coronavirus disease incidence.[12] Of course there was a 65 percent chance that

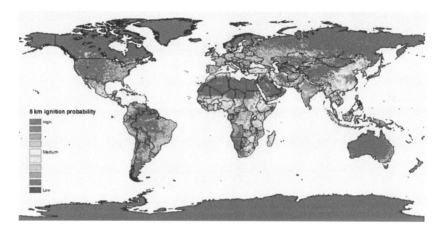

**Figure 8.5**

Map of modeled probability of start country for coronavirus. Permission received from source. Source shared on request.

an outbreak would emerge in another part of the world, but ModelRisk was able to name the index country site where COVID-19 first emerged.

I was duly impressed by their predictive modeling powers. They were correct. Kudos. But it's just like a medical anthropologist to ask, "So what?" The prediction stayed hidden in a 386-page bonds prospectus designed to inform investors about the chances they might lose their principal investment. ModelRisk's prediction did not help human communities better prepare for a coronavirus pandemic. It did not change government policies. It did not save lives. It just gave investors the information they wanted.

## MODELING FOR INVESTOR LOSS

A key to getting investors to invest their money in the World Bank pandemic bonds was showing them their chance of losing it. ModelRisk's job was to bring together the uncertainty of disease and quantify the gamble investors would take if they bought the bonds. The modelers' job, as the World Bank saw it, was to bring what they called "scientific objectivity" to investing in the bonds. Investors wanted that too.

| | Year 1 | Year 2 | Year 3 | Cumulative Term | Cumulative Total | Annualized |
|---|---|---|---|---|---|---|
| Probability of Attachment | 1.17% | 1.81% | 1.80% | 4.78% | 5.43% | 1.81% |
| Expected Loss | 0.19% | 0.30% | 0.30% | 0.80% | 0.90% | 0.30% |
| Probability of Exhaustion | <0.01% | <0.01% | <0.01% | <0.01% | <0.01% | <0.01% |

**Figure 8.6**
ModelRisk's "loss risk" predictions for investors. *Source:* World Bank, *Prospectus Supplement*, June 28, 2017, II-4, https://thedocs.worldbank.org/en/doc/f355aa56988e258a 350942240872e3c5-0240012017/original/PEF-Final-Prospectus-PEF.pdf. See table A.5 in the appendix.

"All numbers are important, but there are three numbers that are super important: (1) the probability of [investors] losing *some* money, (2) the probability of losing *all* of [their] money, and (3) the expected loss," a modeler told me. ModelRisk calculated these three numbers for all six viruses. For coronavirus in the Class A bond, the three numbers were presented in the prospectus as in figure 8.6.

### Probability of Attachment
The probability that investors would lose *any* of their money was modeled at about two chances (1.81%) in a hundred for each year of the three years of the bond. Quite low. "The probability of attachment is the concept that the investment attaches to a payout," a modeler said. Or, in other words, it expresses the chances that investors lose some or all of their principal.

### Expected Loss
The average amount of loss "is always greater than or equal to the probability of losing all your money," a ModelRisk modeler explained. "An expected loss of [0.3%], that means that, if there's $100 at risk, you're expected to [lose less than $1] each year for each of the three years of the bond."

### Probability of Exhaustion
The probability that Class A investors would lose *all* their money was modeled at less than 0.01 percent, meaning that the modeling indicated there was less than 1 chance in 10,000 that they would lose all their money. This made the Class A pandemic bond look like a good bet. Class B investors, though, with a 4.78 percent probability over the three-year life of the bond[13] and

who lost all their money when COVID-19 hit, had reason to be bummed at their bad luck.

## HUMANS MAKING DECISIONS

One of my favorite things about the research I do is finding the humans behind things like "data," "algorithms," "models," even "pricing." Words like those tend to hide the humans and the human decision-making that happens out of public view. As if activities like those could just happen on their own without human intention. That certainly was not the case with the pandemic bonds. Folks at the Bank needed to dispel any impression that the modeling of potential investor loss was "subjective" or biased. Modeling was at the center of the Bank's proof that the bonds were backed up by hard science. For investors, the modeling grounded the bonds in science and math, legitimizing them as a serious investment opportunity.

But the human choices formalizing the bonds as investment vehicles were not easy to make because the bonds had so many moving parts. When one part was adjusted, other parts were thrown out of whack. Designers and modelers had to return to the basic design of the bonds again and again. For the bonds' triggers "we were asking questions like, 'Why 250 cases? Why not 5,000 cases? Why not 10 cases?' But then the bonds would be too expensive. Oh, we spent countless hours," a designer said.

ModelRisk ran thousands of "what if" combinations to set the triggers. According to one modeler, "We weren't trying to sell the Bank that the 250 [deaths] is right or the 750 is right or maybe it should be slightly more or less than that. Our objective was to say our model can estimate these various numbers with reasonable accuracy. All the "what if" options created trigger decision-making logjams that took time to sort out, about two years for the pandemic bonds' design. "In companies, one person has the authority to say yes or no, but the World Bank isn't like that," an insurance broker observed.

TheBrokers personnel weighed in on the triggers too because they were exclusively "market-facing. . . . They are the ones that meet with the investors constantly, even those completely uninterested in the Bank's bonds," a modeler said. One broker told me, "We talked to public health stakeholders who weren't keeping that market-facing lens, who kind of pushed that obligation away, and we had to emphasize, no, you need to intelligently design the structure so that you can get to the point so when it does trigger, like, everybody knows that it is a serious [health] event."

When the Model was done, the World Bank paid for information teams to travel to financial capitals like London, Zurich, Tokyo, and New York in what was called "the investor roadshow." Pandemic bonds developers, including ModelRisk folks, met with investors potentially interested in investing in the pandemic bonds. (For a while, there were pictures online of investors being feted at cocktail parties held by the World Bank. They've since been taken down.) "Investors asked a lot of questions around the data and the veracity of the data and the triggers—because for them, that's what matters the most," a World Bank official explained. Prior to the offering, because the bonds were such a new product, the ModelRisk modelers had a lot of explaining to do. "We had discussions with the investors to tell them what the model does to make sure that they understand the model. Only a couple of them dug really deep, like some kind of test, sending email after email," a modeler said.

### INVESTORS' VIEWS

"The modeling makes you think about the probability of losing your money, right?" a pandemic bond investor said, adding,

> We never have perfect information, right? We certainly hired our experts too, who are experts on pandemic data and WHO information, and what the chain of information looks like in that organization, and how reliable it can be and not, and so on. And then I guess we formed the view that the risk uncertainty is there. But that risk just bumps up the return, right? A good investment transaction is one where there is very little uncertainty and I will say that this one [the pandemic bonds] had a rather big uncertainty and that's one reason why, you know, the [interest] you require is a bit higher . . . assuming the modeling was correct.

"We hope," a modeler said, "that the investors think the model presents a reasonable way to look at the risk metrics." Not all potential investors were convinced. One said that, although they admired the World Bank's "honorable intent to come up with something," they thought the possible profit to be made "obscured the stench of the risk," meaning that the base interest being offered—11.5 percent for Class B bonds, for example—was high because the chance of losing their money was high. "Even when we spent hours on [understanding it], it was still too complex," they continued. "And then how'd you know that the modeling that is presented to us is most faithfully representing what this transaction is structured to achieve? How'd you know that this modeling is good? We just couldn't wrap our heads around it."

Most investors didn't decide to buy the bonds because they actually understood the epidemiological science of disease. Most of them felt they didn't need to. Most investors did not seem to care that ModelRisk had run millions of simulations of the six diseases covered by the bonds, or about the details I've belabored here. It was enough that one million tries seemed like a lot, and it was an impressive amount. They did not need to understand the rationale behind ModelRisk's expansion of the conventional SEIR model to include more compartments because they wanted to estimate the number of asymptomatic people spreading the disease. Health population data was not relevant to their concerns. None of the investors I interviewed wanted to talk about the health data that went into the model. The stories I shared about the on-the-ground collection of health data were treated like interesting but quaint urban myths. Of the investors I talked to who bought the bonds, they just needed to believe that high-quality investor risk loss modeling had been done by the World Bank with data from the WHO. Full stop.

### MODELING FOR THE BONDS' PRICE

Once the triggers and the three "super important" numbers were set, the Bank had to set its "first offer" prices on the bonds. The offering prices needed to be seen by investors as fair assessments of the chance that they might lose their money. An investor told me that ModelRisk "put a probability on a pandemic happening and then investors used that to say, okay, well, if there's a 5 percent probability of the event happening, then I want to get paid X amount in interest, whatever they feel compensates for the risk."

In January 2018, I went to the Bank Treasury unit to learn more about how the pandemic bonds had been priced. It was after the fact—the pandemic bonds had gone through the active pricing and selling stages months before—but I wanted to understand the process. The Treasury official sent to be interviewed by me walked into the meeting clearly stressed. About every ten to twelve minutes, they excused themselves and left. Through the meeting-room glass, I could see them disappear around a bank of cubicles. I learned that they were refreshing their computer screen to check on the pricing of a bond, although they also admitted to running to the restroom for an upset stomach. That morning I happened to be there during the pricing of a World Bank CAD$1 billion Canadian Sustainable Development Bond, reportedly designed to "raise awareness for how empowering women and girls is one of the most effective ways to accelerate economic development, reduce poverty and build sustainable societies around the world."[14] Over the two hours of our interview, the Bank Treasury official began to relax as the price of the bond "tightened" (lowered, meaning that the Bank would be able to pay investors less interest on the bond) and evidence mounted that it would be "comfortably oversubscribed, with more than forty investors placing orders for more than CAD$1.2 billion." A success. So many orders meant that the World Bank had offered a price for the bond that investors found fair and reasonable, something they hadn't known for sure earlier that morning.

I wasn't at the World Bank when the pandemic bonds were pricing, but I learned that on the day they were priced, the process was similar and at least as nerve-wracking. The Bank had used ModelRisk's assessments and input from TheBrokers and ILS investors to decide on an offer price. They did not know for sure ahead of time if the investors would embrace that offer price *or* the pandemic bonds' structures, which had design features never offered to ILS investors before.

The pandemic bonds pricing went three rounds, which means that from that first price offer there was enough demand that the Bank lowered the interest rate for investors twice before investors said, in effect, "We won't buy the bonds if you go lower because, in our judgment, the potential profit will be too low relative to the risk that we'll lose money." But over three rounds, the price tightened, and when bonds sales finalized, relief flooded faces at the World Bank (figure 5.3).

### NOT MODELING TO STOP DISEASE

In my work, I think a lot about opportunity costs. If a lot of time, money, and human energy is being spent on one thing, say, modeling investor loss risk, what is time, money, and human energy *not* being spent on, say, strengthening—or supporting the development of—healthcare systems?

The largest international development bank in the world, under the direction of a medical anthropologist, did not contract modelers for the most effective ways to predict the next pandemics or stop them. The World Bank hired ModelRisk to model how diseases would likely play out, as measured by human death. ModelRisk was not tasked with running country-specific variables to model where or which diseases might jump next from animals to people and then people to people, or what optimal pandemic disease prevention likely looked like, or which public health interventions would most likely stop raging infectious diseases once they started to kill people. Preventing and stopping pandemics wasn't what the World Bank hired ModelRisk to do. Instead, the modeling was done to help investors decide how risky it was to gamble on pandemic bonds.

When I pointed out to World Bank officials that I knew from experience how hard it is to collect the kind of real-time data the Bank used for the bonds even in non-pandemic times, a World Bank official told me that if the modeling was consistent, the data did not matter much. "If people historically and systematically underreport how many cases of Ebola there are, the model could still be accurate. Yeah, it's not really accurate, but the model is still probabilistically making the right determinations." For investors, the Bank official should have added. Investor loss was the Bank's fixation. The time, money, and human energy spent on the pandemic bonds at the World Bank and, by extension, ModelRisk, was focused on investors, but not on how to predict, prevent, or stop the next global pandemic.

# 9   THE DATA: WHO CARES?

A couple of months into my first stay in Sierra Leone, as I climbed down from the flatbed of a small public transport truck, the back of my dress caught on the tow hitch. I dropped, board straight, like a tree being felled, directly into the mud. It was a surprisingly soft landing. Head to toe, the front of my body was inches deep in the wet gooey red laterite clay mud. It was surprisingly warm. My fellow travelers found this uproarious. Young men playacted my fall, teetering, then saving themselves at the last second from my soggy fate. Middle-aged women poked into their bags, pulling out loose bits of fabric for my cleanup. Roadside, I stood like a scarecrow, arms sticking out, as they gently wiped me down, whisking away the biggest mud gobs, trying unsuccessfully to hide their smiles.

That was my most literal contact with rainy season roads in Salone. We passengers had climbed out of the truck that day to lighten its load because it was stuck in the mud. It was the third time we climbed down and pushed the truck out of the squooshy warm goo on the twenty-six-mile journey.

Over that same stretch of road on a motorcycle, I once had three flat tires in a single day, on the same tire. I patched one hole, rode on, and with a pop or hiss, air would spring from a new one. New inner tubes hadn't been in shops for months, and I was using a patch kit long after its expiration date. Another time, further north, maneuvering my motorcycle over slick, wet bedrock, it went down. I jumped off, but it continued down the hill on its own, bumping and spinning for twenty meters, me running helplessly behind it, arms flailing like a windmill, before it came to a stop. I

**Figure 9.1**
Road during the rainy season in West Africa, 2013. Photo credit: Travis Lupik. Used with permission.

was struggling to stand it up when a farmer emerged from a roadside path along a thicket of banana trees to help me get it upright. So kind. The petrol tank—our first concern—was battered but intact, no spillage. Petrol was precious and finding it in rural Sierra Leone was a perennial problem, one that required strategic planning to overcome. I miscalculated once, ran out of gas, stranding myself on a little used road that I hoped would be a shortcut through dense tropical forest. After an hour, a kindly monkey hunter on a motorcycle came by and offered me a ride back to town. I ignored the rifle strung across the handlebars, and hopped on the seat behind him, trying not to lean against the freshly dead monkeys strapped to the back rack. Traveling rural roads was one precarious turn after another.

Roads, fuel, and waterways matter in data collection. This is true everywhere in the world, if what you're after is health data that's as accurate as humanly possible. These particular routes in Sierra Leone became crucially important the minute World Bank officials did two things: started touting Sierra Leone as a likely beneficiary of the bonds and made real-time health data a contingency trigger for millions of dollars of pandemic response, Yet during an interview in Washington, one of the Bank's pandemic bond designers blithely assured me that the data were problem-free, repeating what sounded like a well-worn script, which it was. They had used the same cheery assurances when investors had questions about the bond's trigger data. As our conversation progressed, though, there was some backpedaling.

> **World Bank official (WBO):** In the initial stages, when we were designing the trigger and figuring out how we'll [get data] in real time, we thought, "Okay, maybe we need to get special data from somewhere else," and whatever. And then, ultimately, we settled for WHO's publicly available data. It's the data the WHO puts out . . . there was sufficient comfort, you know, in the data the WHO provides. WHO puts out those numbers in the moment.
>
> **Author:** By the month, or—
>
> **WBO:** No, they take it in real time. You should talk to the [other] team because they're the ones who gave us the assurance that WHO is doing this really in real time.
>
> **Author:** Thank you, yes, I'll follow up. In my research, though, I travel around with the people who collect the numbers for WHO. . . . I mean, I know the guys who collect the numbers in Sierra Leone . . .
>
> **WBO:** Okay . . . all right . . . well . . . I'm a third-party receiver of the numbers. I don't know whether it is a suspected case or a probable case or a confirmed case. I don't track that. That's not my job. It is WHO's job, so we entrusted them with that responsibility. That is the data that we go on. . . . There was sufficient comfort, you know, in the data the WHO provides.

I had this conversation with the World Bank official two years before COVID-19 arrived, and it was Ebola, the Bank's exemplar disease for the bonds, that was on our minds. Ebola, the virus that sparked the West African pandemic in 2014 first emerged in a Guinean town about sixty miles (97 kilometers) east of my muddy faceplant. The first laboratory-confirmed case of Ebola in Sierra Leone was in May 2014, the beginning of the rainy season. The disease spread quickly between July 31 and October 31, with cases rising from 375 confirmed cases to 3,317[1] in the three months. And these were just the laboratory-confirmed cases; there were more cases and deaths that went uncounted and misdiagnosed. When I asked a WHO official working in the Freetown office how the WHO publishes *weekly* disease reports when they compile data *monthly*, they said "Well, we manage," with an awkward laugh. "We fully understand how complicated and difficult it is to collect this data," a Bank designer told me. "If you look at all the [WHO documents], we can see how it rapidly keeps changing. . . . But the WHO has a very elaborate system, so please—the WHO has a whole wing that does nothing but data collection—check with them," they said, instructing me, who had already checked. They didn't know I'd also seen data collection from the seat of a motorcycle, riding on Salone's infamously muddy tracks.

### ENUMERATOR WORK

I've traveled with Sierra Leonean enumerators—the gig-labor cohort of mostly young men and some women—who collect data for Statistics Sierra Leone, the WHO, and NGOs. Sierra Leonean freelance enumerators work on short-term contractual bases for any organization that "needs numbers." For example, an enumerator might be hired to collect data in twenty villages from people who suffer from a disease. Their job is to travel to these villages in, for example, two weeks' time, collect disease data, and usually fill in a survey on a smart phone or tablet. That may sound straightforward, but in actual practice it is not. It's precarious wage labor, complicated by language—in Sierra Leone there are about twenty different languages spoken in an area the size of Scotland. Data have must-receive-by-date schedules, too often put together by people who have never been to Sierra Leone or driven on its roads or understand the precarious rhythms of labor and labor mobility during the dry and rainy seasons. They schedule as if data were not collected by humans obliged to move their bodies through space, time, and muddy roads. As if diseases would not break out during rainy seasons. As if roads do not matter and diagnostic equipment and medical supplies would not be traveling by truck or boat to rural outposts. All this is why the Bank official's comment, "they collect data in real time," struck me as ridiculous.

When enumerators talked[2] about the challenges of collecting data during the rainy season, I felt their grievances in my bones. Riding Salone's roads by motorcycle in the dry season is some of the best fun I've ever had. But during the rainy season, from May to November, it can be like riding through wet concrete. "Health data is usually collected in the rainy season because people are more prone to sickness then," an enumerator told me. "There are some places where [motor]bikes, cars, and boats can't go." "[We] have to go through frightful water, bridges, and bush paths in forests. Dangerous!" another said.

Detailing the challenges of the job, one enumerator said, "The last time I went to Kailahun district [a region where the early Ebola outbreak occurred], I walked twenty-one miles [34 kilometers] to go to a village and twenty-one miles to come back. When you go to the field, your very first problem is how far it is. . . . Just imagine walking twenty-one miles to go and twenty-one to come back, and you have four villages to cover!" Another said, "[My] worst fear is water. Sometimes crossing bodies of water with [our motorcycles] in boats is not safe, and I don't know how to swim." Traveling to Bonthe Island, one of the data collection districts, can take six to eight hours one way by narrow wooden dugout canoes, with an enumerator's motorcycle strapped upright between the seats. Friends have told me stories of it raining hard for the entire trip.

Data is collected on phones and tablets that need to be charged, sometimes from car batteries or small generators. Or an enumerator might be stuck with an old phone or tablet that won't hold a charge at all. Two enumerators who traveled by car reported having to leave the car and then walk forest paths carrying a small but heavy diesel-powered generator on their heads so they would have a reliable charge for their tablets once they reached village data collection sites.

Collecting health data in Sierra Leone is physically and socially demanding work, and more so during an epidemic or pandemic, be it cholera, measles, Ebola, or COVID-19. Exposure to dread diseases is an everyday affair. An NGO worker confessed that he was supposed to travel with Ebola virus samples in a Styrofoam cooler strapped with bungie cords to the back of his motorcycle. He didn't want to go, and it took some time for his colleagues to cajole him into overcoming his fear of contagion from carrying the cooler and talk him into going. But that convincing took some time. He arrived seven hours late with the samples and was fired.

## BEHIND THE NEAT COLUMNS OF WHO NUMBERS

As COVID-19 showed the world,[3] real-time health data collection and analysis is a messy hodgepodge everywhere. Lots of people, including those at the WHO, do the best they can, but official tallies of infectious disease are normally published a year or two after collection because quality data cataloging takes a long time.

Yet, by design, for the World Bank pandemic bonds to release aid monies, they needed current death counts. These kinds of data are not the same as patient treatment records, those paper records that sometimes, still, hang off a clipboard at the ends of hospital beds, or their digitized cousins. The bonds could only trigger if the "third party Event Calculation Agent" (ModelRisk) received WHO data and worked to confirm: How many people were dying? Where were they dying? Crossing borders? How often were they dying? Fast enough?

A North African public health epidemiologist working for the WHO in Freetown explained to me a point I heard repeatedly, "The WHO by itself cannot collect data. [Sierra Leone's] Ministry of Health [and Sanitation] does that." We were chatting midafternoon in a Freetown Cockle Bay neighborhood courtyard, beneficiaries of a balmy breeze coming off the Atlantic Ocean not far away. The WHO epidemiologist continued, saying, "The WHO has no authority over health data in Sierra Leone and relies on what the government can collect. What the WHO does is assign a consultant or someone to support the ministry to compile, organize, and do analysis, things like that. The WHO is only and always just supporting."

On paper, the Sierra Leonean government data stream looks neat and orderly: health data are collected by health workers from patients at more than 1,000 peripheral health units (PHUs) in fourteen districts spread out all over the country. PHUs in rural Sierra Leone—like in the area where Ebola first broke—are a central contact for official health data collection. But, truth be told, they are often short of supplies and staff. Internet service comes and goes.[4] So too does pay. During the Ebola outbreak, health workers throughout the country went for months without pay.[5] "Less than 2 percent of US$3.3 billion" earmarked as Ebola aid went to frontline health workers.[6]

Can't health workers set up a digital network connection, use an app, and submit the data? Yes, that works, especially for some medical facilities closer to Freetown. But personnel in rural outposts have more work to do. Fulsome data reporting, like the kind outsiders expect, presupposes trained staff at all posts and health workers able to navigate both the routine and emergency digital data collection. A lot of the work and transmissions are done on phones or tablets, not computers with serious GPU output. Geeky IT skills, often in short supply in rural outposts, are needed to fix app glitches and troublesome service networks. Anyone in Sierra Leone earnestly trying to meet a deadline cannot rely exclusively on internet connections, which is where the need for enumerators on motorcycles comes in. The data must be driven. Someone must make the often herculean effort to ride the roads to get from point A to point B to submit data. In some rural outposts, data are still entered in big paper ledgers, which may need to be physically carried to a district headquarters compilation point by motorcycle or public transportation. Ledger data are entered into computer programs, sometimes by PHU workers, sometimes by district administrative staff.

From the district, the data are sent, usually electronically, to the health ministry in Freetown, which might send it directly to the WHO in Geneva, but which may send it first to Accra, Ghana, where it may be reviewed by McKinsey, the global management consultant, before sending it on. In Geneva, working with the data they receive, the WHO "pulls all the information together and triangulates it [to try to verify it]," a WHO official told me. At each leg of travel, the data get "cleaned"[7]—the fixing or removing of incorrect, misformatted, duplicate, or incomplete data—processes that are invisible to the ultimate end users of the data, like the World Bank official, who tend to—or need to—take the data at face value.

When the time came for ModelRisk to check the COVID-19 counts, was ModelRisk using real-time WHO data, as the World Bank official first insisted? No, of course not. It couldn't work that way, not with health data from Sierra Leone or from anywhere else in the world. Did Bank officials really expect data to travel "in the moment," without a glitch, collected from the bedsides of sick and dead in a rural area to a government, and from there to the WHO office first in the capital city and then in Geneva, then to the World Bank in Washington or to ModelRisk in Boston? In a time of pandemic emergency? Seriously? Not if you want accurate counts. People might try their best, but it's simply beyond the realm of human possibility to collect and compile sound death-from-disease data that quickly.

### THE FICTION OF "NO GOOD DATA AVAILABLE"

A lot of health data is collected in Sierra Leone. I mean, *a lot*. "There are so many projects in health and they are not integrated. They are independent and duplicating. . . . All the donors are interested in different data and they do different mechanisms to get that data," a Freetown WHO official told me. Their data may or may not get into government databases, but not always because it doesn't meet the measure of high epidemiological standards. The director of one private health clinic in Freetown told me about the health ministry promising to pick up their data monthly, which it did promisingly for several months and then abruptly stopped, with no explanation. The director heard they stopped because the ministry needed bad numbers to qualify for aid. Their clinic data was too good—only two maternal deaths in 2,076 births in two years. That same director told me about the multiple templates she and her Sierra Leonean staff have to prepare each month. It's so time-consuming, she said, because each agency and organization has their own way of "doing data." Sierra Leonean clinic staff must become expert in multiple data record-keeping systems.

In short, the myth of "no good data" in Sierra Leone is a lie. Yes, of course, like everywhere, there is some inadequately collected, shoddily crunched data. But the prevailing belief that poor countries have no good data in 2024 is just not true. The problem is that the well-collected and analyzed health data in Sierra Leone is not in one single database, or ten. Data do not get collected, stored, or used by only the government. Data are stored in computers all over the country. Some are made public; some stays private.

Some data end up in government databases, some does not. Sierra Leone health data also sit in computers all over the world because international aid workers go home, or governments like the United States and the United Kingdom collect health data on the Sierra Leonean programs they fund. Big NGOs like Oxfam, the Red Cross, and the International Rescue Committee collect data for their own data metrics and accounting. Hundreds of smaller organizations, like Marie Stopes, Mercy Ships, and Focus 1000, collect data on their special programs. In the best of times, the health data coming out of Sierra Leone are a smorgasbord of numbers from official government health care providers, private charities, and NGOs just passing through. The WHO in Freetown is not much more than a receiver of data that was first collected by a whole host of folks using a multitude of different formats, some of which make it into the Sierra Leone database that the government faithfully hands over each month to the WHO in Geneva. But this is also true: a lot of sound Sierra Leonean public health data never makes it to Geneva.

Here's something that bears repeating: this is what the privatization of health care has wrought. In poor countries, disparate data caches are just one symptom exacted by—sorry to bring this up yet again—structural adjustment and its progeny promoted by the World Bank and the IMF. An ad hoc health sector produces ad hoc health data. This bears true for the United States as well, as COVID-19 revealed.[8]

"The WHO data" used to trigger the pandemic bonds were an effective illusion. A lot of people involved with the bonds knew this. It was a modeler who told me, "Well, they're the best we've got, and we've got to use something."

## WHAT PEOPLE WERE WILLING TO ADMIT ABOUT THE BONDS' DATA

A retired Bank official who reviewed early drafts of the pandemic bonds design knew the data would not be as dependable as some of their colleagues were saying. "I thought, wait, if there is going to be a payout, it's gonna be a high stakes thing. . . . Are the data systems in these countries really robust enough to support them? I couldn't see it." A Bank interviewee spelled it out for me: higher-ups cared that their technical design *worked*. Data were but a cog in that wheel.

Others at the Bank copped an attitude when I brought up the topic of data during their interviews: Stop with your questions. Don't make me think about this. Talking about this annoys me. As a group, Bank bonds designers didn't much care to hear about Salone's muddy roads or enumerators squeezing themselves and their motorcycles into narrow canoes, afraid of tipping over into ocean currents. Once, after sharing my ethnographic research on the realities of life in the rural health outposts, a World Bank official responded with a long heavy sigh, and then said:

> WBO: That's a hypothetical position that you are taking. I'm sorry, I don't agree with it.
>
> Author: Well, it's not actually something to agree or disagree with. I've traveled to those posts. . . . Enumerators told me what they did to get data, and what they observed their colleagues doing . . .
>
> WBO: We have had this discussion many times [within the Bank], and we don't believe it. What does happen is [long pause] that [pause] the data reporting might not happen at the time, at the same time. It may get reported five days later. It may get reported ten days later.

Another designer, after I shared enumerators' horror stories, said, with a straight face, "That's like a James Bond movie. Sure that can happen, there's underreporting and overreporting. But that's a movie scenario. The probability of that, to me, is like a fraction of a percent. It is not worth worrying about."

But some ILS folks *did* worry about the limitations of the data. "From the data side," one told me, "there are improvements happening on a global scale. . . . But even five years ago, it was pretty not great in terms of, like, just the formatting of what the WHO was putting out. It was all over the place." When I pointed out that the bonds could, in fact, "work" even when the data were incorrect, an ILS expert responded, "Yes. Correct. The hope is that we picked the right variables."

And some potential investors knew, a Bank designer admitted, "A number of investors who are big investors in this market, who buy all our World Bank cat bonds in the natural catastrophe space like earthquake and hurricanes bonds, were not comfortable [with the pandemic bond] because . . .

a lot of them thought there will be this incentive to overreport [the data]. People are saying, 'Well, if you've got fifteen cases and you know you have to get twenty to get a payment you just, you know, bump it up.'" Another said, "If you suddenly scream, 'Hey, we're having Ebola outbreak, we're collecting data!' You know, it's negative and that got some investors uncomfortable, and some just said, 'No, I just can't trust that.' There's the moral hazard of people overreporting. So the data definitely was a big issue."

By design, the pandemic bonds depended on a real-time data stalwartness that simply does not exist. Folks knew. Yet, in World Bank documents, investor synopses, and bond blogs, the data for the bonds' triggers were characterized as clear-cut: "[Pandemic bond] triggers use publicly available and observable data to determine the payment amounts. As these triggers are based on observable data, they provide more transparency, increase the speed of payment, and allow for an objective benchmarking of risk . . . and *indisputable* activation criteria."[9] All things considered, "indisputable" was a pretty galling claim.

### THE KNOWN KNOWN: DISCLAIMING THE BONDS' DATA

If anyone needs more evidence that the data for the pandemic bonds were a known weakness, consider these World Bank, WHO, and ModelRisk disclaimers in the bonds' prospectus setting out their terms and conditions, spelled out in all capital letters, no less:

**World Bank Disclaimer**
"[THE WORLD BANK] ACCEPTS RESPONSIBILITY FOR THE INFORMATION CONTAINED IN THIS PROSPECTUS SUPPLEMENT, EXCEPT FOR THE INFORMATION UNDER THE HEADING "*INFORMATION ABOUT THE WORLD HEALTH ORGANIZATION AND WHO REPORTS.*"[10]

**WHO Disclaimer**
"WHO DISCLAIMS ALL RESPONSIBILITY FOR ANY ERRORS OR OMISSIONS IN THE PREPARATION AND/OR PUBLICATION OF ANY WHO REPORTS."[11]

**ModelRisk Disclaimer**

"[MODELRISK] HAS NOT VERIFIED THE AUTHENTICITY OR ACCURACY OF THE ORIGINAL DATA IN THE HISTORICAL CATALOGS OR OTHER DATA SOURCES USED TO DEVELOP THE [MODELRISK] MODEL.[12] . . . THE RISK ANALYSIS RESULTS REPORTED IN THE AIR EXPERT RISK ANALYSIS REPORT ARE, THEREFORE, SUBJECT TO NUMEROUS ASSUMPTIONS, UNCERTAINTIES AND THE INHERENT LIMITATIONS OF ANY STATISTICAL ANALYSIS. . . . ACTUAL LOSS EXPERIENCE IS INHERENTLY UNPREDICTABLE.[13]

The huge amount of data everywhere is not solving problems really, [because] it's not about having data," a modeler observed. "It's about how to get use of it, how to make it into information that investors need. If we have better data, of course, we can build a better model." But better data and better models targeting *investor interests* are not actually going to fix the big bucket of pandemic funding challenges the world faces.

## "BETTER DATA, BETTER MODELS," A.K.A. MISSING THE POINT

I'm uncomfortable admitting how shocked I was to hear again and again that the accuracy of the data mattered so little. A modeler characterized it like this: "As long as the modeling is consistent with using the same sort of data source over time, whether that data is really right becomes kind of not essential." In short, the data: Who cares?

And yet, so much time and human energy goes into creating data.

Make no mistake, I don't want to live in a world without "the numbers" in global health. To state the obvious, quantitative data can be important for planning and measurement tools that can improve care. In the current system, though, they also operate as essential currency, and are used to determine accountability, project success, failure, credit, and blame. They are the ticket to decision-making tables. They are where the politics of global health gets played out, with human life and death in the balance.

As an anthropologist, I have another reason for liking the numbers. Data are particularly revealing artifacts; they tell us so much about where people's priorities lay.

Recently I attended a talk in a faculty of health sciences by a well-known senior global health consultant who had recently worked at the WHO. They were the kind of person who, for the first seven minutes of their talk, left up a slide with a wall-filling photo of themselves, shoulder-to-shoulder, with the director-general of the WHO as he prepared his 2017 acceptance speech, just the two of them, communicating their status by association. As a personality, their demeanor was not much different from the World Bank consultant at that School of International Studies all those years ago who introduced me to catastrophe bonds. Using enumerative data, the speaker sketched out their WHO work, and encouraged audience members to use data to "measure their health impacts" in a "results-based strategy" using "data and delivery dashboards," emphasizing "results," "targets," "indices," and "outputs." "The way to improve health is through *innovation and the better application of data*," they concluded, using jargon not much different from that used to hype the pandemic bonds.

During the question-and-answer period, I raised my hand and told the story of nurses working in Sierra Leone who are forced to pay so much attention to data collection that they were short on time for patient care (note: their North American counterparts report similar "data burnout"[14]). A Sierra Leonean nurse's wages were garnished for failing to record data properly, though there were no penalties for skimping on patient care. Then I noted in their presentation, that they, the WHO consultant, had not once mentioned the word "care" or presented slides with the word "care," and wasn't it odd that the World Health Organization devoted so much time and energy to "data" but not to "care"? Oh, this last point did not go over well with the speaker, and they spent the next five minutes trying to excoriate me, using empty jargon I've heard hundreds of times before and that always makes me wonder about a speaker's lack of empathy. Why don't they interrogate the data? Why don't they take fuller measure of the human costs of dataworks and the fact that more data does not, in and of itself, equal more care?

During the 2014–2016 Ebola outbreak, PHUs and hospitals in Sierra Leone were overrun and overwhelmed. Collecting data was not top of mind. It couldn't be. Not with so many people dying, including those responsible for care. A fifth of the health care workers in Sierra Leone died of Ebola.[15] Forty-seven PHUs closed.[16] The fact that Ebola data went uncollected and unreported was among the least tragic outcomes.

Likewise, COVID-19 hammered home the realities of health data collection the world over,[17] prompting big questions. How *do* we collect data *in* a pandemic? How *do* we aggregate data from all those different data collection templates from a gazillion health groups on the ground doing different things, using different data collection systems, each with exacting data entry and submission requirements, in a timely way? Then there are the burning Is-this-the-world-we-want? questions: When doctors, nurses, and other health professionals are themselves dying and burning out and there are few personnel left to keep sick patients alive, is it reasonable to expect the practitioners still standing, still treating patients, to keep a running count, to tally the dead too? For a pandemic bond? Really?

* * *

Since 2000, the WHO, World Bank, the Gates Foundation, and others have spent billions in building health data and information systems around the world. In public talks and behind closed doors, their officers bemoan how hard it is to set up data systems in countries like Sierra Leone. But you know what's harder? Establishing a universal healthcare *system*. Sierra Leoneans want it, and they are on the record about how poorly multilateral agencies support them.[18] The country is *still* legally obliged to not prioritize making care systems; any money Salone has must first be spent on loan repayment to the World Bank and the IMF.

Data systems are no proxy for true care, the kinds of care intimacies that heal people, giving people another round among the living. Data can't stand in for the kind of well-governed, well-funded universal systems essential as a first line of defense for human wellness during pandemics and, well, always. Systems that prioritize *care*? Build them first.

# AFTERWORD

The World Bank's pandemic bonds were historic, raising US$132.5 million for pandemic response in poor countries from a previously untapped source—private investors. Bank officials were fond of saying that the pandemic bonds were a test of how private investment could save the world from the risk of dread disease. And then came COVID-19, the pop quiz from hell. No one needs to be reminded that COVID-19 caused twenty million deaths[1] (still counting); that global economic losses from the pandemic have been estimated at over US$12 trillion[2] (still accounting); or that so many countries were so underprepared to face the dread disease.

After years of researching the pandemic bonds, I don't doubt many of the designers' good intentions. The people I met believed the bonds were a moral good. The best of them earnestly aimed to address what they saw as a worrisome and persistent global health problem: the risk that we'd have a pandemic and there'd be no money to quickly address it. For a few, making the bonds was a game they just wanted to win. And for one or two, the bonds were just a job assignment from a boss. For one Bank designer, making the bonds was not a job they understood very well. Still, as a collective, the folks at the Bank and their ILS design crews ultimately masterminded a complex financial instrument and got incongruous parts to work well enough together. The design was, in the end, clunky, but the fact that the designers brought together so many different kinds of experts, each with their own agenda, and got the mechanics to work in financial markets was remarkable. This did not, though, make the bonds fit-for-purpose as a pandemic response payment innovation.

When I started research on the pandemic bonds, because I had a brief career in global affairs, I'd already ridden rainy season roads in West Africa by motorcycle. I already knew the cacophonies and considerable strengths of people working in Sierra Leonean clinics, hospitals, and bureaucracies. Because I had walked the decorous halls of the World Bank before, I knew I'd find both brilliant, likable mensches and cold, condescending dilettantes there. Conducting research again in the *Ordnung* (order) of Germany and in the highbrow and lowbrow parochialisms of Boston was like going home. What I didn't know was that I would become fascinated with catastrophe bonds' technical mechanics, or that I would like so many of the people I met so much. Talking with experts about catastrophe bonds was heady and intellectually exciting. Selling risk itself? An idea born in nerd heaven. It was no stretch for me to become intrigued.

But not all catastrophe bonds are created equal. Human health risks are different from weather risks. Weather perils come, and then they go. A lot of what ILS insures—from hurricanes to cybersecurity hacks to World Cup matches—are one-offs, here for a flash. But pandemics stick around. For years. Infectious diseases take up residence in human communities. Death and bodily disability are discernably different registers of damage and human tragedy compared with property loss. Death was such a crude and offensive trigger for the bonds; death and wind speed are not alike.

The pandemic bonds proved to be a small but illustrative exposé of "the financialization of everything"[3] and "the datafication of everything"[4] coming together in a financial device that aimed to offload the risks of human care from public entities into private hands. Its execution proved challenging. Behind the scenes, I saw people initially excited about the *idea* of making pandemic risk investable, including the president of the World Bank. As the bonds' design phase stretched into years, though, motivation waned. The bonds morphed into an innovation for innovation's sake. A technofutures scholar captured the innovation tic: "Imperfect algorithms, messy data, and unprovable predictions [get] constantly intersected with aspirational visions, human judgment, and a liberal dose of black-boxing."[5] Innovation is like that; Kim said so himself.[6] There was so much attention and excitement at the beginning, but then the adrenaline started to wane. Many at the

Bank lost track of what they had originally said they were trying to do with the bonds. "Saving lives and economies" morphed into protecting investor loss. You can see it in the modeling. Over time, the "innovative" pandemic bonds' design capitulated to conventional capitalist ways and means of doing things. "Pandemic risk" became synonymous with "investor risk," and nobody seemed to notice. The pandemic bonds carved off the risk from the responsibility for implementation and health systems-making, and nobody seemed to care. There's simply no getting around the fact that investors care most about financial returns and their loss risk. The health of populations is not on their radar in a meaningful way because it doesn't have to be. That's why financial innovation is no proxy for health systems; it's too flaky, too mismatched to the task of serving human health over a lifespan, and especially during a pandemic. Episodic fits and starts of financial profit and loss cycles don't meet human care needs. The financialization of human health does not have an impressive track record.[7]

Public health operates, though, on a different register, one designed for the long haul, and for the long-term prevention of human suffering.

To this day, when I think about the pandemic bonds, I am overwhelmed by the wastefulness of so much intellectual horsepower, political will, money, opportunity, and publicity going into a short-term financialized device that has faded to next to nothing. What would have been possible if that massive brain trust had been spent instead on universal health systems–making as a first line of pandemic response? Human health*care* timelines are the opposite of short-term speculative excitements. As the stories of the bonds show, the financialization of health response skews attention away from care, messes with health systems planning and governance, and does little to improve the hard on-the-ground slog of care. Humans need steady, reliable public health services throughout their lives to survive pandemics and thrive thereafter.

After working in West African, European, and North American hospitals and clinics, I know how difficult care systems are to create and sustain. "The best investment of funds and attention is in ensuring adequate and stable financing for core public-health capacities," a conspicuous and vociferous critic of the Bank's bonds argued.[8] The need for serious, ongoing investment in primary healthcare *systems* is venerated in public health circles because it works as a first line of defense for reducing unnecessary human suffering.

The bonds were a misdirection,[9] a distraction away from making universal primary healthcare systems around the world the first line of defense against pandemics. They directed attention to the markets. Look here for the answer, not there. Think this, not that. Stop dwelling on the value[10] of the returns on the "big bets"[11] of healthcare *systems*. Concentrate instead on the miracle of the markets. Ignore the fact that, with markets, there is no social contract to improve human health, no obligation to do good, no constituency committed to minimizing human harm. *Come on*. Governments are imperfect and some are terrible, but the good ones have built-in mechanisms for feedback, change, and *systems of care at scale* unmatchable by private investors.

Some World Bank designers seemed surprised that the pandemic bonds cast a negative light on the Bank's primary approach to problems. Their consternation surprised me. The Bank is a bank is a bank. Not to be confused with a care agency. The Bank favors private over public investment, an aspect often obscured by its grandiose rhetoric about "international development" and "shared prosperity." The Bank prioritizes private investment deals and provisioning even in countries without enough public goods to ensure basic human rights and dignities—or healthcare.

COVID-19 showed the world that most countries have not reckoned enough with the big design questions about who pays for pandemics, and how; and what *is* the optimal balance between governments, banks, and investors? As the pandemic bonds story reveals, growing more dependent on private investors changes whose interests are primary.

There's nothing inevitable about financial arrangements. The Bank called off its planned pandemic bonds 2.0 revision, but can we expect that the World Bank's pandemic bond model will be reanimated at some point in the future? Right now, sentiment runs against using the pandemic bonds 1.0 design to solve our future pandemic payment challenges. Dependency on death data was troubled from the start, for one, and who would pay investor interest in the future? Pandemic bonds 1.0 donors Germany and Japan are unlikely to reenlist, according to insiders. Germany is a hard no; Japan reportedly didn't like the negative publicity of the bonds.

But in February 2024, the World Bank announced "a significant expansion of the use of catastrophe bonds, reinsurance and instruments such as parametric risk transfer for countries exposed to large-scale disasters, with an ambition to embed catastrophe insurance and risk transfer instruments more deeply into [the Bank's] financing operations."[12] The World Bank's pandemic bonds got some negative press, but they have not been forgotten. ILS insiders talk publicly about the future potential of pandemic bonds. Said one, "Obviously, with hindsight, we can always think of things that can be improved in such an ambitious and complex transaction such as this. But the Bank should be applauded for pioneering such very important technology. They've given us a blueprint of how things can be evolved further, and I think once the dust settles, we will see that technology being used again."[13]

This book is a cautionary tale, with a time stamp. It shows what the designers thought they got right in 2017 about making pandemics investable, what COVID-19 proved in 2020 they got wrong, and what it all could mean for the future of global health finance. The World Bank's pandemic bonds were a first go. More of these devices are likely coming. "We think we're going to have to do it again, and again, and again," an ILS executive told me. "We see pandemics as an increasing threat. We see the world needing more capacity for this. We see the capital markets as a good viable source of alternative capacity. So it makes sense to learn from the first one, iterate on it, do something even better next time."

ILS is where the action will be. Watch that space. Because pandemic risk can be priced—ModelRisk showed it can—and investors can decide to cover pandemic risk—they just might again—there could be more pandemic bonds in our future. The next iterations of pandemic bonds could have "better" triggers; they may be redesigned to allow for prevention activities. It's near impossible, though, that future pandemic bond issuers will be any better able to prioritize risks to human life and limb over investor loss; ILS bonds are not built to deliver care, they're built so investors will invest. Modelers love to say, "All the models are wrong, but some of them are useful." Now we know for whom.

# Appendix

**Table A.1**

The number of people required to die from coronavirus before the pandemic bonds paid out

| | Aggregate number of confirmed deaths within IBRD/IDA countries | | |
|---|---|---|---|
| **Coronavirus maximum. Coverage: $195.83 million** | **At 250** | **At 750** | **At 2,500** |
| **Regional (outbreaks affecting two to seven countries)** | 29% (US$56.25 million) | 57% (US$112.5 million) | 100% (US$195.83 million) |
| **Global (outbreaks affecting eight or more countries)** | 34% (US$65.63 million) | 67% (US$131.25 million) | 100% (US$195.83 million) |

*Source:* World Bank, *Operations Manual: Pandemic Emergency Financing Facility*, 2019, p. 8, https://thedocs .worldbank.org/en/doc/842101571243529089-0090022019/original/PEFOperationsManualapproved10.15 .18.pdf, accessed May 4, 2023.

**Table A.2**

World Bank pandemic bonds investors by type and location

| Distribution by investor type | Class A | Class B |
|---|---|---|
| Dedicated catastrophe bond investor | 61.7% | 35.3% |
| Endowment | 3.3% | 6.3% |
| Asset manager | 20.0% | 10.3% |
| Pension fund | 14.4% | 42.1% |

**Table A.2 (continued)**

| Distribution by investor location | Class A | Class B |
|---|---|---|
| United States | 27.9% | 15.0% |
| Europe | 71.8% | 82.9% |
| Bermuda | 0.1% | 2.1% |
| Japan | 0.2% | 0.0% |

*Source:* World Bank Group, "World Bank Launches First-Ever Pandemic Bonds to Support $500 Million Pandemic Emergency Financing Facility," press release, June 28, 2017, https://www.worldbank.org/en/news/press-release/2017/06/28/world-bank-launches-first-ever-pandemic-bonds-to-support-500-million-pandemic-emergency-financing-facility, accessed July 16, 2024.

**Table A.3**

Pandemic Emergency Financing Facility (PEF) country allocations (updated February 2021)

| Country | PEF funds (US$) | Fund recipient |
|---|---|---|
| Afghanistan | 8,869,070.67 | UNICEF; WHO |
| Bangladesh | 14,872,047.79 | UNFPA; WFP |
| Benin | 1,000,000.00 | Government |
| Bhutan | 1,000,000.00 | Government |
| Bolivia* | 1,500,000.00 | UNICEF; WFP; WHO |
| Burkina Faso | 4,715,073.93 | UNICEF |
| Burundi | 1,632,612.21 | UNICEF |
| Cabo Verde | 1,000,000.00 | Government |
| Cambodia | 1,213,332.35 | Government |
| Cameroon | 7,392,057.22 | UNFPA; UNICEF; WFP; WHO |
| Central African Republic | 1,000,000.00 | IFRC |
| Chad | 2,322,283.54 | UNFPA; UNICEF |
| Congo, Dem Rep of | 13,181,549.40 | UNFPA; UNICEF; WHO |
| Congo, Rep of | 1,286,905.17 | UNFPA; UNICEF; WHO |
| Cote d'Ivoire | 2,818,731.45 | IFRC; WHO |
| Djibouti | 1,000,000.00 | Government |
| Dominica | 1,000,000.00 | WHO |
| Ethiopia | 7,236,953.41 | UNICEF |
| Fiji | 1,000,000.00 | Government |
| Gambia, The | 1,000,000.00 | Government |
| Ghana | 3,287,552.45 | FAO; IFRC; UNFPA; UNICEF; WFP; WHO |
| Grenada | 1,000,000.00 | Government |
| Guinea | 1,700,796.38 | WHO |
| Guinea-Bissau | 1,000,000.00 | Government |
| Guyana | 1,000,000.00 | WHO |
| Haiti | 1,775,022.46 | UNICEF |

**Table A.3 (continued)**

| Country | PEF funds (US$) | Fund recipient |
|---|---|---|
| Honduras | 1,264,937.69 | WHO |
| Kenya | 3,720,494.41 | Government |
| Kosovo | 2,231,507.98 | Government |
| Kyrgyz Republic | 1,000,000.00 | UNICEF |
| Lao | 1,000,000.00 | UNIEF; WHO |
| Liberia | 1,000,000.00 | UNICEF; WHO |
| Madagascar | 1,861,843.59 | Government |
| Malawi | 1,200,913.39 | WHO |
| Maldives | 1,000,000.00 | Government |
| Mali | 3,566,451.53 | Government |
| Mauritania | 1,000,000.00 | WHO |
| Moldova | 3,666,157.78 | Government |
| Mongolia | 1,000,000.00 | Government |
| Mozambique | 1,965,017.90 | UNFPA; UNICEF; WHO |
| Myanmar | 8,068,249.01 | Government |
| Nepal | 1,877,536.40 | UNICEF |
| Nicaragua | 1,000,000.00 | UNICEF |
| Niger | 5,347,241.39 | UNICEF; WHO |
| Nigeria | 15,000,000,00 | Government |
| Pakistan | 15,000,000.00 | INICEF |
| Papua New Guinea | 1,252,504.28 | Government |
| Rwanda | 1,000,000.00 | Government |
| São Tomé and Príncipe | 1,000,000.00 | Government |
| Senegal | 1,564,968.47 | UNICEF; WHO |
| Sierra Leone | 1,000,000.00 | UNICEF |
| Somalia | 3,076,207.76 | UNICEF; WHO |
| South Sudan | 1,581,306.85 | WHO |
| Sri Lanka* | 1,809,695.98 | Government |
| St. Lucia | 1,000,000.00 | Government |
| St. Vincent and the Grenadines | 1,000,000.00 | WHO |
| Tanzania | 3,986,804.71 | Government |
| Timor-Leste | 1,000,000.00 | Government |
| Togo | 1,000,000.00 | WHO |
| Uganda | 2,845,574.63 | Government |
| Uzbekistan | 4,294,607.48 | Government |
| Vietnam* | 6,549,215.23 | Government |
| Yemen | 4,075,242.12 | WHO |
| Zambia | 1,217,199.54 | UNICEF |
| **64** | **195,827,666.55** | |

*Source:* World Bank, "Pandemic Emergency Financing Facility (PEF), Updated February 2021," https://pubdocs.worldbank.org/en/140481591710249514/pdf/PEF-country-allocations-table.pdf.
* As per the PEF Framework, a PEF-eligible country is any IDA member country that is an IDA-eligible country (i.e., IDA only or blend country) either or both (a) under the IDA seventeenth replenishment (IDA17), or/ and (b) at the time of submission of a request for funds. Although Bolivia, Sri Lanka, and Vietnam are no longer IDA countries under IDA18, they were IDA countries under IDA17; therefore, they continue to be PEF-eligible countries.

**Table A.4**

Major variables included in the [ModelRisk] pandemic model

| | |
|---|---|
| Start location | The location of the first case whose model assumptions were based on past experience and exposure to zoonotic reservoirs. |
| Transmission rate | Expected rate of new cases per case at time t=0. Modeled using binominal distribution and varies based on seasonality and country latitude. Effective rate of transmission is impacted by the number of susceptible people in the population. |
| Case fatality rate (CFR) | Provides the estimated rate of death per case. CFR is event and country specific (e.g., industrialized vs. nonindustrialized). |
| Travel patterns | Modeled using the travel patterns between cities. Includes international air travel data, border crossing data (nonair), commuter flow data (where available), and gravity flow model (where commuter flow is not available). |
| Time until active containment | Represents modeling of the number of days it takes for active containment by national and international health organizations to take effect. Not applicable to influenza. |
| Transmission rate following active containment | Expected rate of new cases per case following active containment. Not applicable to influenza. |
| Vaccine production | Represents modeling of the number of days it takes for vaccine production to begin. Applicable to influenza only. |
| Country-specific variables | Consideration of country-specific factors such as economic development (e.g., GDP per capita), health metrics (e.g., Hospital beds per capita), and cultural practices. |

*Note:* This is a copy of a publicly available online slide, modified to maintain the anonymity of the pandemic bond modeler. The words "cultural practices" were highlighted by author. Permission received from source. Source shared on request.

**Table A.5**

ModelRisk's "loss risk" predictions for investors

| | Year 1 | Year 2 | Year 3 | Cumulative ter | Cumulative total | Annualized |
|---|---|---|---|---|---|---|
| **Probability of attachment** | 1.17% | 1.18% | 1.80% | 4.78% | 5.43% | 1.81% |
| **Expected loss** | 0.19% | 0.30% | 0.30% | 0.80% | 0.90% | 0.30% |
| **Probability of exhaustion** | <0.01% | <0.01% | <0.01% | <0.01% | <0.01% | <0.01% |

*Source:* World Bank, *Prospectus Supplement*, June 28, 2017, II-4, https://thedocs.worldbank.org/en/doc /f355aa56988e258a350942240872e3c5-0240012017/original/PEF-Final-Prospectus-PEF.pdf.

| Source | Description |
|---|---|
| OAG Aviation Worldwide | Passenger origin and destination statistics |
| UN Population Division | Trends in International Migrants by Destination and Origin |
| US Census | Daily commuter rate statistics and demographic information for US |
| UN Food and Agriculture Organization | Global gridded density of domestic poultry and pig populations (~5km) |
| LandScan | Global gridded human population (~1km) |
| World Bank | Geographic distribution of age/sex cohorts and GDP |
| The World Health Organization | Geographic distribution of hospital beds and physicians per capita |
| Global Register of Migration Species (GROMS) | Migratory waterfowl population data |
| Global Cover | Land Use/Land cover data |
| UN FAO Emergency Prevention System for Animal Health | Reported cases of influenza in wild birds, domestic birds, and swine |
| Scientific Literature | Epidemiological and biological research on: the dynamics, disease spread, governing parameters (e.g. transmissibility, virulence, etc.), historical impact, mitigation impact, temporal data sets, etc. of the relevant pathogens |

**Figure A.1**

Major data sources for modeling the World Bank pandemic bonds. *Source:* World Bank, *Prospectus Supplement*, June 28, 2017, I-4, https://thedocs.worldbank.org/en/doc/f355aa 56988e258a350942240872e3c5-0240012017/original/PEF-Final-Prospectus-PEF.pdf.

| Country | Modeled Probability[1] |
|---|---|
| China | 17% |
| India | 17% |
| Pakistan | 4% |
| Iran | 3% |
| Nigeria | 3% |
| Other | 55% |

(1) May not add to 100% due to rounding

**Figure A.2**

ModelRisk's modeled probability of start country for coronavirus. *Source:* World Bank, *Prospectus Supplement*, June 28, 2017, I-23, https://thedocs.worldbank.org/en/doc/f355aa56988e 258a350942240872e3c5-0240012017/original/PEF-Final-Prospectus-PEF.pdf.

# Notes

**AUTHOR'S NOTE**

1. The World Bank is the subject of chapter 4; see https://www.worldbank.org/en/home.

2. Jacob Stern, "Online Betting Has Gone Off the Deep End," *The Atlantic*, October 13, 2023, https://www.theatlantic.com/technology/archive/2023/10/novelty-betting-regulation /675633/; on Canadian students betting: Alexander Osipovich, "How Betting on U.S. Politics Is Getting Big," September 10, 2024, in *The Journal*, podcast, https://gimletmedia.com /shows/the-journal/gmhnago7/how-betting-on-us-politics-is-getting.

3. Lawrence Paul Yuxweluptun is a Cowichan and Okanagan artist living in Vancouver, Canada, internationally renowned for his hard-hitting political modern and surrealist art.

4. "In 1990, Yuxweluptun painted the futility of a tower of scientists attempting to repair the environmental destruction caused through greedy resource extraction. . . . The teetering scientists are performing mere maintenance, however, and poorly, as they try to use the same modes of knowledge that led us to the problems in the first place." Karen Duffek and Tania Willard, *Lawrence Paul Yuxweluptun: Unceded Territories* (Vancouver: Figure 1 Publishing, 2016), 27.

5. Finance has become a subject of inquiry for anthropologists relatively recently; see, for example, the following books: Arjun Appadurai, *Banking on Words: The Failure of Language in the Age of Derivative Finance* (Chicago: University of Chicago Press, 2015); David Graeber, *Debt: The First 5,000 Years* (Brooklyn, NY: Melville House, 2011); Jane I. Guyer, *Marginal Gains: Monetary Transactions in Atlantic Africa* (Chicago: University of Chicago Press, 2004); Karen Ho, *Liquidated: An Ethnography of Wall Street* (Durham, NC: Duke University Press, 2009); Bill Maurer, *Mutual Life, Limited: Islamic Banking, Alternative Currencies, Lateral Reason* (Princeton, NJ: Princeton University Press, 2005); Kristin Peterson, *Speculative Markets: Drug Circuits and Derivative Life in Nigeria* (Durham, NC: Duke University Press, 2014); Annelise Riles, *Collateral Knowledge: Legal Reasoning in the Global Financial Markets* (Chicago: University of Chicago Press, 2011); Caroline Schuster, *Forecasts: A Story of Weather and Finance at the Edge of Disaster* (Toronto: University of Toronto Press, 2023); Gillian Tett, *Fool's*

*Gold: How Unrestrained Greed Corrupted a Dream, Shattered Global Markets and Unleashed a Catastrophe* (New York: Abacus, 2009); and Caitlin Zaloom, *Out of the Pits: Traders and Technology from Chicago to London* (Chicago: University of Chicago Press, 2010).

6. I've been writing about global health finance for over a decade. See also Susan L. Erikson, "Global Health Business: The Production and Performativity of Statistics in Sierra Leone and Germany," *Medical Anthropology* 31, no. 4 (2012): 367–384, https://doi.org/10.1080/0145 9740.2011.621908; Susan L. Erikson, "Secrets from Whom? Following the Money in Global Health Finance," *Current Anthropology* 56, no. S12 (December 2015): S306–S316, https:// doi.org/10.1086/683271; and Susan L. Erikson, "Metrics and Market Logics of Global Health," in *Metrics: What Counts in Global Health*, ed. Vincanne Adams (Durham, NC: Duke University Press, 2016), 147–162.

7. Susan L. Erikson, "Global Ethnography: Problems of Theory and Method," in *Globalization, Reproduction, and the State*, ed. Carole H. Browner and Carolyn F. Sargent (Durham, NC: Duke University Press, 2011), 23–37.

8. George E. Marcus, "Ethnography in/of the World System: The Emergence of Multi-Sited Ethnography," *Annual Review of Anthropology* 24 (October 1995): 106–108, https://doi .org/10.1146/annurev.an.24.100195.000523.

9. Stacy Leigh Pigg, "On Sitting and Doing: Ethnography as Action in Global Health," *Social Science & Medicine* 99 (December 2013): 127–134, https://doi.org/10.1016/j .socscimed.2013.07.018.

## CHAPTER 1

1. The World Bank is a large and complex international financial institution, described in greater detail in chapters 4 and 6. At the time the pandemic bonds were being created, it had two express goals: (1) to end extreme poverty by decreasing the number of people living on less than $1.90 a day to below 3 percent of the world population, and (2) to increase overall prosperity by increasing income growth in the bottom 40 percent of every country in the world by 2030. "World Bank Group," World Bank Group, accessed July 18, 2023, https:// www.worldbank.org/en/home. In 2023, it revised its mission statement: "To create a world free of poverty—on a livable planet." Ajay Banga, "2023 Annual Meetings Plenary Remarks," October 13, 2023, https://www.worldbank.org/en/news/speech/2023/10/13/remarks-by -world-bank-group-president-ajay-banga-at-the-2023-annual-meetings-plenary.

2. World Bank Group, "World Bank Group President Calls for New Global Pandemic Emergency Facility," *World Bank Group*, October 10, 2014, https://www.worldbank.org/en/news /press-release/2014/10/10/world-bank-group-president-calls-new-global-pandemic -emergency-facility. A World Bank PowerPoint presentation on the pandemic bonds in select circulation and not made public around May 2015 promised to deliver "more preparedness," "better response," and "a quick dispersing mechanism" for pandemics.

3. Jim Yong Kim, "What Ebola Taught the World One Year Later," *Time*, March 24, 2015, https://time.com/3755178/ebola-lessons/.

4. Swiss Re, *Resilience in Action: 2017 Financial Report* (Zurich: Swiss Re, 2018), 11, https://reports.swissre.com/2017/servicepages/downloads/files/2017_financial_report_swissre_ar17.pdf.

5. I use the December 31, 2019, date as my reference point, acknowledging that some scientists estimate COVID-19 had been spreading from early October 2019 or mid-November 2019—e.g., David L. Roberts, Jeremy S. Rossman, and Ivan Jarić, "Dating First Cases of COVID-19," *PLOS Pathogens* 17, no. 6 (September 2020): 1, https://doi.org/10.1371/journal.ppat.1009620, and Zaheer Allam, "The First 50 Days of COVID-19: A Detailed Chronological Timeline and Extensive Review of Literature Documenting the Pandemic," *Surveying the Covid-19 Pandemic and Its Implications* (July 2020): 1, https://doi.org/10.1016/B978-0-12-824313-8.00001-2. But the widely accepted start date is December 31, 2019, when Chinese health authorities officially announced the disease, as reported in Hengbo Zhu, Li Wei, and Ping Niu, "The Novel Coronavirus Outbreak in Wuhan, China," *Global Health Research and Policy* 5, no. 6 (March 2020): 1, https://doi.org/10.1186/s41256-020-00135-6.

6. World Bank Group, "World Bank Group Launches Groundbreaking Financing Facility to Protect Poorest Countries against Pandemics," *World Bank Group*, May 21, 2016, https://www.worldbank.org/en/news/press-release/2016/05/21/world-bank-group-launches-groundbreaking-financing-facility-to-protect-poorest-countries-against-pandemics.

7. World Health Organization, *Coronavirus Disease (Covid-19): Situation Report—116*, May 15, 2020, https://www.who.int/docs/default-source/coronaviruse/situation-reports/20200515-covid-19-sitrep-116.pdf?sfvrsn=8dd60956_2.

8. Mark Baker, "Saving the World, One Bond at a Time," *Euromoney*, July 12, 2017, https://www.euromoney.com/article/b13szgmbqtg6dn/saving-the-world-one-bond-at-a-time.

9. Gillian Tett, "A Little Market Medicine to Prevent the Next Pandemic," *Financial Times*, January 22, 2015, https://www.ft.com/content/114a5aa2-a21f-11e4-bbb8-00144feab7de.

10. World Bank Group, "World Bank Launches First-Ever Pandemic Bonds to Support $500 Million Pandemic Emergency Financing Facility," *World Bank Group*, June 28, 2017, https://www.worldbank.org/en/news/press-release/2017/06/28/world-bank-launches-first-ever-pandemic-bonds-to-support-500-million-pandemic-emergency-financing-facility.

11. Larry Summers, "Pandemic Bonds Have Potential to Be Win-Win," *Financial Times*, October 14, 2015, https://www.ft.com/content/00784360-52d1-3104-9e3f-56987e3defcd.

12. Michael Igoe, "World Bank Pandemic Facility 'An Embarrassing Mistake,' Says Former Chief Economist," *Devex*, April 12, 2019, https://www.devex.com/news/world-bank-pandemic-facility-an-embarrassing-mistake-says-former-chief-economist-94697.

13. Olga Jonas, "Pandemic Bonds: Designed to Fail in Ebola," *Nature* 572, no. 7769 (August 2019): 285, https://doi.org/10.1038/d41586-019-02415-9.

14. Tracy Alloway and Tasos Vossos, "How Pandemic Bonds Became the World's Most Controversial Investment," *Bloomberg*, December 9, 2020, https://www.bloomberg.com/news

/features/2020-12-09/covid-19-finance-how-the-world-bank-s-pandemic-bonds-became -controversial.

15. Anna Szymanski, "Breakingviews—Pandemic Bonds Are the Sick Man of Finance," *Reuters*, February 26, 2020, https://www.reuters.com/article/us-china-health-breakingviews -idINKCN20K350.

16. Karen McVeigh, "World Bank's $500m Pandemic Scheme Accused of 'Waiting for People to Die,'" *The Guardian*, February 28, 2020, https://www.theguardian.com/global-develop ment/2020/feb/28/world-banks-500m-coronavirus-push-too-late-for-poor-countries -experts-say.

17. Drew Hinshaw and Leslie Scism, "Pandemic Insurance Has Yet to Pay Out to Poor Countries," *Wall Street Journal*, April 10, 2020, https://www.wsj.com/articles/pandemic-insurance -has-yet-to-pay-out-to-poor-countries-11586546397.

18. Dror Etzion, Bernard Forgues, and Emmanuel Kyrpraios, "Pandemic Bonds: The Financial Cure We Need for Covid-19?," *The Conversation*, March 29, 2020, https://theconversation .com/pandemic-bonds-the-financial-cure-we-need-for-covid-19-134503.

19. Medical anthropologist and physician Paul Farmer made "staff, stuff, space, and systems" a mantra of his life's work in clinical care; see also Paul Farmer, *Fevers, Feuds, and Diamonds: Ebola and the Ravages of History* (New York: Picador Paper Press, 2020). Partners in Health, the global health organization Farmer cofounded, recently added a fifth "s," "social support," to the mantra. See also Partners in Health, "Building Strong Health Systems," accessed October 31, 2023, https://www.pih.org/our-approach.

20. Throughout the book, I use "Wall Street" as metonymical shorthand for capital markets, inclusive of multiple global-capital market sites where people, institutions, and corporations can buy, sell, and trade financial instruments. Wall Street is, literally, is a very short street in New York City's financial hub on the island of Manhattan. But it is also synonymous for what is now a huge global financial network, otherwise known as the "capital market." Like Amsterdam, the City of London, and Istanbul, New York City's Wall Street is one of the places in the world where money was exchanged between people who had money and people who needed money. They used to be physical city centers. These capital or "money" markets now also exist virtually.

The pandemic bonds were issued online and sold to investors located in Europe, North America, Japan, and Bermuda. At least the digital signal when they bought the bonds had IP addresses from those places, though if they were using VPNs, who knows where in the world they were, where they were registered, or where their money came from. Investing has changed a lot in a very short period of time. All of which speaks to why I needed a single term—Wall Street—to refer to those once-physical-now-digital virtual spaces all over the world and in the cloud where financial products are bought and sold.

21. Michael Lewis, "In Nature's Casino," *New York Times Magazine*, August 26, 2007, https:// www.nytimes.com/2007/08/26/magazine/26neworleans-t.html.

22. Artemis, *Q4 2023 Catastrophe Bond and ILS Market Report: An Unprecedented Year of New Risks, Records, and Huge Market Growth*, December 29, 2023, https://www.artemis.bm/wp-content/uploads/2023/12/catastrophe-bond-ils-market-report-q4-2023.pdf.

23. Evan Osnos, "The Getty Family's Trust Issues," *New Yorker*, January 23, 2023, https://www.newyorker.com/magazine/2023/01/23/the-getty-familys-trust-issues.

24. The money released totaled US$194.86 million. US$132.5 million from the bonds, which are the subject of this book, and US$63.34 million were from a different financial mechanism called swaps, which I do not cover. The bonds and the swaps had similar trigger criteria but were different investor vehicles. I could study the contractual conditions of the bonds because a lot of their contractual conditions were made public in a World Bank investor prospectus. The swaps contracts, in contrast, were a special, nondisclosed arrangement between the World Bank and the private investors, out of public view.

25. World Bank, *Pandemic Emergency Financing Facility (PEF) Country Allocations*, February 2021, https://pubdocs.worldbank.org/en/140481591710249514/pdf/PEF-country-allocations-table.pdf.

26. Alloway and Vossos, "Pandemic Bonds."

27. Risk is—and has been—many things. See Ying Li, Thomas Hills, and Ralph Hertwig, "A Brief History of Risk," *Cognition* 203, no. 104344 (October 2020): 1–11, https://doi.org/10.1016/j.cognition.2020.104344.

28. Ramsay MacMullen, *Roman Social Relations: 50 B.C. to A.D. 284* (New Haven: Yale University Press, 1974), 38.

29. Peter S. Goodman, *Davos Man: How the Billionaires Devoured the World* (New York: Custom House, 2022), 2.

30. Lauren J. Wallace et al., "The Role of the Private Sector in the Covid-19 Pandemic: Experiences from Four Health Systems," *Frontiers in Public Health* 10, no. 878225 (May 2022): 1–16, https://doi.org/10.3389/fpubh.2022.878225; Lynn Unruh et al., "A Comparison of 2020 Health Policy Responses to the Covid-19 Pandemic in Canada, Ireland, the United Kingdom, and the United States of America," *Health Policy* 126, no. 5 (May 2022): 427–437, https://doi.org/10.1016/j.healthpol.2021.06.012.

31. Tung Thanh et al., "The Covid-19 Vaccine Development Landscape," *Nature* 19 (April 2020): 305–306, https://www.nature.com/articles/d41573-020-00073-5.

32. For example, Veronica Vecchi, Niccolò Cusumano, and Eric J. Boyer, "Medical Supply Acquisition in Italy and the United States in the Era of Covid-19: The Case for Strategic Procurement and Public-Private Partnerships," *American Review of Public Administration* 50, nos. 6–7 (July 2020): 642–649, https://doi.org/10.1177/0275074020942061.

33. Pfizer, *Pfizer Reports Fourth-Quarter and Full-Year 2021 Results*, December 2021, accessed February 14, 2022, https://s28.q4cdn.com/781576035/files/doc_financials/2021/q4/Q4-2021-PFE-Earnings-Release.pdf.

34. Grant Robertson, "'Without Early Warning You Can't Have Early Response': How Canada's World-Class Pandemic Alert System Failed," *Globe and Mail*, July 25, 2020, https://www.theglobeandmail.com/canada/article-without-early-warning-you-cant-have-early-response-how-canadas/.

35. Laurie Garrett, "Trump Has Sabotaged America's Coronavirus Response," *Foreign Policy*, January 31, 2020, https://foreignpolicy.com/2020/01/31/coronavirus-china-trump-united-states-public-health-emergency-response/.

36. World Health Organization, "Influenza (Avian and Other Zoonotic)," https://www.who.int/europe/health-topics/Influenza-avian-and-other-zoonotic.

37. Ramon Pacheco Pardo et al., "Learning and Remembering: How East Asia Prepared for Covid-19 over the Years," *Global Policy*, May 27, 2020, https://www.globalpolicyjournal.com/blog/27/05/2020/learning-and-remembering-how-east-asia-prepared-covid-19-over-years.

38. Vicente Navarro, "Why Asian Countries Are Controlling the Pandemic Better than the United States and Western Europe," *International Journal of Health Services* 51, no. 2 (March 2021): 261–264, https://doi.org/10.1177/0020731421999930.

39. Africa Centers for Disease Control, "About Us," accessed October 31, 2023, https://africacdc.org/about-us/.

40. "The Federal Response to Covid-19, Data through 1/31/2023," USAspending.gov, accessed March 23, 2023, https://www.usaspending.gov/disaster/covid-19?publicLaw=all.

41. World Bank, "(PEF) Country Allocations."

42. The Bill and Melinda Gates Foundation, "Funding Commitments to Fight Covid-19," *Bill & Melinda Gates Foundation*, January 12, 2022, accessed March 23, 2023, https://www.gatesfoundation.org/ideas/articles/covid19-contributions.

43. Tracey Elizabeth Claire Jones-Konneh et al., "Impact of Health Systems Reform on COVID-19 Control in Sierra Leone: A Case Study," *Tropical Medicine and Health* 51, no. 1 (May 2023): 1, https://doi.org/10.1186/s41182-023-00521-z.

44. "Universal Declaration of Human Rights," United Nations, accessed October 31, 2023, https://www.un.org/en/about-us/universal-declaration-of-human-rights.

45. Decades of social science research show the devastating impacts neoliberal political economy practices had on the health of human communities. For example, James Pfeiffer and Rachel Chapman, "Anthropological Perspectives on Structural Adjustment and Public Health," *Annual Review of Anthropology* 39, no. 1 (October 2010), https://doi.org/10.1146/annurev.anthro.012809.105101; Ellen Shaffer and Joseph Brenner, "Trade and Health Care: Corporatizing Vital Human Services," in *Sickness and Wealth: The Corporate Assault on Global Health*, ed. Meredith Fort, Mary Anne Mercer, and Oscar Gish (Cambridge, MA: South End Press, 2004); and Ronald Labonte, "International Governance and World Trade Organization (WTO) Reform," *Critical Public Health* 12, no. 1 (2002): 65–86, https://doi.org/10.1080/09581590110113312. See also Sanjay Basu, Megan A. Carney, and Nora J. Kenworthy, eds., "Ten Years after the Financial Crisis: The Long Reach of Austerity and Its Global Impacts

on Health," special issue, *Social Science & Medicine* 187 (2017), https://doi.org/10.1016/j
.socscimed.2017.06.026; David Stuckler and Sanjay Basu, *The Body Economic: Why Austerity
Kills: Recessions, Budget Battles, and the Politics of Life and Death* (Toronto: HarperCollins,
2013); Benjamin M. Hunter and Susan F. Murray, "Deconstructing the Financialization
of Healthcare," *Development and Change* 50, no. 5 (June 2019): 1263–1287, https://doi
.org/10.1111/dech.12517.

46. David Harvey critiqued the limitations of neoliberalism as an approach to common social
good in Harvey, *A Brief History of Neoliberalism* (Oxford: Oxford University Press, 2005),
2–3.

47. For example, among the gravest of these gaps relative to human dignity is the provision of a
basic human need: shelter. Aaron Glantz, *Homewreckers: How a Gang of Wall Street Kingpins,
Hedge Fund Magnates, Crooked Banks, and Vulture Capitalists Suckered Millions Out of Their
Homes and Demolished the American Dream* (New York: Custom House, 2019).

48. Gary Gerstle, *The Rise and Fall of the Neoliberal Order: America and the World in the Free
Market Era* (Oxford: Oxford University Press, 2022).

49. Ilene Grabel, *When Things Don't Fall Apart: Global Financial Governance and Development
Finance in the Age of Productive Incoherence* (Cambridge, MA: MIT Press, 2018).

50. Gillian Tett, *Fool's Gold*, 83–85; Benjamin Lee and Randy Martin, eds., *Derivatives and the
Wealth of Societies* (Chicago: University of Chicago Press, 2016).

51. Adam Tooze, *Crashed: How a Decade of Financial Crises Changed the World* (New York: Viking,
2018).

52. Jill Lepore, "The Disruption Machine," *New Yorker*, June 16, 2014, https://www.newyorker
.com/magazine/2014/06/23/the-disruption-machine.

53. Andrew Leyshon and Nigel Thrift, "The Capitalization of Almost Everything: The Future of
Finance and Capitalism," *Theory, Culture & Society* 24, nos. 7–8 (December 2007): 97–115,
https://doi.org/10.1177/0263276407084699; *The Economist*, "Bonds That Rock and Roll,"
May 7, 1998, https://www.economist.com/finance-and-economics/1998/05/07/bonds
-that-rock-and-roll.

54. Thomas Piketty, *Capital in the Twenty-First Century* (Cambridge, MA: Harvard University
Press, 2014).

55. Paul Farmer and Jim Yong Kim, "2017 AM: 116th Annual Meeting Opening Keynote:
Bending the Arc of Change," American Anthropological Association, January 18, 2018,
YouTube video, 1:00:35, https://www.youtube.com/watch?v=uwCIfJkUVNE.

56. Michael Lewis in *The Fifth Risk: Undoing Democracy* (New York: W. W. Norton, 2018) is
illuminating on this point.

57. Joan Tronto, *Caring Democracy: Markets, Equality, Justice* (New York: New York University
Press, 2013); Deva Woodly et al., "The Politics of Care," *Contemporary Political Theory* 20,
no. 4 (August 2021): 890–925, https://doi.org/10.1057/s41296-021-00515-8.

58. Camilla Hodson, "World Bank Ditches Second Round of Pandemic Bonds," *Financial Times*, July 5, 2020, https://www.ft.com/content/949adc20-5303-494b-9cf1-4eb4c8b6aa6b.

59. For summaries of "failure" see, e.g., Hodson, "World Bank Ditches"; Alloway and Vossos, "Pandemic Bonds"; Robin Kaiser-Schatzlein, "No Pain, No Gain: Pandemic Bonds and the Privatization of Public Health," *Harper's Magazine*, July 2022, https://harpers.org /archive/2022/07/pandemic-bonds-and-the-privatization-of-public-health-world-bank -pandemic-emergency-financing-facility/.

60. Hinshaw and Scism, "Pandemic Insurance."

61. Artemis, "COVID 19 Outlook for Insurance, Reinsurance, & Insurance-Linked Securities— Prospectus 2021 Conference," January 15, 2021, in *Artemis Live*, podcast, episode no. 34, 39:00, https://audioboom.com/posts/7773074-covid-19-outlook-for-insurance-reinsur ance-ils-prospectus-2021-conference.

62. Artemis, "COVID 19 Outlook," 38:30.

**CHAPTER 2**

1. Farmer and Kim, "Annual Meeting Opening Keynote," at 56:35 min.

2. Stacy Vanek Smith and Cardiff Garcia, "Pandemic Bonds," March 24, 2020, in *The Indicator from Planet Money, National Public Radio*, podcast, https://www.npr.org/transcripts/821000049.

3. Kate Allen, "'Pandemic Bonds' Are the Latest Idea to Beat Disease," *Financial Times*, June 28, 2017, https://www.ft.com/content/487b0d00-5c26-11e7-b553-e2df1b0c3220.

4. World Bank, *The Pandemic Emergency Financing Facility*, 2018, accessed May 4, 2023, https://thedocs.worldbank.org/en/doc/763521516900352855-0090022018/original /EnglishPEFBrochure.pdf.

5. Tett, "A Little Market Medicine."

6. Igoe, "'An Embarrassing Mistake.'"

7. Jonas, "Pandemic Bonds."

8. Alloway and Vossos, "Pandemic Bonds."

9. Landon Thomas, "The World Bank Is Remaking Itself as a Creature of Wall Street," *New York Times*, January 28, 2018, https://www.nytimes.com/2018/01/25/business/world-bank-jim -yong-kim.html.

10. Susan Erikson, "Financial Experimentality: Ebola Bonds and New Forms of Global Health Pandemic Financing," keynote for "Post Ebola: Knowledge Production and the Limitations of Translation," Max-Planck-Institut für ethnologische Forschung, Halle, Germany, October 28, 2015; Susan Erikson, "The Financialization of Ebola," *Somatosphere*, November 11, 2015, http://somatosphere.net/2015/11/the-financialization-of-ebola.html.

11. Jim Yong Kim et al., eds., *Dying for Growth: Global Inequality and the Health of the Poor* (Monroe, ME: Common Courage Press, 2000).

12. World Bank Group, "Groundbreaking Financing Facility."

13. World Bank Group, "Groundbreaking Financing Facility."

14. World Bank, "World Bank Issues Its First Ever Catastrophe Bond Linked to Natural Hazard Risks in Sixteen Caribbean Countries," June 30, 2014, https://www.worldbank.org/en/news /press-release/2014/06/30/world-bank-issues-its-first-ever-catastrophe-bond-linked-to -natural-hazard-risks-in-sixteen-caribbean-countries.

15. A good primer on World Bank trust funds is Janelle Winters and Devi Sridhar's "Earmarking for Global Health: Benefits and Perils of the World Bank's Trust Fund Model," *BMJ* 358, no. j3394 (August 2017): 1–5, https://doi.org/10.1136/bmj.j3394.

16. A good primer on the PEF is Felix Stein and Devi Sridhar's "Health as a 'Global Public Good': Creating a Market for Pandemic Risk," *BMJ* 358, no. j3397 (August 2017): 1–4, https://doi.org/10.1136/bmj.j3397.

17. Cash grants in the PEF were available on an "as needed" basis via an approval process of the World Bank's PEF Steering Committee. By December 31, 2019, with taxpayers' money donated by Germany (US$56.95 million) and Australia (US$7.05 million) plus investment income earned and minus administration fees, the PEF disbursed a cash grant total of US$61.40 million, primarily for the Ebola outbreak in the Democratic Republic of Congo, as detailed in World Bank, *Pandemic Emergency Financing Facility Financial Report*, December 31, 2019, https://fiftrustee.worldbank.org/content/dam/fif/funds/pef/TrusteeReports /PEF_TR_12_19.pdf.

18. The World Bank introduced swaps to the financial world in 1981. The pandemic bond swaps are described in World Bank, *Prospectus Supplement*, June 28, 2017, PT-73, https://thedocs .worldbank.org/en/doc/f355aa56988e258a350942240872e3c5-0240012017/original/PEF -Final-Prospectus-PEF.pdf. A general introduction to swaps, albeit quite technical, is in Nurgül Reçber Chambers, "Swaps," *Öneri Dergisi* 1, no. 5 (June 1996): 139–143, https:// doi.org/10.14783/maruoneri.703453.

19. For the official World Bank accounting, see also World Bank, *Pandemic Emergency Financing Facility Financial Report*, April 30, 2021, 9, https://fiftrustee.worldbank.org/content/dam /fif/funds/pef/TrusteeReports/PEF_TF_04_30_2021.pdf.

20. Christine I. Wallich, "The World Bank's Currency Swaps," *Finance & Development* June (1984): 15–19, https://www.elibrary.imf.org/view/journals/022/0021/002/article-A004-en.xml.

21. Artemis, "World Bank Adds $105m of Pandemic Swaps to $320m of PEF Cat Bonds," June 29, 2017, https://www.artemis.bm/news/world-bank-adds-105m-of-pandemic-swaps-to -320m-of-pef-cat-bonds/.

22. Steve Evans, "Coronavirus May Trigger $196m World Bank Cat Bond & Swap Payout," March 23, 2020, https://www.artemis.bm/news/coronavirus-may-trigger-196m-world-bank-cat -bond-swap-payout/.

23. For the official World Bank accounting, see also World Bank, *Financial Report*, April 30, 2021, 9.

24. Evans, "Coronavirus."

25. Tett, "A Little Market Medicine."

26. "IDA Borrowing Countries," World Bank, accessed April 27, 2023, https://ida.worldbank .org/en/about/borrowing-countries.

27. World Bank, *Financial Report*, April 30, 2021, 9.

28. For example, Laurie Garrett, "The World Bank Has the Money to Fight Ebola but Won't Use It," *Foreign Policy*, July 22, 2019, https://foreignpolicy.com/2019/07/22/the-world -bank-has-the-money-to-fight-ebola-but-wont-use-it/.

29. "Covered territories" are listed in appendix 1 to annex A in World Bank, *Prospectus*. For a list of IDA countries, see "IDA Member Countries," World Bank, last modified November 9, 2023, https://www.worldbank.org/en/about/leadership/members#ida.

30. World Bank, *Prospectus*.

31. Garrett, "Money to Fight Ebola."

32. Felix Stein and Devi Sridhar identify this as a weak design feature in Stein and Sridhar, "'Global Public Good.'"

33. "AP3," AP3, accessed February 24, 2024, https://www.ap3.se/en.

34. AP3, *Third National Swedish Pension Fund: Annual Report 2017*, 2018, https://a.storyblok .com/f/257759/x/7fd361cde5/ap3_annualreport2017.pdf.

35. An SEC-accredited investor must have earned at least US$200,000 in each of the prior two years and have a net worth over US$1 million. Banks, partnerships, corporations, nonprofits, and trusts may be accredited investors if their total assets exceed US$5 million or if all of the equity owners are SEC-accredited investors. The link at the time of the pandemic bonds was "Investor Bulletin: Accredited Investors," Investor.gov, US Securities and Exchange Commission, September 23, 2013, https://www.investor.gov/additional-resources/news-alerts /alerts-bulletins/investor-bulletin-accredited-investors. This link has been updated to "Accredited Investors—Updated Investor Bulletin," Investor.gov, US Securities and Exchange Commission, April 14, 2021, https://www.investor.gov/introduction-investing/general-resources /news-alerts/alerts-bulletins/investor-bulletins/updated-3.

36. "Accredited Investors—Updated Investor Bulletin," US Securities and Exchange Commission, April 14, 2021, accessed May 25, 2023, https://www.sec.gov/node/172921.

37. AP3, *Annual Report 2017*, 23.

38. On its website, Artemis provides two general lists of ILS investors, which includes Coca-Cola, the BBC, and IBM pension funds, accessed March 7, 2024, https://www.artemis.bm /pension-funds-investing-in-insurance-linked-securities-ils/ and https://www.artemis.bm /ils-fund-managers/.

39. Steve Evans, "Pandemic Cat Bond Secondary Price Reacts as Coronavirus Cases Rise," *Artemis*, February 17, 2020, https://www.artemis.bm/news/pandemic-cat-bond-secondary-price -reacts-as-coronavirus-cases-rise/.

40. Steve Evans, "Pandemic Cat Bond Price Plummets on Growing Coronavirus Threat," *Artemis*, March 2, 2020, https://www.artemis.bm/news/pandemic-cat-bond-price-plummets-on -growing-coronavirus-threat/.

41. In many conversations since 2017, Gary Parker, a Simon Fraser University professor in the statistics and actuarial science department, graciously helped me with general information about the bonds and their financial calculations. Any mistakes are mine.

42. LIBOR—the London Inter-Bank Offered Rate—was a rate of interest (standard in the industry until June 30, 2023) between banks for when they loaned money to each other. The LIBOR rate paid by the bonds was the one used for six-month loans.

43. The –0.4% is a funding margin charged to investors, which likely represents a cost of doing business.

44. Artemis, "AP3 a Lead Investor in World Bank Pandemic Catastrophe Bond," August 24, 2017, https://www.artemis.bm/news/ap3-a-lead-investor-in-world-bank-pandemic -catastrophe-bond/.

## CHAPTER 3

1. World Bank Group, "Groundbreaking Financing Facility."

2. Notable fights for local sovereignty include 1790 and 1898 conflicts with British authority. The divide-and-conquer administrative strategy of the British—setting ethnic groups against one another during the slave trade and colonial eras—set the stage for political rivalries at independence in 1961, which are still evident in contemporary Sierra Leonean politics. T. Risely Griffith, "Sierra Leone: Past, Present and Future," *Proceedings of the Royal Colonial Institute* 13 (1881–1882): 58, 59; Arthur Abraham, "Bureh, the British, and the Hut Tax War," *International Journal of African Historical Studies* 7, no. 1 (1974): 99–106, https://doi .org/10.2307/216556.

3. Adia Benton, *HIV Exceptionalism: Development through Disease in Sierra Leone* (Minneapolis: University of Minnesota Press, 2015).

4. A. B. Zack-Williams, "Sierra Leone: Crisis and Despair," *Review of African Political Economy*, no. 49 (Winter 1990): 22, https://www.jstor.org/stable/4005975.

5. During the time that I lived in the comparatively well-off Mende town, rumors circulated that the Sierra Leonean president, Stevens, had become the seventh richest person in the world. Locally, it was assumed that he was profiting from illegally selling diamonds mined close by, but his corruptions ran deeper. See also Sama Banya, *Looking Back—My Life and Times* (Freetown: Sierra Leonean Writers Series, 2015); Solomon E. Berewa, *A New Perspective on Governance, Leadership, Conflict and Nation Building in Sierra Leone* (Bloomington, IN: AuthorHouse, 2011); William Reno, *Corruption and State Politics in Sierra Leone* (Cambridge: Cambridge University Press, 1995). Stevens left office in 1985 with reportedly over US$1.5 billion, which, calculated for inflation, is over US$3.7 billion today.

6.  A. B. Zack-Williams, "Crisis and Structural Adjustment in Sierra Leone: Implications for Women," in *Women Pay the Price: Structural Adjustment in Africa and the Caribbean*, ed. Gloria Thomas-Emeagwali (Trenton, NJ: Africa World Press, 1995), 54.

7.  Bret Benjamin, *Invested Interests: Capital, Culture, and the World Bank* (Minneapolis: University of Minnesota Press, 2007), 35.

8.  Some additional money would also have come in from West African regional projects. "Projects," Project List, World Bank, accessed July 22, 2023, https://projects.worldbank.org/en/projects-operations/projects-list.

9.  Paul Cadario, interview by Charles Ziegler, *World Bank Group Archives Oral History Project*, April 4, 17, 22, and 30, 2013, https://oralhistory.worldbank.org/transcripts/transcript-oral-history-interview-paul-cadario-held-april-4-17-22-30-2013.

10. Dr. John Karefa-Smart, Sierra Leone Minister of External Affairs, 1961, BACS Productions, "Sierra Leone with Sir Milton Margai," uploaded November 24, 2013, YouTube video, at 6:50, https://www.youtube.com/watch?v=ztUXY_IYT0U.

11. "British West African Pound," Wikipedia, last modified February 14, 2024, https://en.wikipedia.org/wiki/British_West_African_pound.

12. "Currency Converter," OANDA, accessed September 10, 2024, https://www.oanda.com/currency-converter/en/?from=GBP&to=SLE&amount=1.

13. *Bending the Arc*, directed by Kief Davidson and Pedro Kos (New York: Impact Partners, 2017).

14. Caroline Doggart, "From Reconstruction to Development in Europe and Japan," in *The Evolving Role of the World Bank*, ed. K. Sarwar Lateef (Washington, DC: World Bank, 1995), 37–67, 67n6.

15. World Bank, "Heavily Indebted Poor Countries (HIPC) Initiative," accessed September 10, 2024, https://www.worldbank.org/en/topic/debt/brief/hipc.print.

16. Elkyn Chaparro, interview by Richard Webb and Devesh Kapur, *World Bank Group Archives Oral History Project*, June 29, 1992, p. 4, https://oralhistory.worldbank.org/transcripts/transcript-oral-history-interview-elkyn-chaparro-june-29-1992-washington-dc.

17. Chaparro, *Oral History Project*.

18. Chaparro, *Oral History Project*.

19. Devesh Kapur, John P. Lewis, and Richard C. Webb, *The World Bank: Its First Half Century* (Washington, DC: Brookings Institution Press, 1997), 507.

20. Zack-Williams, "Sierra Leone: Crisis and Despair," 29.

21. OANDA, "Currency Converter." In 2022, Sierra Leone recalibrated its currency, "knocking three zeros off its bank notes"; see https://www.aljazeera.com/economy/2022/7/1/sierra-leone-knocks-zeros-off-bank-notes-in-currency-re-calibration.

22. Peter Griffiths, *The Economist's Tale: A Consultant Encounters Hunger and the World Bank* (London: Zed Books, 2003).

23. The World Bank was not the only international financial institution to loan Sierra Leone money. See also a ledger of International Monetary Fund (IMF) loans to Sierra Leone. "Sierra Leone: Transactions with the Fund from May 01, 1984 to June 30, 2023," International Monetary Fund, accessed July 23, 2023, https://www.imf.org/external/np/fin/tad/extrans1 .aspx?memberKey1=850&endDate=2099%2D12%2D31&finposition_flag=YES. Note that for some loans, Sierra Leone paid more to the IMF in principal, interest, and fees than it originally borrowed.

24. Pfeiffer and Chapman, "Structural Adjustment"; Megan A. Carney and Nora J. Kenworthy, eds., "Austerity, Health and Wellbeing: Transnational Perspectives," special issue, *Social Science and Medicine* 187 (August 2017): 203–312, https://www.sciencedirect.com/journal /social-science-and-medicine/vol/187, including Basu, Carney, and Kenworthy, "Long Reach of Austerity," 203–207.

25. Alexander Kentikelenis et al., "The International Monetary Fund and the Ebola Outbreak," *Lancet Global Health* 3, no. 2 (December 2014): E69–E70, https://doi.org/10.1016/S2214 -109X(14)70377-8; A. B. Zack-Williams, ed., *When the State Fails: Studies on Intervention in the Sierra Leone Civil War* (London: Pluto Press, 2012). Also, in 1995, the World Trade Organization (WTO) used its General Agreement on Trade and Services (GATS) to make health services a tradeable commodity and shrink national health systems further. See Shaffer and Brenner, "Trade and Health Care"; and Labonte, "International Governance."

26. Farmer, *Fever, Feuds, and Diamonds*.

27. Throughout the book, when I've used "healthcare" as a single word, it refers to organized systems and services. But millions of people throughout the world do not have access to organized care. Nerdy medical anthropologist of global health that I am, I use "health care" as two words to indicate three things: (1) health *care* takes many forms throughout the world; (2) not all of it is organized by nation-states and regional authorities; and (3) sometimes health care, as two words, is an artifact of a global political economy that constrains universal health systems development, as in the case in Sierra Leone.

28. Sierra Leone Ministry of Health and Sanitation 2013, as cited in Ibrahim Abdullah and Ismail Rashid, eds., *Understanding West Africa's Ebola Epidemic: Towards a Political Economy* (London: Zed Books, 2017). See also in the same volume Ibrahim Abdullah and Abou Bakarr Kamara, "Confronting Ebola with Bare Hands: Sierra Leone's Health Sector on the Eve of the Ebola Epidemic," for an additional example of World Bank involvement that impacted health outcomes. See also Ellen Foley's *Your Pocket Is What Cures You: The Politics of Health in Senegal* (New Brunswick, NJ: Rutgers University Press, 2009).

29. Universal health systems around the world are hugely varied. Some, like with the UK's National Health Service, make governments the employer, hiring practitioners and running health services as a branch of government. Others, like in Germany, make government the

managers and regulators of the system but not the actual employer. Germany's *Krankenkassen* operate something like insurance companies but are not-for-profit. Inefficient systems, like those in the Unites States, which spends the most per person but has many of the worst population health outcomes among wealthy countries, have a hodgepodge of private and public services and a profit-making insurance industry. The best health outcomes in the world have been shown to emerge from systems where governments are clearly the boss, even when system elements are a mix of both public and private provisioning.

30. Caroline Huber, Lyn Finelli, and Warren Stevens, "The Economic and Social Burden of the 2014 Ebola Outbreak in West Africa," *Journal of Infectious Diseases* 218, no. 5 (October 2018): S698–S704, https://doi.org/10.1093/infdis/jiy213.

31. World Bank, "(PEF) Country Allocations."

## CHAPTER 4

1. The World Bank Group describes itself as "a unique global partnership: five institutions working for sustainable solutions that reduce poverty and build shared prosperity in developing countries" in "Who We Are," World Bank Group, accessed July 23, 2023, https://www.worldbank.org/en/who-we-are. Its five institutions include an investors' court that serves as an arbitration tribunal for disputes between poor countries and corporations and an investment services corporation that secures proprietary protections for private investors. Although the World Bank Group is now five institutions under one name, in this book, my use of "World Bank" refers primarily to the activities of the International Bank for Reconstruction and Development (IBRD), the original institution as set out in the Bretton Woods Agreement, and the issuer of the pandemic bonds.

2. Katherine Marshall, *The World Bank: From Reconstruction to Development to Equity* (New York: Routledge, 2008).

3. Former World Bank economist William Easterly wrote *The Elusive Quest for Growth* (Cambridge, MA: MIT Press, 2002), which presented an argument decisively against the kind of aid doled out by the World Bank.

4. Democracy Now, "60 Years Is Enough: Thousands Protest the IMF and World Bank," *Democracy Now*, April 30, 2004, https://www.democracynow.org/2004/4/30/60_years_is_enough _thousands_protest.

5. Former World Bank economist Joseph E. Stiglitz, *Globalization and Its Discontents* (New York: W. W. Norton, 2002).

6. Urban Dictionary, s.v., "world bank," by Luther Bliss, January 29, 2018, https://www.urban dictionary.com/define.php?term=world%20bank.

7. Ngaire Woods, *The Globalizers: The IMF, the World Bank, and Their Borrowers* (Ithaca, NY: Cornell University Press, 2006).

8. Benjamin, *Invested Interests*, xvi.

9. Michael Goldman, *Imperial Nature: The World Bank and Struggles for Social Justice in the Age of Globalization* (New Haven, CT: Yale University Press, 2005), xi.

10. Ed Conway, *The Summit: The Biggest Battle of the Second World War—Fought behind Closed Doors* (London: Little, Brown, 2014).

11. The quote and images of the placards are also included here: World Bank Group, *World Bank Group Archives Exhibit Series: Bretton Woods Monetary Conference, July 1–22, 1944*, January 2016, https://documents1.worldbank.org/curated/en/538791468000300309/pdf/104697 -WP-PUBLIC-2008-07-Bretton-Woods-Monetary-Conf.pdf.

12. World Bank Group, *Exhibit Series*.

13. See Steve Gloyd, "Sapping the Poor: The Impact of Structural Adjustment Programs," in *Sickness and Wealth: The Corporate Assault on Global Health*, ed. Meredith Fort, Mary Anne Mercer, and Oscar Gish (Cambridge, MA: South End Press, 2004), 43–54.

14. Pfeiffer and Chapman, "Structural Adjustment"; Salmaan Keshavjee, *Blind Spot: How Neoliberalism Infiltrated Global Health* (Oakland: University of California Press, 2014); Kim et al., *Dying for Growth*; Carney and Kenworthy, "Austerity, Health and Wellbeing"; including Basu, Carney, and Kenworthy, "Long Reach of Austerity," 203–207.

15. Lisa Smirl, "Drive by Development," *Spaces of Aid*, March 11, 2014, https://spacesofaid .wordpress.com/2014/03/11/drive-by-development-the-role-of-the-suv-in-international -humanitarian-assistance/.

16. I left the job after two years when I could no longer bear the cognitive dissonance of my commitments to local sovereignty and decision-making—born of my hardscrabble time spent in Sierra Leone—and the US government's foreign policies and practices that consistently denied people the right to make their own decisions under the guise of "development."

17. *Bending the Arc*, 27:40.

18. Kapur, Lewis, and Webb, *World Bank*, 912–913n29.

19. Conway, *Summit*, 268.

20. Kapur, Lewis, and Webb, *World Bank*, 3.

21. Richard H. Demuth, "A Look Backward," *International Bank Notes: The First Fifteen Years* 15, no. 6 (June 1961): 6, https://documents1.worldbank.org/curated/en/483041468914423403 /pdf/International-Bank-notes.pdf.

22. Richard Demuth, interview by Robert W. Oliver, *World Bank Group Archives Oral History Program*, August 10, 1961, 11, https://documents1.worldbank.org/curated/en/62354146 8147539954/pdf/789850TRN0Demu0view0August010001961.pdf.

23. Demuth, "A Look Backward," 6.

24. Conway, *Summit*, 296.

25. Demuth, *Oral History Program*, 6.

26. World Bank, *70 Years: Connecting Capital Markets to Development*, 2018, 70, https://
thedocs.worldbank.org/en/doc/905031541023749461-0340022018/original/70yearscon
nectingcapitalmarketstodevelopment.pdf.

27. World Bank, *70 Years*, 70.

28. World Bank, *70 Years*, 40.

29. Demuth, "A Look Backward," 6–7.

30. "What We Do," US Securities and Exchange Commission, last modified April 6, 2023,
https://www.sec.gov/about/what-we-do.

31. Kapur, Lewis, and Webb, *World Bank*, 918nn49–50.

32. World Bank, "Over 70 Years of Innovation in the Global Capital Markets," accessed February
24, 2024, https://treasury.worldbank.org/en/about/unit/treasury/about#2.

33. Michael Lewis, *The Big Short: Inside the Doomsday Machine* (New York: W. W. Norton, 2010).

34. Sydney Cope, interview by Robert Oliver, *World Bank Group Oral History Program*, August
9, 1961, p. 26, https://documents.worldbank.org/en/publication/documents-reports
/documentdetail/608111468124481188/main-report.

35. International Bank for Reconstruction and Development, *Technical Report on the French
West African Railways*, May 24, 1953, https://documents1.worldbank.org/curated/en
/618181468032414631/pdf/multi0page.pdf.

36. International Bank for Reconstruction and Development, *Twenty-Eighth Special Meeting of
the Executive Directors: Loans to the Kingdom of Belgium and the Belgian Congo*, September
13, 1952, 4, 5, 15, http://documents1.worldbank.org/curated/en/442661468013865834
/pdf/658270BR0P03730Congo000Sept01301951.pdf.

37. World Bank, *Loans to Kingdom of Belgium and to the Belgian Congo*, September 13, 1951,
https://documents1.worldbank.org/curated/en/353751468003920929/pdf/Loan-0048
-Belgium-Belgian-Congo-Development-Plan-Project-Loan-Agreement.pdf.

38. International Bank for Reconstruction and Development, *Loans to the Kingdom*, 4.

39. PBS, "Africa's Greatest Civilizations: The City of M'banza-Kongo," February 27, 2017,
video, 2:15, https://www.pbs.org/video/africas-great-civilizations-city-mbanza-kongo
-africas-great-civilizations/.

40. International Bank for Reconstruction and Development, *Loans to the Kingdom*, 5.

41. International Bank for Reconstruction and Development, *Twenty-Eighth Special Meeting*,
15-16.

42. See Galit A. Sarfaty, *Values in Translation: Human Rights and the Culture of the World Bank*
(Stanford, CA: Stanford University Press, 2012).

43. Daniel Crena de Longh, interview by Oral History Research Office, Columbia University,
*World Bank Group Oral History Program*, August 1, 1961, 16, https://documents1.worldbank

.org/curated/en/932021468148171738/pdf/789700v20TRN0C0rview0August01001961
.pdf.

44. William Clark, "Robert McNamara at the World Bank," *Foreign Affairs* 60, no. 1 (Fall 1981): 174, https://doi.org/10.2307/20040995.

45. Adrian Robert Bazbauers, "The Wolfensohn, Wolfowitz, and Zoellick Presidencies: Revitalising the Neoliberal Agenda of the World Bank," *Forum for Development Studies* 41, no. 1 (March 2014): 91, https://doi.org/10.1080/08039410.2013.868821.

46. Barack Obama, "President Obama Nominates Jim Yong Kim for World Bank President," The Obama White House, March 23, 2010, YouTube video, 6:39, https://www.youtube .com/watch?v=UmRlhxhXClE.

47. Sophie Edwards, "As Jim Kim Steps Down, a Tumultuous World Bank Presidency Comes to an End," *Devex*, February 4, 2019, https://www.devex.com/news/as-jim-kim-steps-down -a-tumultuous-world-bank-presidency-comes-to-an-end-94247.

48. World Bank, "Maximizing Finance for Development," April 11, 2018, YouTube video, https://www.youtube.com/watch?v=sdzttzJphsE.

49. "Search Results," Open Knowledge Repository Beta, accessed August 5, 2021, https://open knowledge.worldbank.org/home.

50. World Bank, "Maximizing Finance for Development," infographic, April 10, 2018, https:// www.worldbank.org/en/news/infographic/2018/04/10/maximizing-finance-for -development.

51. World Bank, *From Billions to Trillions: MDB [Multilateral Development Bank] Contributions to Financing for Development*, July 2015, https://documents1.worldbank.org/curated /en/602761467999349576/pdf/98023-BR-SecM2015-0233-IDA-SecM2015-0147-IFC -SecM2015-0105-MIGA-SecM2015-0061-Box391499B-OUO-9.pdf.

52. World Bank, Open Learning Campus, https://ppp.worldbank.org/public-private-partner ship/library/world-bank-group-open-learning-campus-olc. The twenty-three-video webinar on public-private partnerships was publicly available when I accessed it on August 5, 2021. It is now password-protected and no longer publicly available.

53. UNCTAD, "Developing Countries Face $2.5 Trillion Annual Investment Gap in Key Sustainable Development Sectors, UNCTAD Report Estimates," *UNCTAD*, June 24, 2014, https://unctad.org/press-material/developing-countries-face-25-trillion-annual -investment-gap-key-sustainable.

54. Jim Yong Kim, "Speech at the 2017 Annual Meetings Plenary," October 13, 2017, https:// www.worldbank.org/en/news/speech/2017/10/13/wbg-president-jim-yong-kim-speech -2017-annual-meetings-plenary-session; Jim Yong Kim, "Rethinking Development Finance: LSE Public Lecture," April 11, 2017, in *LSE Public Event*, podcast, https://www.lse.ac.uk /lse-player?id=3802.

55. World Bank Group, "Public-Private Partnerships," accessed March 6, 2024, https://ppp .worldbank.org/public-private-partnership/about-us/about-public-private-partnerships.

56. Mariana Mazzucato explains the problem of governments not requiring some kind of return on government investments in *The Entrepreneurial State: Debunking Public vs. Private Sector Myths* (New York: PublicAffairs, 2015).

57. James Leigland, "Public-Private Partnerships in Developing Countries: The Emerging Evidence-Based Critique," *World Bank Research Observer* 33, no. 1 (February 2018): 103–134, https://doi.org/10.1093/wbro/lkx008; Arne Ruckert and Ronald Labonté, "Public-Private Partnerships (PPPs) in Global Health: The Good, the Bad and the Ugly," *Third World Quarterly* 35, no. 9 (November 2014): 1598–1614, https://doi.org/10.1080/01436597.2014 .970870; Judith Richter, "Public-Private Partnerships for Health: A Trend with No Alternatives?," *Development* 47 (June 2004): 43–48, https://doi.org/https://doi.org/10.1057 /palgrave.development.1100043; Michael R. Reich, "Public-Private Partnerships for Public Health," *Nature Medicine* 6 (June 2000): 617–620, https://doi.org/10.1038/76176.

58. Manjari Mahajan, "Philanthropy and the Nation-State in Global Health: The Gates Foundation in India," *Global Public Health* 13, no. 10 (December 2017): 1357–1368, https://doi .org/10.1080/17441692.2017.1414286.

59. Arwen Barr et al., "Health Sector Fragmentation: Three Examples from Sierra Leone," *Globalization and Health* 15, no. 8 (January 2019): 1–8, https://doi.org/10.1186/s12992 -018-0447-5.

60. Enthusiasm for blended finance has since been tempered. One study found that US$1 raised only 75 cents on average, only 37 cents in the world's poorest countries (Samantha Attridge and Lars Engen, *Blended Finance in the Poorest Countries: The Need for a Better Approach*, April 2019, http://cdn-odi-production.s3-website-eu-west-1.amazonaws.com /media/documents/12666.pdf). Maria José Romero, "Development Finance Takes 'Private Turn': Implications and Challenges Ahead," *Development* 59 (May 2017): 59–65, https:// doi.org/10.1057/s41301-017-0074-0, raises other concerns explaining that at the core of blended finance is a perverse logic: private investors are believed to take the greatest risk, even as governments and philanthropies backstop their losses. With blended finance, taxpayers and donors prop up private investment instead of investing public monies directly to improve societal essentials like health, education, and social protections. Blended finance instruments and impact investing (including by other names) have targeted labor, health, education, and social welfare problems, with varying degrees of success (Susan L. Erikson, "Global Health Futures? Reckoning with a Pandemic Bond," *Medicine Anthropology Theory* 6, no. 3 (October 2019): 1–32, https://doi.org/10.17157/mat.6.3.664).

61. Gillian Tett, "Blended Finance, the Spinach of Investing, Will Make Us Stronger," *Financial Times*, February 25, 2021, https://www.ft.com/content/16885bf1-b172-4dcc-b7f8 -0b32798563c6.

62. Milton Friedman, "A Friedman Doctrine—The Social Responsibility of Business Is to Increase Its Profits," *New York Times Magazine*, September 13, 1970.

63. Greta Krippner, *Capitalizing on Crisis: The Political Origins of the Rise of Finance* (Cambridge, MA: Harvard University Press, 2012); Rana Foroohar, *Makers and Takers: How Wall Street Destroyed Main Street* (New York: Crown, 2017).

64. Kim et al., *Dying for Growth.*

65. Felix Stein and Devi Sridhar, "The World Bank Reinvents Itself—And Puts Poverty Reduction at Risk," *The Conversation*, June 16, 2017, https://theconversation.com/the-world-bank-reinvents-itself-and-puts-poverty-reduction-at-risk-79403; K.S. Jomo and Anis Chowdhury, "World Bank Financializing Development," *Development* 62, no. 1 (September 2019): 147–153, https://doi.org/10.1057/s41301-019-00206-3.

66. Ève Chiapello, Anita Engels, and Eduardo Gonçalves Gresse. *Financializations of Development: Global Games and Local Experiments* (New York: Routledge, 2023).

67. World Bank, "Projects."

## CHAPTER 5

1. Gillian Tett, *Anthro-Vision: How Anthropology Can Explain Business and Life* (New York: Random House Business, 2021).

2. Fred Martineau, Annie Wilkinson, and Melissa Parker, "Epistemologies of Ebola: Reflections on the Experience of the Ebola Response Anthropology Platform," *Anthropology Quarterly* 90, no. 2 (Spring 2017): 475–494, https://doi.org/10.1353/anq.2017.0027.

3. Twelve years before becoming World Bank president, Kim coedited a book that indicted the World Bank for global poverty. See Kim et al., *Dying for Growth.*

4. Jim Yong Kim, "The David Rubenstein Show: Dr. Jim Yong Kim," interview by David Rubenstein, September 5, 2018, YouTube video, 11:16, https://www.youtube.com/watch?v=2HBzTz4c3SU.

5. Jim Yong Kim, "World Bank President Jim Yong Kim: The VICE News Interview," *Vice News*, April 25, 2015, YouTube video, 0:06, https://www.youtube.com/watch?v=619qFMXneeU.

6. Kim, "VICE News Interview," 1:48, 7:35.

7. Thomas, "Creature of Wall Street."

8. Jim Yong Kim, "Billions to Trillions: Idea to Action," July 13, 2015, https://www.worldbank.org/en/news/speech/2015/07/13/billions-trillions-ideas-action-event.

9. World Bank, "World Bank Launches First Ever Pandemic Bonds to Support PEF," World Bank Treasury, June 28, 2017, YouTube video, 3:48, https://www.youtube.com/watch?v=RgmBjDGHAAI.

10. Jim Yong Kim, "We Need a New Global Response to Pandemics," *World Economic Forum*, January 20, 2015, https://www.weforum.org/agenda/2015/01/we-need-a-new-global-response-to-pandemics/.

11. Kim, "What Ebola Taught."

12. Sophie Edwards, "Pandemic Response a Cycle of 'Panic and Neglect,' Says World Bank President," *Devex*, April 5, 2017, https://www.devex.com/news/pandemic-response-a-cycle-of-panic-and-neglect-says-world-bank-president-89995.

13. Jim Yong Kim, "Speech: Rethinking Development Finance," April 17, 2017, https://www.worldbank.org/en/news/speech/2017/04/11/speech-by-world-bank-group-president-jim-yong-kim-rethinking-development-finance.

14. Farmer and Kim, "Annual Meeting Opening Keynote," at 59:13.

15. Sarah Boseley, "Escalation of Ebola Crisis Could Have Been Avoided, Says World Bank President," *The Guardian*, July 18, 2016, https://www.theguardian.com/global-development/2016/jul/18/ebola-escalation-could-have-been-avoided-world-bank-president-jim-young-kim-pandemic-financing-facility; emphasis mine.

16. Lant Prichett, "Why Obama's World Bank Pick Is Proving So Controversial," *New Republic,* April 10, 2012, https://newrepublic.com/article/102624/why-obamas-world-bank-pick-proving-so-controversial; Robert H. Wade, "US Keeps Control of the World Bank," *Le Monde Diplomatique*, October 24, 2012, https://mondediplo.com/outsidein/us-keeps-control-of-the-world-bank.

17. Jim Yong Kim, "Doesn't Everyone Deserve a Chance at a Good Life?," TED talk, July 19, 2017, YouTube video, 22:12, https://www.youtube.com/watch?v=Fc1yN6uxZfQ.

18. Kim, "The David Rubenstein Show," 12:59.

19. Jim Yong Kim, "Get to Know Jim Yong Kim," interview by Eric Nam, *I Think You're Dope*, DIVE Studios, January 6, 2021, YouTube video, 1:12:28, https://www.youtube.com/watch?v=JiwvibnE2TQ.

20. Jim Yong Kim, "Dr. Jim Yong Kim on Global Health," interview by Bill Moyers, *Bill Moyers Journal*, September 11, 2009, video, 24:12, https://billmoyers.com/content/dr-jim-yong-kim-on-global-health/.

21. "Countries," Partners in Health, accessed July 24, 2023, https://www.pih.org/countries.

22. Tracy Kidder, *Mountains beyond Mountains: The Quest of Dr. Paul Farmer, a Man Who Would Cure the World* (New York: Random House, 2003), 99.

23. Kim, "The David Rubenstein Show," 10:12.

24. Kim, "The David Rubenstein Show," 9:30.

25. Kidder, *Mountains beyond Mountains*, 169.

26. Pfeiffer and Chapman, "Structural Adjustment"; Glen Biglaiser and Ronald J McGauvran, "The Effects of IMF Loan Conditions on Poverty in the Developing World," *Journal of International Relations and Development* 25 (2022): 806–833.

27. See James Pfeiffer and Rachel Chapman, "The Art of Medicine: An Anthropology of Aid in Africa," *The Lancet* 385 (May 2015): 2144–2145, https://www.thelancet.com/pdfs/journals/lancet/PIIS0140-6736(15)61013-3.pdf.

28. Kidder, *Mountains beyond Mountains*, 123.

29. Kidder, *Mountains beyond Mountains*, 144.

30. Kidder, *Mountains beyond Mountains*, 145.

31. Jim Yong Kim, "Jim Yong Kim on Global Futures," Global Georgetown, February 9, 2017, YouTube video, 37:45, https://www.youtube.com/watch?v=Z0PLnyLVByo.

32. Kidder, *Mountains beyond Mountains*, 143.

33. Kidder, *Mountains beyond Mountains*, 149.

34. *Bending the Arc*, 36:20.

35. A former Harvard Medical School student of Kim's wrote a particularly scathing rebuke of their ethics. Sam Dubal, "Renouncing Paul Farmer: A Desperate Plea for Radical Political Medicine," *Being Ethical in an Unethical World* (blog), May 17, 2012, https://samdubal .blogspot.com/2012/05/renouncing-paul-farmer-desperate-plea.html.

There was also a lively scholarly debate in a top-tier medical anthropology journal in the early 2000s about the approach taken by the Farmer-Kim-Harvard cohort, which was seen as ethnocentric and self-righteous. See also Leslie Butt, "The Suffering Stranger: Medical Anthropology and International Morality," *Medical Anthropology* 21, no. 1 (2002): 1–24, https://doi.org/10.1080/01459740210619; followed by a reply from Alec Irwin et al., "Suffering, Moral Claims, and Scholarly Responsibility: A Response to Leslie Butt," *Medical Anthropology* 21, no. 1 (2002): 25–30, https://doi.org/10.1080/01459740210621; followed by a final comment from Leslie Butt, "Reply to Alec Irwin, Joyce Millen, Jim Kim, John Gershman, Brooke G. Schoepf, and Paul Farmer," *Medical Anthropology* 21, no. 1 (2002): 31–33, https://doi.org/10.1080/01459740210622.

36. Irene M. Wielawski, "Taking Charge," *Dartmouth Alumni Magazine*, September 2009, https://dartmouthalumnimagazine.com/articles/taking-charge.

37. Kidder, *Mountains beyond Mountains*, 170.

38. Wielawski, "Taking Charge."

39. Kim, "Get to Know Jim Yong Kim," 23:55.

40. Kidder, *Mountains beyond Mountains*, 173.

41. Wielawski, "Taking Charge."

42. Kidder, *Mountains beyond Mountains*, 174.

43. Kim, "Get to Know Jim Yong Kim," edited for brevity, 13:25.

44. Kim, "Get to Know Jim Yong Kim," 23:40.

45. Kidder, *Mountains beyond Mountains*, 170.

46. Kim, "Get to Know Jim Yong Kim," edited for brevity, 22:20.

47. Kim, "Get to Know Jim Yong Kim," edited for brevity, 23:00.

48. Kim, "Get to Know Jim Yong Kim," edited for brevity, 13:40.

49. Kim, "The David Rubenstein Show," 12:52.

50. Andrew Rice, "The Evolution of an Idealist," *Foreign Policy*, no. 218 (May/June 2016): 55, https://www.jstor.org/stable/44843425.

51. Brian Solomon, "Me-First Leadership: Jim Yong Kim's Unfulfilled Promise at Dartmouth," *Forbes*, March 23, 2012, https://www.forbes.com/sites/briansolomon/2012/03/23/me-first -leadership-jim-yong-kims-unfulfilled-promise-at-dartmouth/?sh=71e9c8d75e52.

52. Solomon, "Me-First Leadership."

53. Janet Reitman, "Confessions of an Ivy League Frat Boy: Inside Dartmouth's Hazing Abuses," *Rolling Stone*, March 28, 2012, https://www.rollingstone.com/feature/confessions-of-an-ivy -league-frat-boy-inside-dartmouths-hazing-abuses-238604/.

54. Susan Adams, "Harvard Professor Slams Obama's World Bank Nomination," *Forbes*, March 23, 2012, https://www.forbes.com/sites/susanadams/2012/03/23/harvard-professor -slams-obamas-world-bank-nomination/?sh=469070d43db1.

55. Andrew Rice, "How the World Bank's Biggest Critic Became Its President," *The Guardian*, August 11, 2016, https://www.theguardian.com/news/2016/aug/11/world-bank-jim -yong-kim.

56. Adams, "Harvard Professor Slams."

57. Rice, "World Bank's Biggest Critic."

58. Jim Yong Kim, "Defeating Covid-19—A 5 Part Plan w. Dr. Jim Yong Kim and Marshall Goldsmith," interview by Marshall Goldsmith and Sanyin Siang, Marshall Goldsmith, May 1, 2020, YouTube video, 54:36, https://www.youtube.com/watch?v=gDTRoodVXWo.

59. McKinsey has been making inroads—and finding clients—in global health for many years. See Julia Belluz and Marine Buissonniere, "How McKinsey Infiltrated the World of Global Public Health," *Vox*, December 13, 2019, https://www.vox.com/science-and -health/2019/12/13/21004456/bill-gates-mckinsey-global-public-health-bcg; see also Mariana Mazzucato and Rosie Collington, *The Big Con: How the Consulting Industry Weakens Our Businesses, Infantilizes Our Governments, and Warps Our Economies* (New York: Penguin Press, 2023).

60. McKinsey & Company, "Organizational Health Index," accessed July 24, 2023, https:// www.mckinsey.com/solutions/orgsolutions/overview/organizational-health-index.

61. World Bank Group, *2013 Employee Engagement Survey Summary of Results*, 2013, p. 25, https://www.brettonwoodsproject.org/wp-content/uploads/2014/03/EES2013_WBG _SummaryReport-staff-survey.pdf.

62. World Bank Group, *2014 Staff Survey*, 2014, https://s3.documentcloud.org/documents /2107735/world-bank-2014-sraff-survey.pdf; World Bank Group, *Engagement Survey 2015*, 2015, https://www.documentcloud.org/documents/2119278-world-bank-staff-survey -comments.html; Jeff Tyson, "World Bank Staff Survey Highlights Discontent with Senior Management," *Devex*, June 22, 2015, https://www.devex.com/news/world-bank-staff-survey

-highlights-discontent-with-senior-management-86384; Jeff Tyson, "Why the World Bank's Staff Survey Is Delayed," *Devex*, December 23, 2014, https://www.devex.com/news/why-the-world-bank-s-staff-survey-is-delayed-85111.

63. Annie Lowrey, "World Bank, Rooted in Bureaucracy, Proposes a Sweeping Reorganization," *New York Times*, October 6, 2013, https://www.nytimes.com/2013/10/07/business/interna tional/world-bank-rooted-in-bureaucracy-proposes-a-sweeping-reorganization.html.

64. Annie Lowrey, "World Bank Revamping Is Rattling Employees," *New York Times*, May 27, 2014, https://www.nytimes.com/2014/05/28/business/international/world-bank-revamping-is-rattling-employees.html.

65. World Bank, "World Bank Group President: No More Business as Usual," October 11, 2013, https://www.worldbank.org/en/news/press-release/2013/10/11/world-bank-group-president-annual-meetings-plenary.

66. Shawn Donnan, "World Bank Chief Dogged by Staff Anger," *Financial Times*, October 8, 2014, https://www.ft.com/content/b7b8e8c0-4e75-11e4-bfda-00144feab7de.

67. *The Economist*, "Opprobrium from the Atrium," November 8, 2014, 74, https://www.economist.com/finance-and-economics/2014/11/08/opprobrium-from-the-atrium.

68. Rice, "World Bank's Biggest Critic."

69. Edwards, "Jim Kim Steps Down."

70. Jim Yong Kim, "Preventing the Next Pandemic: A Conversation with the World Bank President," interview by J. Stephen Morrison, Center for Strategic & International Studies, June 2, 2016, YouTube video, 18:24, https://www.youtube.com/watch?v=tXWJWHkgl8k.

71. Sasha Chavkin and Ben Hallman, "World Bank Workers Losing Faith in Leadership, Survey Reveals," *International Consortium of Investigative Journalists*, June 22, 2015, https://www.icij.org/inside-icij/2015/06/world-bank-workers-losing-faith-leadership-survey-reveals/.

72. Rice, "World Bank's Biggest Critic."

73. Claire Provost, "A World Bank of Trouble?," *The Guardian*, December 4, 2014, https://www.theguardian.com/global-development-professionals-network/2014/dec/04/a-world-bank-of-trouble.

74. Lowrey, "World Bank, Rooted in Bureaucracy."

75. Robin Harding, "World Bank: Man on a Mission," *Financial Times*, April 7, 2014, https://www.ft.com/content/012f15d6-b8fa-11e3-98c5-00144feabdc0.

76. *Financial Times*, "The World Bank Risks Sliding into Irrelevance," November 20, 2014, https://www.ft.com/content/0953c8cc-70bc-11e4-9129-00144feabdc0.

77. Thomas, "Creature of Wall Street."

78. Rice, "World Bank's Biggest Critic."

79. Rice, "World Bank's Biggest Critic."

80. Thomas, "Creature of Wall Street."

81. Jim Yong Kim, "LinkedIn Speaker Series: Dr. Jim Yong Kim," interview by Allen Blue, LinkedIn, September 12, 2018, YouTube video, 22:50, https://www.youtube.com/watch?v=yDkqhSOUVo4.

82. World Bank Treasury, "Milestones in World Bank Bonds History: 1947–2017," October 16, 2017, YouTube video, 2:57, https://www.youtube.com/watch?v=TAJOZEaPJoA.

83. Sophie Edwards, "As Jim Kim Steps Down, a Tumultuous World Bank Presidency Comes to an End," *Devex*, February 4, 2019, https://www.devex.com/news/as-jim-kim-steps-down-a-tumultuous-world-bank-presidency-comes-to-an-end-94247; Mark Vandevelde, James Politi, and Sam Fleming, "Why Jim Yon Kim's Move Has Shaken Up the World Bank," *Financial Times*, January 11, 2019, https://www.ft.com/content/44dd27d8-158d-11e9-a581-4ff78404524e; John Zarocostas, "Jim Yong Kim Steps Down from the World Bank," *Lancet*, 393 (January 26, 2019): 305–306; *The Economist*, "The World Bank's President Resigns Abruptly," January 12, 2019, 66; Ronald C. Machen et al., "Investigation of Data Irregularities in *Doing Business 2018* and *Doing Business 2020: Investigation Findings and Report to the Board of Executive Directors*," WilmerHale, September 15, 2021.

84. Amy Maxmen, "Why the World Bank Ex-Chief Is on a Mission to End Coronavirus Transmission," *Nature*, April 22, 2020, https://www.nature.com/articles/d41586-020-01218-7. Also in Jim Yong Kim, "100 Coaches Live," interview by Marshall Goldsmith and Sanyin Siang, April 30, 2020, LinkedIn video, https://www.linkedin.com/video/live/urn:li:ugcPost:6661647942627143680/.

85. Jim Yong Kim, "A Conversation with Jim Yong Kim '82, Vice Chairman and Partner at Global Infrastructure Partners," interview by Edward Steinfeld, Watson Institute for International and Public Affairs, February 13, 2019, YouTube video, 1:20:09, https://www.youtube.com/watch?v=wxEUCvvrCnM.

**CHAPTER 6**

1. I have long drawn inspiration for thinking about how people, places, and things get "made up" from Ian Hacking's "Making Up People," *London Review of Books* 28, no. 16 (August 2006), https://www.lrb.co.uk/the-paper/v28/n16/ian-hacking/making-up-people.

2. Claire L. Wendland, *Partial Stories: Maternal Death from Six Angles* (Chicago: University of Chicago Press, 2022).

3. World Bank Treasury, "About," accessed July 25, 2023, https://treasury.worldbank.org/en/about/unit/treasury/about.

4. World Bank Treasury, "Create, Don't Just Participate. The World Bank Student Careers," August 25, 2020, YouTube video, 1:57, https://www.youtube.com/watch?v=RdLvR0mfMPk&list=PLuz9mCSZhLGlRp5Qa_ZSX0DJd_xNB8ZGj.

5. World Bank, "Building Human Capital Starts with Health," *World Bank Blogs*, December 12, 2018, https://blogs.worldbank.org/health/building-human-capital-starts-health.

6. World Bank, "Development Finance (DFi)," accessed July 25, 2023, https://www.worldbank.org/en/about/unit/dfi.

## CHAPTER 7

1. Paula Jarzabkowski, Rebecca Bednarek, and Paul Spee, *Making a Market for Acts of God: The Practice of Risk-Trading in the Global Reinsurance Industry* (Oxford: Oxford University Press, 2015), 166–170.

2. "Catastrophe Bonds and ILS Issuance by Trigger and by Year," Artemis, accessed March 2, 2024, https://www.artemis.bm/dashboard/cat-bonds-ils-by-trigger-by-year/.

3. Steve Evans, "25 years of Artemis, over $170bn of Deal Directory of Transactions Tracked," *Artemis*, May 20, 2024, https://www.artemis.bm/news/25-years-of-artemis-over-170bn-of-deal-directory-transactions-tracked/.

4. Artemis, "Golden Goal Finance Ltd.," accessed March 2, 2024, https://www.artemis.bm/deal-directory/golden-goal-finance-ltd/.

5. Artemis, "World Bank Hails First Cat Bond from New Capital-at-Risk Notes Program," July 1, 2014, https://www.artemis.bm/news/world-bank-hails-first-cat-bond-from-new-capital-at-risk-notes-program/.

6. Karen A. Grépin, "International Donations to the Ebola Virus Outbreak: Too Little, Too Late?," *BMJ* 350, no. h376 (February 2015): 1–5, https://doi.org/10.1136/bmj.h376.

7. Veronica Scotti, "Lessons for a Post-Covid-19 World," *Swiss Re*, April 27, 2020, https://www.swissre.com/our-business/public-sector-solutions/contributing-to-the-global-debate/covid-19-pandemic-emergency-funding.html.

## CHAPTER 8

1. I've derived the company's pseudonym, ModelRisk, from its catastrophe risk modeling focus.

2. World Bank, *Prospectus*, 6.

3. World Bank, *Prospectus*, I-1 to II-35.

4. CDC, "New Modeling Tool for Response to Ebola Virus Disease," last modified September 23, 2014, https://archive.cdc.gov/#/details?url=https://www.cdc.gov/media/releases/2014/s0923-ebola-model-Factsheet.html.

5. In "How Computer Modelers Took on the Ebola Outbreak," *IEEE Spectrum*, May 28, 2015, https://spectrum.ieee.org/how-computer-modelers-took-on-the-ebola-outbreak, David Brown explains that "The CDC built a model that assumed more than half of cases were unreported. . . . [T]he high forecasts were really worst-case scenarios. They assumed that additional treatment centers wouldn't open up, contact tracing wouldn't improve, and burial practices wouldn't get safer. But all of those improvements were in fact taking place."

6. Cristina Carias et al., "Forecasting the 2014 West African Ebola Outbreak," *Epidemiologic Reviews* 41, no. 1 (November 2019): 34, https://doi.org/10.1093/epirev/mxz013; Sebastian

Funk et al., "Assessing the Performance of Real-Time Epidemic Forecasts: A Case Study of Ebola in the Western Area Region of Sierra Leone, 2014–15," *PLOS Computational Biology* 15, no. 2 (February 2019): 1–17, https://doi.org/10.1371/journal.pcbi.1006785.

7. IBM, "What Is Monte Carlo Simulation?," accessed July 26, 2023, https://www.ibm.com/cloud/learn/monte-carlo-simulation.

8. Anthropologists aim to make descriptive sense of the "whole cloth" of a problem, not just the threads that can be enumerated. Our strength is in using words to describe and analyze. For examples of excellent collections of anthropological research on an infectious disease pandemic, see Mary Moran and Daniel Hoffman, "Ebola in Perspective," *Hot Spots, Fieldsights*, October 7, 2014, https://culanth.org/fieldsights/series/ebola-in-perspective; Catherine Bolten and Susan Shepler, eds., "Producing Ebola: Creating Knowledge in and about an Epidemic," special issue, *Anthropology Quarterly* 90, no. 2 (Spring 2017): 349–569, https://muse.jhu.edu/issue/36572/online. See also the American Anthropological Association, *Strengthening West African Health Care Systems to Stop Ebola: Anthropologists Offer Insights*, November 18, 2014, https://pure.mpg.de/rest/items/item_2096578/component/file_2103624/content.

9. Erikson, "Global Health Business."

10. Ronald Ross, "An Application of the Theory of Probabilities to the Study of A Priori Pathometry—Part I," *Proceedings of the Royal Society A* 92, no. 638 (February 1916): 204–230, https://doi.org/10.1098/rspa.1916.0007. See Fred Brauer, "Mathematical Epidemiology: Past, Present, and Future," *Infectious Disease Modeling* 2, no. 2 (May 2017): 113–127, https://doi.org/10.1016/j.idm.2017.02.001.

11. World Bank, *Prospectus*, I-8.

12. World Bank, *Prospectus*, I-23.

13. World Bank, *Prospectus*, II-5.

14. World Bank, "World Bank Sustainable Development Bond Raises Awareness for Women and Girls' Empowerment," *World Bank*, January 9, 2018, https://www.worldbank.org/en/news/press-release/2018/01/09/world-bank-sustainable-development-bond-raises-awareness-for-women-and-girls-empowerment.

**CHAPTER 9**

1. CDC, "2014 Ebola Outbreak in West Africa Epidemic Curves, Ebola (Ebola Virus Disease)," last modified April 3, 2019, https://www.cdc.gov/vhf/ebola/history/2014-2016-outbreak/cumulative-cases-graphs.html.

2. Some of these on-the-ground examples are from ethnographic research conducted by a member of our research team, Sam Eglin, who was an MSc student at Simon Fraser University at the time.

3. The COVID-19 pandemic tested data systems worldwide. For an explanation of US COVID-19 data collection, see Michael Lewis, *The Premonition: A Pandemic Story* (New York: W. W. Norton, 2021).

4.  Vijay Narayan, "Sierra Leone's Health Workforce Crisis: Drivers of Suboptimal Distribution and Poor Retention of Primary Healthcare Workers in Rural Areas" (MPH thesis, University of Washington, 2015), 20–21, http://hdl.handle.net/1773/33072.

5.  Amy Maxmen, *Ebola's Unpaid Heroes: How Billions in Aid Skips over Those at the Frontline* (New York: Newsweek Insights, 2015), Kindle.

6.  Susan Shepler, "We Know Who Is Eating the Ebola Money! Corruption, the State, and the Ebola Response," in "Producing Ebola: Creating Knowledge in and about an Epidemic," ed. Catherine Bolten and Susan Shepler, special issue, *Anthropological Quarterly* 90, no. 2 (Spring 2017): 465, https://doi.org/10.1353/anq.2017.0026.

7.  See Cal (Crystal) Biruk, *Cooking: Culture and Politics in an African Research World* (Durham, NC: Duke University Press, 2018), 135, 146, and 166–167.

8.  Lewis, *The Premonition*.

9.  World Bank, *Pandemic Emergency Financing Facility—Global Pandemic Response through a Financial Intermediary Fund*, May 3, 2016, 13–14, https://documents1.worldbank.org /curated/en/354341467990992248/pdf/104838-BR-R2016-0071-Box394885B-OUO-9 .pdf; emphasis mine.

10.  World Bank, *Prospectus*, 3; emphasis in original.

11.  World Bank, *Prospectus*, 10.

12.  World Bank, *Prospectus*, 7.

13.  World Bank, *Prospectus*, 6.

14.  National Academies of Sciences, Engineering, and Medicine, *Taking Action against Clinician Burnout: A Systems Approach to Professional Well-Being* (Washington, DC: National Academies Press, 2019), chap. 4, "Factors Contributing to Clinician Burnout and Professional Well-Being," https://doi.org/10.17226/25521; Jeffrey Budd, "Burnout Related to Electronic Health Record Use in Primary Care," *Journal of Primary Care & Community Health* 14 (2023): 1–7, https://doi.org/10.1177/21501319231166921.

15.  Joanna Raven, Haja Wurie, and Sophie Witter, "Health Workers' Experiences of Coping with the Ebola Epidemic in Sierra Leone's Health System: A Qualitative Study," *BMC Health Services Research* 18 (April 2018): 1–9, https://doi.org/10.1186/s12913-018-3072-3.

16.  Government of Sierra Leone, *National Ebola Recovery Strategy for Sierra Leone: 2015–2017*, July 2015, 25, https://ebolaresponse.un.org/sites/default/files/sierra_leone_recovery _strategy_en.pdf.

17.  The COVID-19 pandemic challenged data systems worldwide. For an discussion of COVID-19 data collection in the United States, see Lewis, *The Premonition*.

18.  World Health Organization, *What Worked? What Didn't? What's Next? 2023 Progress Report on the Global Action Plan for Healthy Lives and Well-Being for All*, 2023, 12, https://iris.who .int/bitstream/handle/10665/367422/9789240073371-eng.pdf.

## AFTERWORD

1. *The Economist*, "The Pandemic's True Death Toll," last modified July 18, 2023, https://www.economist.com/graphic-detail/coronavirus-excess-deaths-estimates.

2. Reuters, "IMF Sees Cost of COVID Pandemic Rising beyond $12.5 Trillion Estimate," January 20, 2022, https://www.reuters.com/business/imf-sees-cost-covid-pandemic-rising-beyond-125-trillion-estimate-2022-01-20/.

3. Harvey, *A Brief History of Neoliberalism*, 33; Servaas Storm, "Financialization and Economic Development: A Debate on the Social Efficiency of Modern Finance," *Development and Change* 49, no. 2 (2018): 302–329, https://doi.org/10.1111/dech.12385.

4. Barbara Prainsack, "The Political Economy of Digital Data: Introduction to the Special Issue," in "The Political Economy of Digital Data," ed. Barbara Prainsack, special issue, *Policy Studies* 41, no. 5 (2020): 439–446, https://doi.org/10.1080/01442872.2020.1723519.

5. Sun-ha Hong, *Technologies of Speculation: The Limits of Knowledge in a Data-Driven Society* (New York: New York University Press, 2020), 3.

6. Kim, "Get to Know Jim Yong Kim," edited for brevity, 23:00.

7. For example, Sarah Hughes-McLure and Emma Mawdsley, "Innovative Finance for Development? Vaccine Bonds and the Hidden Costs of Financialization," *Economic Geography* 98, no. 2 (March 2022): 145–169, https://doi.org/10.1080/00130095.2021.2020090; Felix Stein, "Risky Business: COVAX and the Financialization of Global Vaccine Equity," *Globalization and Health* 17, no. 112 (September 2021): 1–11, https://doi.org/10.1186/s12992-021-00763-8; Felix Stein and Devi Sridhar, "The Financialization of Global Health," *Wellcome Open Research* 3, no. 17 (February 2018): 1–4, https://doi.org/10.12688/wellcomeopenres.13885.1.

8. Jonas, "Pandemic Bonds."

9. I am grateful to Koen Peeters and the Oxford-Amsterdam group for the conversations about misdirection as an applied theoretical framework. Koen Peeters Grietens et al., eds., "Misdirection in Global Health: Creating the Illusion of (Im)possible Alternatives in Global Health Research and Practice," special issue, *Science & Technology Studies* 35, no. 2 (May 2022): 2–119, https://sciencetechnologystudies.journal.fi/issue/view/7770.

10. Mariana Mazzucato, *The Value of Everything: Making and Taking in the Global Economy* (New York: PublicAffairs, 2018).

11. Rajiv Shah, *Big Bets: How Large-Scale Change Really Happens* (New York: S&S/Simon Element, 2023); Nick Romeo, *The Alternative: How to Build a Just Economy* (Cambridge, MA: MIT Press, 2023).

12. Steve Evans, "World Bank to Scale-Up Access to Catastrophe Bonds and Reinsurance Capital," *Artemis*, February 2, 2024, https://www.artemis.bm/news/world-bank-to-scale-up-access-to-catastrophe-bonds-and-reinsurance-capital/.

13. Artemis, "COVID 19 Outlook," 38:30.

# Bibliography

Abdullah, Ibrahim, and Abou Bakarr Kamara. "Confronting Ebola with Bare Hands: Sierra Leone's Health Sector on the Eve of the Ebola Epidemic." In *Understanding West Africa's Ebola Epidemic: Towards a Political Economy*, edited by Ibrahim Abdullah and Ismail Rashid, 112–138. London: Zed Books, 2017.

Abdullah, Ibrahim, and Ismail Rashid, eds. *Understanding West Africa's Ebola Epidemic: Towards a Political Economy*. London: Zed Books, 2017.

Abraham, Arthur. "Bureh, the British, and the Hut Tax War." *International Journal of African Historical Studies* 7, no. 1 (1974): 99–106. https://doi.org/10.2307/216556.

Adams, Susan. "Harvard Professor Slams Obama's World Bank Nomination." *Forbes*, March 23, 2012. https://www.forbes.com/sites/susanadams/2012/03/23/harvard-professor-slams-obamas-world-bank-nomination/?sh=469070d43db1.

Adams, Vincanne, ed. *Metrics: What Counts in Global Health*. Durham, NC: Duke University Press, 2016.

Africa Centers for Disease Control. "About Us." Accessed October 31, 2023. https://africacdc.org/about-us/.

Allam, Zaheer. "The First 50 Days of COVID-19: A Detailed Chronological Timeline and Extensive Review of Literature Documenting the Pandemic." *Surveying the Covid-19 Pandemic and Its Implications* (July 2020): 1–7. https://doi.org/10.1016/B978-0-12-824313-8.00001-2.

Allen, Kate. "'Pandemic Bonds' Are the Latest Idea to Beat Disease." *Financial Times*, June 28, 2017. https://www.ft.com/content/487b0d00-5c26-11e7-b553-e2df1b0c3220.

Alloway, Tracy, and Tasos Vossos. "How Pandemic Bonds Became the World's Most Controversial Investment." *Bloomberg*, December 9, 2020. https://www.bloomberg.com/news/features/2020-12-09/covid-19-finance-how-the-world-bank-s-pandemic-bonds-became-controversial.

American Anthropological Association. *Strengthening West African Health Care Systems to Stop Ebola: Anthropologists Offer Insights*. November 18, 2014. https://pure.mpg.de/rest/items/item_2096578/component/file_2103624/content.

AP3. "AP3." Accessed February 24, 2024. https://www.ap3.se/en.

AP3. *Third National Swedish Pension Fund: Annual Report 2017.* 2018. https://a.storyblok.com/f/257759/x/7fd361cde5/ap3_annualreport2017.pdf.

Appadurai, Arjun. *Banking on Words: The Failure of Language in the Age of Derivative Finance.* Chicago: University of Chicago Press, 2015.

Artemis. "AP3 a Lead Investor in World Bank Pandemic Catastrophe Bond." August 24, 2017. https://www.artemis.bm/news/ap3-a-lead-investor-in-world-bank-pandemic-catastrophe-bond/.

Artemis. "Catastrophe Bonds and ILS Issuance by Trigger and by Year." Accessed March 2, 2024. https://www.artemis.bm/dashboard/cat-bonds-ils-by-trigger-by-year/.

Artemis. "COVID 19 Outlook for Insurance, Reinsurance, & Insurance-Linked Securities—Prospectus 2021 Conference." *Artemis Live,* no. 34, January 15, 2021. Podcast, 39:00. https://audioboom.com/posts/7773074-covid-19-outlook-for-insurance-reinsurance-ils-prospectus-2021-conference.

Artemis. "Golden Goal Finance Ltd." Accessed March 2, 2024. https://www.artemis.bm/deal-directory/golden-goal-finance-ltd/.

Artemis. "IBRD CAR 111–112—World Bank Pandemic Catastrophe Bond." Accessed June 8, 2023. https://www.artemis.bm/deal-directory/ibrd-car-111-112/.

Artemis. *Q4 2023 Catastrophe Bond and ILS Market Report: An Unprecedented Year of New Risks, Records, and Huge Market Growth.* December 29, 2023. https://www.artemis.bm/wp-content/uploads/2023/12/catastrophe-bond-ils-market-report-q4-2023.pdf.

Artemis. "World Bank Adds $105m of Pandemic Swaps to $320m of PEF Cat Bonds." June 29, 2017. https://www.artemis.bm/news/world-bank-adds-105m-of-pandemic-swaps-to-320m-of-pef-cat-bonds/.

Artemis. "World Bank Hails First Cat Bond from New Capital-at-Risk Notes Program." July 1, 2014. https://www.artemis.bm/news/world-bank-hails-first-cat-bond-from-new-capital-at-risk-notes-program/.

Attridge, Samantha, and Lars Engen. *Blended Finance in the Poorest Countries: The Need for a Better Approach.* April 2019. http://cdn-odi-production.s3-website-eu-west-1.amazonaws.com/media/documents/12666.pdf.

Baker, Mark. "Saving the World, One Bond at a Time." *Euromoney,* July 12, 2017. https://www.euromoney.com/article/b13szgmbqtg6dn/saving-the-world-one-bond-at-a-time.

Banga, Ajay. "2023 Annual Meetings Plenary Remarks." *World Bank,* October 13, 2023. https://www.worldbank.org/en/news/speech/2023/10/13/remarks-by-world-bank-group-president-ajay-banga-at-the-2023-annual-meetings-plenary.

Banya, Sama. *Looking Back—My Life and Times.* Freetown: Sierra Leonean Writers Series, 2015.

Barr, Arwen, Lauryn Garrett, Robert Marten, and Sowmya Kadandale. "Health Sector Fragmentation: Three Examples from Sierra Leone." *Globalization and Health* 15, no. 8 (January 2019): 1–8. https://doi.org/10.1186/s12992-018-0447-5.

Basu, Sanjay, Megan A. Carney, and Nora J. Kenworthy. "Ten Years after the Financial Crisis: The Long Reach of Austerity and Its Global Impacts on Health." In "Austerity, Health and Wellbeing: Transnational Perspectives," edited by Megan A. Carney and Nora J. Kenworthy. Special issue, *Social Science & Medicine* 187 (August 2017): 203–207. https://doi.org/10.1016/j.socscimed.2017.06.026.

Bazbauers, Adrian Robert. "The Wolfensohn, Wolfowitz, and Zoellick Presidencies: Revitalising the Neoliberal Agenda of the World Bank." *Forum for Development Studies* 41, no. 1 (March 2014): 91–114. https://doi.org/10.1080/08039410.2013.868821.

Belluz, Julia, and Marine Buissonniere. "How McKinsey Infiltrated the World of Global Public Health." *Vox*, December 13, 2019. https://www.vox.com/science-and-health/2019/12/13/21004456/bill-gates-mckinsey-global-public-health-bcg.

Benjamin, Bret. *Invested Interests: Capital, Culture, and the World Bank*. Minneapolis: University of Minnesota Press, 2007.

Benton, Adia. *HIV Exceptionalism: Development through Disease in Sierra Leone*. Minneapolis: University of Minnesota Press, 2015.

Berewa, Solomon E. *A New Perspective on Governance, Leadership, Conflict and Nation Building in Sierra Leone*. Bloomington, IN: AuthorHouse, 2011.

Biglaiser, Glen, and Ronald J. McGauvran. "The Effects of IMF Loan Conditions on Poverty in the Developing World." *Journal of International Relations and Development* 25 (June 2022): 806–833. https://doi.org/10.1057/s41268-022-00263-1.

Bill & Melinda Gates Foundation. "Funding Commitments to Fight COVID-19." *Bill & Melinda Gates Foundation*, January 12, 2022, accessed March 23, 2023. https://www.gatesfoundation.org/ideas/articles/covid19-contributions.

Biruk, Cal (Crystal). *Cooking Data: Culture and Politics in an African Research World*. Durham, NC: Duke University Press.

Bolten, Catherine, and Susan Shepler, eds. "Producing Ebola: Creating Knowledge in and about an Epidemic." Special issue, *Anthropology Quarterly* 90, no. 2 (Spring 2017): 349–569. https://muse.jhu.edu/issue/36572/online.

Boseley, Sarah. "Escalation of Ebola Crisis Could Have Been Avoided, Says World Bank President." *The Guardian*, July 18, 2016. https://www.theguardian.com/global-development/2016/jul/18/ebola-escalation-could-have-been-avoided-world-bank-president-jim-young-kim-pandemic-financing-facility.

Brauer, Fred. "Mathematical Epidemiology: Past, Present, and Future." *Infectious Disease Modeling* 2, no. 2 (May 2017): 113–127. https://doi.org/10.1016/j.idm.2017.02.001.

Brown, David. "How Computer Modelers Took on the Ebola Outbreak." *IEEE Spectrum*, May 28, 2015. https://spectrum.ieee.org/how-computer-modelers-took-on-the-ebola-outbreak.

Budd, Jeffrey. "Burnout Related to Electronic Health Record Use in Primary Care." *Journal of Primary Care & Community Health* 14 (2023): 1–7. https://doi.org/10.1177/21501319231166921.

Butt, Leslie. "Reply to Alec Irwin, Joyce Millen, Jim Kim, John Gershman, Brooke G. Schoepf, and Paul Farmer." *Medical Anthropology* 21, no. 1 (2002): 31–33. https://doi.org/10.1080 /01459740210622.

Butt, Leslie. "The Suffering Stranger: Medical Anthropology and International Morality." *Medical Anthropology* 21, no. 1 (2002): 1–24. https://doi.org/10.1080/01459740210619.

Cadario, Paul. Interview by Charles Ziegler. *World Bank Group Archives Oral History Project*, April 4, 17, 22, and 30, 2013. https://oralhistory.worldbank.org/transcripts/transcript-oral-history -interview-paul-cadario-held-april-4-17-22-30-2013.

Card, Kiffer G., and Kirk J. Hepburn. "Is Neoliberalism Killing Us? A Cross Sectional Study of the Impact of Neoliberal Beliefs on Health and Social Wellbeing in the Midst of the COVID-19 Pandemic." *International Journal of Social Determinants of Health and Health Services* 53, no. 3 (2023): 363–373. https://doi.org/10.1177/00207314221134040.

Carias, Cristina, Justin J. O'Hagan, Manoj Gambhir, Emily B. Kahn, David L. Swerdlow, and Martin I. Meltzer. "Forecasting the 2014 West African Ebola Outbreak." *Epidemiologic Reviews* 41, no. 1 (January 2019): 34–50. https://doi.org/10.1093/epirev/mxz013.

Carney, Megan A., and Nora J. Kenworthy, eds. "Austerity, Health and Wellbeing: Transnational Perspectives." Special issue, *Social Science and Medicine* 187 (August 2017): 203–312. https://www .sciencedirect.com/journal/social-science-and-medicine/vol/187.

CDC. "2014 Ebola Outbreak in West Africa Epidemic Curves, Ebola (Ebola Virus Disease)." Last modified April 3, 2019. https://www.cdc.gov/vhf/ebola/history/2014-2016-outbreak /cumulative-cases-graphs.html.

CDC. "New Modeling Tool for Response to Ebola Virus Disease." Last modified September 23, 2014. https://archive.cdc.gov/#/details?url=https://www.cdc.gov/media/releases/2014/s0923 -ebola-model-Factsheet.html.

Chaparro, Elkyn. Interview by Richard Webb and Devesh Kapur. *World Bank Group Archives Oral History Project*, June 29, 1992. https://oralhistory.worldbank.org/transcripts/transcript-oral -history-interview-elkyn-chaparro-june-29-1992-washington-dc.

Chavkin, Sasha, and Ben Hallman. "World Bank Workers Losing Faith in Leadership, Survey Reveals." *International Consortium of Investigative Journalists*, June 22, 2015. https://www.icij.org /inside-icij/2015/06/world-bank-workers-losing-faith-leadership-survey-reveals/.

Chiapello, Ève, Anita Engels, and Eduardo Gonçalves Gresse. *Financializations of Development: Global Games and Local Experiments*. New York: Routledge, 2023.

Clark, William. "Robert McNamara at the World Bank." *Foreign Affairs* 60, no. 1 (Fall 1981): 167–184. https://doi.org/10.2307/20040995.

Conway, Ed. *The Summit: The Biggest Battle of the Second World War—Fought behind Closed Doors*. London: Little, Brown, 2014.

Cope, Sydney. Interview by Robert Oliver. *World Bank Group Oral History Program*, August 9, 1961. https://documents.worldbank.org/en/publication/documents-reports/documentdetail /608111468124481188/main-report.

Crena de Longh, Daniel. Interview by Oral History Research Office, Columbia University. *World Bank Group Oral History Program*, August 1, 1961. https://documents1.worldbank.org/curated /en/93202146814817738/pdf/789700v20TRN0C0rview0August01001961.pdf.

Davidson, Kief, and Pedro Kos, dirs. *Bending the Arc*. New York: Impact Partners, 2017.

Democracy Now. "60 Years Is Enough: Thousands Protest the IMF and World Bank." *Democracy Now*, April 30, 2004. https://www.democracynow.org/2004/4/30/60_years_is_enough _thousands_protest.

Demuth, Richard. Interview by Robert W. Oliver. *World Bank Group Archives Oral History Program*, August 10, 1961. https://documents1.worldbank.org/curated/en/623541468147539954 /pdf/789850TRN0Demu0view0August010001961.pdf.

Demuth, Richard H. "A Look Backward." *International Bank Notes: The First Fifteen Years* 15, no. 6 (June 1961): 6–10. https://documents1.worldbank.org/curated/en/483041468914423403/pdf /International-Bank-notes.pdf.

Doggart, Caroline. "From Reconstruction to Development in Europe and Japan." In *The Evolving Role of the World Bank*, edited by K. Sarwar Lateef, 37–67. Washington, DC: World Bank, 1995.

Donnan, Shawn. "World Bank Chief Dogged by Staff Anger." *Financial Times*, October 8, 2014. https://www.ft.com/content/b7b8e8c0-4e75-11e4-bfda-00144feab7de.

Dubal, Sam. "Renouncing Paul Farmer: A Desperate Plea for Radical Political Medicine." *Being Ethical in an Unethical World* (blog), May 17, 2012. https://samdubal.blogspot.com/2012/05 /renouncing-paul-farmer-desperate-plea.html.

Duffek, Karen, and Tania Willard. *Lawrence Paul Yuxweluptun: Unceded Territories*. Vancouver: Figure 1 Publishing, 2016.

Easterly, William. *The Elusive Quest for Growth*. Cambridge, MA: MIT Press, 2002.

*The Economist*. "Bonds That Rock and Roll." May 7, 1998. https://www.economist.com/finance -and-economics/1998/05/07/bonds-that-rock-and-roll.

*The Economist*. "The World Bank's President Resigns Abruptly." January 12, 2019. https://www .economist.com/finance-and-economics/2019/01/12/the-world-banks-president-resigns-abruptly.

*The Economist*. "Opprobrium from the Atrium." November 8, 2014. https://www.economist.com /finance-and-economics/2014/11/08/opprobrium-from-the-atrium.

*The Economist*. "The Pandemic's True Death Toll." Last modified February 18, 2024. https://www .economist.com/graphic-detail/coronavirus-excess-deaths-estimates.

Edwards, Sophie. "As Jim Kim Steps Down, a Tumultuous World Bank Presidency Comes to an End." *Devex*, February 4, 2019. https://www.devex.com/news/as-jim-kim-steps-down-a-tumul tuous-world-bank-presidency-comes-to-an-end-94247.

Edwards, Sophie. "Pandemic Response a Cycle of 'Panic and Neglect,' Says World Bank President." *Devex*, April 5, 2017. https://www.devex.com/news/pandemic-response-a-cycle-of-panic-and -neglect-says-world-bank-president-89995.

Erikson, Susan L. "Financial Experimentality: Ebola Bonds and New Forms of Global Health Pandemic Financing." Keynote for "Post Ebola: Knowledge Production and the Limitations of Translation," Max-Planck-Institut für ethnologische Forschung, Halle, Germany, October 28, 2015.

Erikson, Susan L. "The Financialization of Ebola." *Somatosphere*, November 11, 2015. http://somatosphere.net/2015/11/the-financialization-of-ebola.html.

Erikson, Susan L. "Global Ethnography: Problems of Theory and Method." In *Globalization, Reproduction, and the State*, edited by Carole H. Browner and Carolyn F. Sargent, 23–37. Durham, NC: Duke University Press, 2011.

Erikson, Susan L. "Global Health Business: The Production and Performativity of Statistics in Sierra Leone and Germany." *Medical Anthropology* 31, no. 4 (2012): 367–384. https://doi.org/10.1080/01459740.2011.621908.

Erikson, Susan L. "Global Health Futures? Reckoning with a Pandemic Bond." *Medicine Anthropology Theory* 6, no. 3 (October 2019): 1–32. https://doi.org/10.17157/mat.6.3.664.

Erikson, Susan L. "Metrics and Market Logics of Global Health." In *Metrics: What Counts in Global Health*, edited by Vincanne Adams, 147–162. Durham, NC: Duke University Press, 2016.

Erikson, Susan L. "Secrets from Whom? Following the Money in Global Health Finance." *Current Anthropology* 56, no. S12 (December 2015): S306–S316. https://doi.org/10.1086/683271.

Etzion, Dror, Bernard Forgues, and Emmanuel Kyrpraios. "Pandemic Bonds: The Financial Cure We Need for Covid-19?" *The Conversation*, March 29, 2020. https://theconversation.com/pandemic-bonds-the-financial-cure-we-need-for-covid-19-134503.

Evans, Steve. "Coronavirus May Trigger $196m World Bank Cat Bond & Swap Payout." *Artemis*, March 23, 2020. https://www.artemis.bm/news/coronavirus-may-trigger-196m-world-bank-cat-bond-swap-payout/.

Evans, Steve. "Pandemic Cat Bond Price Plummets on Growing Coronavirus Threat." *Artemis*, March 2, 2020. https://www.artemis.bm/news/pandemic-cat-bond-price-plummets-on-growing-coronavirus-threat/.

Evans, Steve. "Pandemic Cat Bond Secondary Price Reacts as Coronavirus Cases Rise." *Artemis*, February 17, 2020. https://www.artemis.bm/news/pandemic-cat-bond-secondary-price-reacts-as-coronavirus-cases-rise/.

Evans, Steve. "World Bank Pandemic Bonds & Swaps Triggered, Will Pay Out $195.84m." *Artemis*, April 17, 2020. https://www.artemis.bm/news/world-bank-pandemic-bonds-swaps-triggered-will-pay-out-195-84m/.

Evans, Steve. "World Bank to Scale-Up Access to Catastrophe Bonds and Reinsurance Capital." *Artemis*, February 2, 2024. https://www.artemis.bm/news/world-bank-to-scale-up-access-to-catastrophe-bonds-and-reinsurance-capital/.

Farmer, Paul. *Fevers, Feuds, and Diamonds: Ebola and the Ravages of History*. New York: Picador Paper Press, 2020.

Farmer, Paul, and Jim Yong Kim, "2017 AM: 116th Annual Meeting Opening Keynote: Bending the Arc of Change." American Anthropological Association, January 18, 2018, YouTube video, 1:00:35. https://www.youtube.com/watch?v=uwCIfJkUVNE.

*Financial Times*. "The World Bank Risks Sliding into Irrelevance." November 20, 2014. https://www.ft.com/content/0953c8cc-70bc-11e4-9129-00144feabdc0.

Foley, Ellen. *Your Pocket Is What Cures You: The Politics of Health in Senegal*. New Brunswick, NJ: Rutgers University Press, 2009.

Foroohar, Rana. *Makers and Takers: How Wall Street Destroyed Main Street*. New York: Crown, 2017.

Funk, Sebastian, Anton Camacho, Adam J. Kucharski, Rachel Lowe, Rosalind M. Eggo, and W. John Edmunds. "Assessing the Performance of Real-Time Epidemic Forecasts: A Case Study of Ebola in the Western Area Region of Sierra Leone, 2014–15." *PLOS Computational Biology* 15, no. 2 (February 2019): 1–17. https://doi.org/10.1371/journal.pcbi.1006785.

Garrett, Laurie. "Trump Has Sabotaged America's Coronavirus Response." *Foreign Policy*, January 31, 2020. https://foreignpolicy.com/2020/01/31/coronavirus-china-trump-united-states-public-health-emergency-response/.

Garrett, Laurie. "The World Bank Has the Money to Fight Ebola but Won't Use It." *Foreign Policy*, July 22, 2019. https://foreignpolicy.com/2019/07/22/the-world-bank-has-the-money-to-fight-ebola-but-wont-use-it/.

Gerstle, Gary. *The Rise and Fall of the Neoliberal Order: America and the World in the Free Market Era*. Oxford: Oxford University Press, 2022.

Glantz, Aaron. *Homewreckers: How a Gang of Wall Street Kingpins, Hedge Fund Magnates, Crooked Banks, and Vulture Capitalists Suckered Millions Out of Their Homes and Demolished the American Dream*. New York: Custom House, 2019.

Gloyd, Steve. "Sapping the Poor: The Impact of Structural Adjustment Programs." In *Sickness and Wealth: The Corporate Assault on Global Health*, edited by Meredith Fort, Mary Anne Mercer, and Oscar Gish, 43–54. Cambridge, MA: South End Press, 2004.

Goldman, Michael. *Imperial Nature: The World Bank and Struggles for Social Justice in the Age of Globalization*. New Haven, CT: Yale University Press, 2005.

Goodman, Peter S. *Davos Man: How the Billionaires Devoured the World*. New York: Custom House, 2022.

Government of Sierra Leone. *National Ebola Recovery Strategy for Sierra Leone: 2015–2017*. July 2015, 25. https://ebolaresponse.un.org/sites/default/files/sierra_leone_recovery_strategy_en.pdf.

Grabel, Ilene. *When Things Don't Fall Apart: Global Financial Governance and Development Finance in the Age of Productive Incoherence*. Cambridge, MA: MIT Press, 2018.

Graeber, David. *Debt: The First 5,000 Years*. Brooklyn, NY: Melville House, 2011.

Grépin, Karen A. "International Donations to the Ebola Virus Outbreak: Too Little, Too Late?" *BMJ* 350, no. h376 (February 2015): 1–5. https://doi.org/10.1136/bmj.h376.

Griffith, T. Risely. "Sierra Leone: Past, Present and Future." *Proceedings of the Royal Colonial Institute* 13 (1881–1882): 58, 59.

Griffiths, Peter. *The Economist's Tale: A Consultant Encounters Hunger and the World Bank.* London: Zed Books, 2003.

Guyer, Jane I. *Marginal Gains: Monetary Transactions in Atlantic Africa.* Chicago: University of Chicago Press, 2004.

Hacking, Ian. "Making Up People." *London Review of Books* 28, no. 16 (August 2006). https://www.lrb.co.uk/the-paper/v28/n16/ian-hacking/making-up-people.

Harding, Robin. "World Bank: Man on a Mission." *Financial Times*, April 7, 2014. https://www.ft.com/content/012f15d6-b8fa-11e3-98c5-00144feabdc0.

Harvey, David. *A Brief History of Neoliberalism.* Oxford: Oxford University Press, 2005.

Hinshaw, Drew, and Leslie Scism. "Pandemic Insurance Has Yet to Pay Out to Poor Countries." *Wall Street Journal*, April 10, 2020. https://www.wsj.com/articles/pandemic-insurance-has-yet-to-pay-out-to-poor-countries-11586546397.

Ho, Karen. *Liquidated: An Ethnography of Wall Street.* Durham, NC: Duke University Press, 2009.

Hodgson, Camilla. "World Bank Ditches Second Round of Pandemic Bonds." *Financial Times*, July 5, 2020. https://www.ft.com/content/949adc20-5303-494b-9cf1-4eb4c8b6aa6b.

Hong, Sun-ha. *Technologies of Speculation: The Limits of Knowledge in a Data-Driven Society.* New York: New York University Press, 2020.

Huber, Caroline, Lyn Finelli, and Warren Stevens. "The Economic and Social Burden of the 2014 Ebola Outbreak in West Africa." *Journal of Infectious Diseases* 218, no. 5 (October 2018): S698–S704. https://doi.org/10.1093/infdis/jiy213.

Hughes-McLure, Sarah, and Emma Mawdsley. "Innovative Finance for Development? Vaccine Bonds and the Hidden Costs of Financialization." *Economic Geography* 98, no. 2 (March 2022): 145–169. https://doi.org/10.1080/00130095.2021.2020090.

Hunter, Benjamin M., and Susan F. Murray. "Deconstructing the Financialization of Healthcare." *Development and Change* 50, no. 5 (June 2019): 1263–1287. https://doi.org/10.1111/dech.12517.

IBM. "What Is Monte Carlo Simulation?" Accessed July 26, 2023. https://www.ibm.com/cloud/learn/monte-carlo-simulation.

Igoe, Michael. "World Bank Pandemic Facility 'An Embarrassing Mistake,' Says Former Chief Economist." *Devex*, April 12, 2019. https://www.devex.com/news/world-bank-pandemic-facility-an-embarrassing-mistake-says-former-chief-economist-94697.

International Bank for Reconstruction and Development. *Technical Report on the French West African Railways.* May 24, 1953. https://documents1.worldbank.org/curated/en/618181468032414631/pdf/multi0page.pdf.

International Bank for Reconstruction and Development. *Twenty-Eighth Special Meeting of the Executive Directors: Loans to the Kingdom of Belgium and the Belgian Congo.* September 13,

1952. http://documents1.worldbank.org/curated/en/442661468013865834/pdf/658270BR0P03730Congo000Sept01301951.pdf.

International Monetary Fund. "Sierra Leone: Transactions with the Fund from May 01, 1984 to June 30, 2023." Accessed July 23, 2023. https://www.imf.org/external/np/fin/tad/extrans1.aspx?memberKey1=850&endDate=2099%2D12%2D31&finposition_flag=YES.

Investor.gov, US Securities and Exchange Commission. "Accredited Investors—Updated Investor Bulletin." Last modified April 14, 2021. https://www.investor.gov/additional-resources/news-alerts/alerts-bulletins/investor-bulletin-accredited-investors.

Irwin, Alec, Joyce Millen, Jim Kim, John Gershman, Brooke G. Schoepf, and Paul Farmer. "Suffering, Moral Claims, and Scholarly Responsibility: A Response to Leslie Butt." *Medical Anthropology* 21, no. 1 (2002): 25–30. https://doi.org/10.1080/01459740210621.

Jarzabkowski, Paula, Rebecca Bednarek, and Paul Spee. *Making a Market for Acts of God: The Practice of Risk-Trading in the Global Reinsurance Industry*. Oxford: Oxford University Press, 2015.

Jomo, K. S., and Anis Chowdhury. "World Bank Financializing Development." *Development* 62, no. 1 (September 2019): 147–153. https://doi.org/10.1057/s41301-019-00206-3.

Jonas, Olga. "Pandemic Bonds: Designed to Fail in Ebola." *Nature* 572, no. 7769 (August 2019): 285. https://doi.org/10.1038/d41586-019-02415-9.

Jones, Lee, and Shahar Hameiri. "COVID-19 and the Failure of the Neoliberal Regulatory State." *Review of International Political Economy* 29, no. 4 (2022): 1027–1052. https://doi.org/10.1080/09692290.2021.1892798.

Jones-Konneh, Tracey Elizabeth Claire, Angella Isata Kaikai, Ibrahim Borbor Bah, Daisuke Nonaka, Rie Takeuchi, and Jun Kobayashi. "Impact of Health Systems Reform on COVID-19 Control in Sierra Leone: A Case Study." *Tropical Medicine and Health* 51, no. 1 (May 2023): 1–13. https://doi.org/10.1186/s41182-023-00521-z.

Kaiser-Schatzlein, Robin. "No Pain, No Gain: Pandemic Bonds and the Privatization of Public Health." *Harper's Magazine*, July 2022. https://harpers.org/archive/2022/07/pandemic-bonds-and-the-privatization-of-public-health-world-bank-pandemic-emergency-financing-facility/.

Kapur, Devesh, John P. Lewis, and Richard C. Webb. *The World Bank: Its First Half Century*. Washington, DC: Brookings Institution Press, 1997.

Karefa-Smart, Dr. John, Sierra Leone Minister of External Affairs. 1961. BACS Productions, "Sierra Leone with Sir Milton Margai." Uploaded November 24, 2013. YouTube video, at 6:50. https://www.youtube.com/watch?v=ztUXY_IYT0U.

Kentikelenis, Alexander, Lawrence King, Martin McKee, and David Stuckler. "The International Monetary Fund and the Ebola Outbreak." *Lancet Global Health* 3, no. 2 (December 2014): E69–E70. https://doi.org/10.1016/S2214-109X(14)70377-8.

Keshavjee, Salmaan. *Blind Spot: How Neoliberalism Infiltrated Global Health*. Oakland: University of California Press, 2014.

Kidder, Tracy. *Mountains beyond Mountains: The Quest of Dr. Paul Farmer, a Man Who Would Cure the World.* New York: Random House, 2003.

Kim, Jim Yong. "100 Coaches Live." Interview by Marshall Goldsmith and Sanyin Siang. April 30, 2020, LinkedIn video. https://www.linkedin.com/video/live/urn:li:ugcPost:66616479 42627143680/.

Kim, Jim Yong. "Billions to Trillions: Idea to Action." July 13, 2015. https://www.worldbank.org /en/news/speech/2015/07/13/billions-trillions-ideas-action-event.

Kim, Jim Yong. "A Conversation with Jim Yong Kim '82, Vice Chairman and Partner at Global Infrastructure Partners." Interview by Edward Steinfeld. Watson Institute for International and Public Affairs. February 13, 2019, YouTube video, 1:20:09. https://www.youtube.com /watch?v=wxEUCvvrCnM.

Kim, Jim Yong. "The David Rubenstein Show: Dr. Jim Yong Kim." Interview by David Rubenstein. September 5, 2018, YouTube video, 24:03. https://www.youtube.com/watch?v=2HBzTz 4c3SU.

Kim, Jim Yong. "Defeating COVID-19—A 5 Part Plan w. Dr. Jim Yong Kim and Marshall Goldsmith." Interview by Marshall Goldsmith and Sanyin Siang. Marshall Goldsmith. May 1, 2020, YouTube video, 54:36. https://www.youtube.com/watch?v=gDTRoodVXWo.

Kim, Jim Yong. "Doesn't Everyone Deserve a Chance at a Good Life?" TED talk. July 19, 2017, YouTube video, 22:12. https://www.youtube.com/watch?v=Fc1yN6uxZfQ.

Kim, Jim Yong. "Dr. Jim Yong Kim on Global Health." Interview by Bill Moyers. *Bill Moyers Journal.* September 11, 2009, video, 24:12. https://billmoyers.com/content/dr-jim-yong-kim-on -global-health/.

Kim, Jim Yong. "Dr. Jim Yong Kim on Leading Efforts to Fight COVID-19 and 'Bending the Arc.'" Interview by Eric Nam. *I Think You're Dope*, DIVE Studios. January 6, 2021, YouTube video, 1:12:28. https://www.youtube.com/watch?v=JiwvibnE2TQ.

Kim, Jim Yong. "Jim Yong Kim on Global Futures." Global Georgetown. February 9, 2017, YouTube video, 37:45. https://www.youtube.com/watch?v=Z0PLnyLVByo.

Kim, Jim Yong. "LinkedIn Speaker Series: Dr. Jim Yong Kim." Interview by Allen Blue. LinkedIn, September 12, 2018, YouTube video, 22:50. https://www.youtube.com/watch?v=yDkqh SOUVo4.

Kim, Jim Yong. "Preventing the Next Pandemic: A Conversation with the World Bank President." Interview by J. Stephen Morrison. Center for Strategic & International Studies. June 2, 2016, YouTube video, 18:24. https://www.youtube.com/watch?v=tXWJWHkgl8k.

Kim, Jim Yong. "Rethinking Development Finance: LSE Public Lecture." *LSE Public Event*, April 11, 2017. Podcast, 1:26:46. https://www.lse.ac.uk/lse-player?id=3802.

Kim, Jim Yong. "Speech at the 2017 Annual Meetings Plenary." *World Bank.* October 13, 2017. https://www.worldbank.org/en/news/speech/2017/10/13/wbg-president-jim-yong-kim-speech -2017-annual-meetings-plenary-session.

Kim, Jim Yong. "Speech: Rethinking Development Finance." *World Bank.* April 17, 2017. https://www.worldbank.org/en/news/speech/2017/04/11/speech-by-world-bank-group-president-jim-yong-kim-rethinking-development-finance.

Kim, Jim Yong. "We Need a New Global Response to Pandemics." *World Economic Forum*, January 20, 2015. https://www.weforum.org/agenda/2015/01/we-need-a-new-global-response-to-pandemics/.

Kim, Jim Yong. "What Ebola Taught the World One Year Later." *Time*, March 24, 2015. https://time.com/3755178/ebola-lessons/.

Kim, Jim Yong. "World Bank President Jim Yong Kim: The VICE News Interview." Vice News. April 25, 2015, YouTube video, 8:07. https://www.youtube.com/watch?v=619qFMXneeU.

Kim, Jim Yong, Joyce V. Millen, Alec Irwin, and John Gershman, eds. *Dying for Growth: Global Inequality and the Health of the Poor.* Monroe, ME: Common Courage Press, 2000.

Krippner, Greta. *Capitalizing on Crisis: The Political Origins of the Rise of Finance.* Cambridge, MA: Harvard University Press, 2012.

Labonte, Ronald. "International Governance and World Trade Organization (WTO) Reform." *Critical Public Health* 12, no. 1 (2002): 65–86. https://doi.org/10.1080/09581590110113312.

Le, Tung Thanh, Zacharias Andreadakis, Arun Kumar, Raúl Gómez Román, Stig Tollefsen, Melanie Saville, and Stephen Mayhew. "The COVID-19 Vaccine Development Landscape." *Nature* 19 (April 2020): 305–306. https://www.nature.com/articles/d41573-020-00073-5.

Lee, Benjamin, and Randy Martin, eds. *Derivatives and the Wealth of Societies.* Chicago: University of Chicago Press, 2016.

Leigland, James. "Public-Private Partnerships in Developing Countries: The Emerging Evidence-Based Critique." *World Bank Research Observer* 33, no. 1 (February 2018): 103–134. https://doi.org/10.1093/wbro/lkx008.

Lepore, Jill. "The Disruption Machine." *New Yorker*, June 16, 2014. https://www.newyorker.com/magazine/2014/06/23/the-disruption-machine.

Lewis, Michael. *The Big Short: Inside the Doomsday Machine.* New York: W. W. Norton, 2010.

Lewis, Michael. *The Fifth Risk: Undoing Democracy.* New York: W. W. Norton, 2018.

Lewis, Michael. "In Nature's Casino." *New York Times Magazine*, August 26, 2007. https://www.nytimes.com/2007/08/26/magazine/26neworleans-t.html.

Lewis, Michael. *The Premonition: A Pandemic Story.* New York: W. W. Norton, 2021.

Leyshon, Andrew, and Nigel Thrift. "The Capitalization of Almost Everything: The Future of Finance and Capitalism." *Theory, Culture & Society* 24, nos. 7–8 (December 2007): 97–115. https://doi.org/10.1177/0263276407084699.

London School of Economics and Political Science. "World Bank Pandemic Financing Scheme Serves Private Sector Interests over Global Health Security, New LSE Analysis Suggests." *LSE News*, October 18, 2019. https://www.lse.ac.uk/News/Latest-news-from-LSE/2019/j-October-2019

/World-Bank-pandemic-financing-scheme-serves-private-sector-interests-over-global-health
-security-new-LSE-analysis-suggests.

Lowrey, Annie. "World Bank Revamping is Rattling Employees." *New York Times*, May 27, 2014. https://www.nytimes.com/2014/05/28/business/international/world-bank-revamping-is -rattling-employees.html.

Lowrey, Annie. "World Bank, Rooted in Bureaucracy, Proposes a Sweeping Reorganization." *New York Times*, October 6, 2013. https://www.nytimes.com/2013/10/07/business/international/world -bank-rooted-in-bureaucracy-proposes-a-sweeping-reorganization.html.

Machen, Ronald C., Matthew T. Jones, George P. Varghese, and Emily L. Stark. *Investigation of Data Irregularities in Doing Business 2018* and *Doing Business 2020: Investigation Findings and Report to the Board of Executive Directors*. WilmerHale. September 15, 2021. https://www.scribd .com/document/525676025/DB-Investigation-Findings-and-Report-to-the-Board-of-Executive -Directors-September-15-2021.

Mahajan, Manjari. "Philanthropy and the Nation-State in Global Health: The Gates Foundation in India." *Global Public Health* 13, no. 10 (December 2017): 1357–1368. https://doi.org/10.1080 /17441692.2017.1414286.

Marcus, George E. "Ethnography in/of the World System: The Emergence of Multi-Sited Ethnography." *Annual Review of Anthropology* 24 (October 1995): 95–117. https://doi.org/10.1146 /annurev.an.24.100195.000523.

Marshall, Katherine. *The World Bank: From Reconstruction to Development to Equity*. New York: Routledge, 2008.

Martineau, Fred, Annie Wilkinson, and Melissa Parker. "Epistemologies of Ebola: Reflections on the Experience of the Ebola Response Anthropology Platform." *Anthropology Quarterly* 90, no. 2 (Spring 2017): 475–494. https://doi.org/10.1353/anq.2017.0027.

Maurer, Bill. *Mutual Life, Limited: Islamic Banking, Alternative Currencies, Lateral Reason*. Princeton, NJ: Princeton University Press, 2005.

Maxmen, Amy. *Ebola's Unpaid Heroes: How Billions in Aid Skips over Those at the Frontline*. New York: Newsweek Insights, 2015. Kindle.

Maxmen, Amy. "Why the World Bank Ex-Chief Is on a Mission to End Coronavirus Transmission." *Nature*, April 22, 2020. https://www.nature.com/articles/d41586-020-01218-7.

Mazzucato, Mariana. *The Entrepreneurial State: Debunking Public vs. Private Sector Myths*. New York: PublicAffairs, 2015.

Mazzucato, Mariana. *The Value of Everything: Making and Taking in the Global Economy*. New York: PublicAffairs, 2018.

Mazzucato, Mariana, and Rosie Collington. *The Big Con: How the Consulting Industry Weakens Our Businesses, Infantilizes Our Governments, and Warps Our Economies*. New York: Penguin Press, 2023.

McKinsey & Company. "Organizational Health Index." Accessed July 24, 2023. https://www .mckinsey.com/solutions/orgsolutions/overview/organizational-health-index.

McVeigh, Karen. "World Bank's $500m Pandemic Scheme Accused of 'Waiting for People to Die.'" *The Guardian*, February 28, 2020. https://www.theguardian.com/global-development/2020/feb/28/world-banks-500m-coronavirus-push-too-late-for-poor-countries-experts-say.

Moran, Mary, and Daniel Hoffman. "Ebola in Perspective." *Hot Spots, Fieldsights*, October 7, 2014. https://culanth.org/fieldsights/series/ebola-in-perspective.

Narayan, Vijay. "Sierra Leone's Health Workforce Crisis: Drivers of Suboptimal Distribution and Poor Retention of Primary Healthcare Workers in Rural Areas." MPH thesis, University of Washington, 2015. http://hdl.handle.net/1773/33072.

National Academies of Sciences, Engineering, and Medicine. *Taking Action against Clinician Burnout: A Systems Approach to Professional Well-Being*. Washington, DC: National Academies Press, 2019. https://doi.org/10.17226/25521.

Navarro, Vicente. "The Consequences of Neoliberalism in the Current Pandemic." *International Journal of Health Services* 50, no. 3 (May 2020): 271–275. https://doi.org/10.1177/0020731420925449.

Navarro, Vicente. "Why Asian Countries Are Controlling the Pandemic Better than the United States and Western Europe." *International Journal of Health Services* 51, no. 2 (March 2021): 261–264. https://doi.org/10.1177/0020731421999930.

OANDA. "Currency Converter." Accessed May 23, 2022. https://www1.oanda.com/currency/converter/.

Obama, Barack. "President Obama Nominates Jim Yong Kim for World Bank President." The Obama White House, March 23, 2010, YouTube video, 6:39. https://www.youtube.com/watch?v=UmRlhxhXClE.

Osnos, Evan. "The Getty Family's Trust Issues." *New Yorker*, January 23, 2023. https://www.newyorker.com/magazine/2023/01/23/the-getty-familys-trust-issues.

Pardo, Ramon Pacheco, Mauricio Avendano-Pabon, Xuechen Chen, Bo-jiun Jing, Takuya Matsuda, Jeong-ho Lee, Joshua Ting, and Kaho Yu. "Learning and Remembering: How East Asia Prepared for COVID-19 over the Years." *Global Policy*, May 27, 2020. https://www.globalpolicyjournal.com/blog/27/05/2020/learning-and-remembering-how-east-asia-prepared-covid-19-over-years.

Partners in Health. "Building Strong Health Systems." Accessed October 31, 2023. https://www.pih.org/our-approach.

Partners in Health. "Countries." Accessed July 24, 2023. https://www.pih.org/countries.

PBS. "Africa's Greatest Civilizations: The City of M'banza-Kongo." February 27, 2017, video, 2:15. https://www.pbs.org/video/africas-great-civilizations-city-mbanza-kongo-africas-great-civilizations/.

Peeters Grietens, Koen, Phoebe Friesen, Rene Gerrets, Gustav Kuhn, Patricia Kingori, and Rachel Douglas-Jones, eds. "Misdirection in Global Health: Creating the Illusion of (Im)possible Alternatives in Global Health Research and Practice." Special issue, *Science & Technology Studies* 35, no. 2 (May 2022): 2–119. https://sciencetechnologystudies.journal.fi/issue/view/7770.

Peterson, Kristin. *Speculative Markets: Drug Circuits and Derivative Life in Nigeria.* Durham, NC: Duke University Press, 2014.

Pfeiffer, James, and Rachel Chapman. "Anthropological Perspectives on Structural Adjustment and Public Health." *Annual Review of Anthropology* 39, no. 1 (October 2010): 149–165. https://doi.org/10.1146/annurev.anthro.012809.105101.

Pfeiffer, James, and Rachel Chapman. "The Art of Medicine: An Anthropology of Aid in Africa." *Lancet* 385 (May 2015): 2144–2145. https://www.thelancet.com/pdfs/journals/lancet/PIIS0140-6736(15)61013-3.pdf.

Pfizer. *Pfizer Reports Fourth-Quarter and Full-Year 2021 Results.* December 2021. Accessed February 14, 2022. https://s28.q4cdn.com/781576035/files/doc_financials/2021/q4/Q4-2021-PFE-Earnings-Release.pdf.

Pigg, Stacy Leigh. "On Sitting and Doing: Ethnography as Action in Global Health." *Social Science & Medicine* 99 (December 2013): 127–134. https://doi.org/10.1016/j.socscimed.2013.07.018.

Piketty, Thomas. *Capital in the Twenty-First Century.* Cambridge, MA: Harvard University Press, 2014.

Politi, James, Sam Fleming, and Mark Vandevelde. "Why Jim Yon Kim's Move Has Shaken Up the World Bank." *Financial Times*, January 11, 2019. https://www.ft.com/content/44dd27d8-158d-11e9-a581-4ff78404524e.

Prainsack, Barbara. "The Political Economy of Digital Data: Introduction to the Special Issue." In "The Political Economy of Digital Data," edited by Barbara Prainsack. Special Issue, *Policy Studies* 41, no. 5 (2020): 439–446. https://doi.org/10.1080/01442872.2020.1723519.

Prichett, Lant. "Why Obama's World Bank Pick Is Proving So Controversial." *New Republic*, April 10, 2012. https://newrepublic.com/article/102624/why-obamas-world-bank-pick-proving-so-controversial.

Provost, Claire. "A World Bank of Trouble?" *The Guardian*, December 4, 2014. https://www.theguardian.com/global-development-professionals-network/2014/dec/04/a-world-bank-of-trouble.

Raven, Joanna, Haja Wurie, and Sophie Witter. "Health Workers' Experiences of Coping with the Ebola Epidemic in Sierra Leone's Health System: A Qualitative Study." *BMC Health Services Research* 18 (April 2018): 1–9. https://doi.org/10.1186/s12913-018-3072-3.

Reçber Chambers, Nurgül. "Swaps." *Öneri Dergisi* 1, no. 5 (June 1996): 139–143. https://doi.org/10.14783/maruoneri.703453.

Reich, Michael R. "Public-Private Partnerships for Public Health." *Nature Medicine* 6 (June 2000): 617–620. https://doi.org/10.1038/76176.

Reitman, Janet. "Confessions of an Ivy League Frat Boy: Inside Dartmouth's Hazing Abuses." *Rolling Stone*, March 28, 2012. https://www.rollingstone.com/feature/confessions-of-an-ivy-league-frat-boy-inside-dartmouths-hazing-abuses-238604/.

Reno, William. *Corruption and State Politics in Sierra Leone*. Cambridge: Cambridge University Press, 1995.

Reuters. "IMF Sees Cost of COVID Pandemic Rising beyond $12.5 Trillion Estimate." *Reuters*, January 20, 2022. https://www.reuters.com/business/imf-sees-cost-covid-pandemic-rising-beyond -125-trillion-estimate-2022-01-20/.

Rice, Andrew. "The Evolution of an Idealist." *Foreign Policy*, no. 218 (May/June 2016): 52–59. https://www.jstor.org/stable/44843425.

Rice, Andrew. "How the World Bank's Biggest Critic Became Its President." *The Guardian*, August 11, 2016. https://www.theguardian.com/news/2016/aug/11/world-bank-jim-yong-kim.

Richter, Judith. "Public-Private Partnerships for Health: A Trend with No Alternatives?" *Development* 47 (June 2004): 43–48. https://doi.org/10.1057/palgrave.development.1100043.

Riles, Annelise. *Collateral Knowledge: Legal Reasoning in the Global Financial Markets*. Chicago: University of Chicago Press, 2011.

Roberts, David L., Jeremy S. Rossman, and Ivan Jarić. "Dating First Cases of COVID-19." *PLOS Pathogens* 17, no. 6 (September 2020): 1–10. https://doi.org/10.1371/journal.ppat.1009620.

Robertson, Grant. "'Without Early Warning You Can't Have Early Response': How Canada's World-Class Pandemic Alert System Failed." *Globe and Mail*, July 25, 2020. https://www.theglobe andmail.com/canada/article-without-early-warning-you-cant-have-early-response-how-canadas/.

Romeo, Nick. *The Alternative: How to Build a Just Economy*. Cambridge, MA: MIT Press, 2023.

Romero, Maria José. "Development Finance Takes 'Private Turn': Implications and Challenges Ahead." *Development* 59 (May 2017): 59–65. https://doi.org/10.1057/s41301-017-0074-0.

Ross, Ronald. "An Application of the Theory of Probabilities to the Study of A Priori Pathometry— Part I." *Proceedings of the Royal Society A* 92, no. 638 (February 1916): 204–230. https://doi .org/10.1098/rspa.1916.0007.

Ruckert, Arne, and Ronald Labonté. "Public-Private Partnerships (PPPs) in Global Health: The Good, the Bad and the Ugly." *Third World Quarterly* 35, no. 9 (November 2014): 1598–1614. https://doi.org/10.1080/01436597.2014.970870.

Sarfaty, Galit A. *Values in Translation: Human Rights and the Culture of the World Bank*. Stanford, CA: Stanford University Press, 2012.

Schuster, Caroline. *Forecasts: A Story of Weather and Finance at the Edge of Disaster*. Toronto: University of Toronto Press, 2023.

Schwab, Tim. *The Bill Gates Problem: Reckoning with the Myth of the Good Billionaire*. New York: Metropolitan Books, 2023.

Scotti, Veronica. "Lessons for a Post-COVID-19 World." *Swiss Re*, April 27, 2020. https://www .swissre.com/our-business/public-sector-solutions/contributing-to-the-global-debate/covid-19 -pandemic-emergency-funding.html.

Shaffer, Ellen, and Joseph Brenner. "Trade and Health Care: Corporatizing Vital Human Services." In *Sickness and Wealth: The Corporate Assault on Global Health*, edited by Meredith Fort, Mary Anne Mercer, and Oscar Gish, 79–94. Cambridge, MA: South End Press, 2004.

Shah, Rajiv. *Big Bets: How Large-Scale Change Really Happens*. New York: S&S/Simon Element, 2023.

Shepler, Susan. "'We Know Who Is Eating the Ebola Money!' Corruption, the State, and the Ebola Response." In "Producing Ebola: Creating Knowledge in and about an Epidemic," edited by Catherine Bolten and Susan Shepler. Special issue, *Anthropological Quarterly* 90, no. 2 (Spring 2017): 451–473. https://doi.org/10.1353/anq.2017.0026.

Smirl, Lisa. "Drive by Development." *Spaces of Aid*, March 11, 2014. https://spacesofaid.word press.com/2014/03/11/drive-by-development-the-role-of-the-suv-in-international-humanitarian -assistance/.

Smith, Stacy Vanek, and Cardiff Garcia. "Pandemic Bonds." *The Indicator from Planet Money, National Public Radio*, March 24, 2020. Podcast. https://www.npr.org/transcripts/821000049.

Solomon, Brian. "Me-First Leadership: Jim Yong Kim's Unfulfilled Promise at Dartmouth." *Forbes*, March 23, 2012. https://www.forbes.com/sites/briansolomon/2012/03/23/me-first-leadership -jim-yong-kims-unfulfilled-promise-at-dartmouth/?sh=71e9c8d75e52.

Stein, Felix. "Risky Business: COVAX and the Financialization of Global Vaccine Equity." *Globalization and Health* 17, no. 112 (September 2021): 1–11. https://doi.org/10.1186/s12992-021 -00763-8.

Stein, Felix, and Devi Sridhar. "The Financialization of Global Health." *Wellcome Open Research* 3, no. 17 (February 2018): 1–4. https://doi.org/10.12688/wellcomeopenres.13885.1.

Stein, Felix, and Devi Sridhar. "Health as a 'Global Public Good': Creating a Market for Pandemic Risk." *BMJ* 358, no. j3397 (August 2017): 1–4. https://doi.org/10.1136/bmj.j3397.

Stein, Felix, and Devi Sridhar. "The World Bank Reinvents Itself—And Puts Poverty Reduction at Risk." *The Conversation*, June 16, 2017. https://theconversation.com/the-world-bank-reinvents -itself-and-puts-poverty-reduction-at-risk-79403.

Stern, Jacob. "Online Betting Has Gone Off the Deep End." *The Atlantic*, October 13, 2023. https://www.theatlantic.com/technology/archive/2023/10/novelty-betting-regulation/675633/.

Stiglitz, Joseph E. *Globalization and Its Discontents*. New York: W. W. Norton, 2002.

Storm, Servaas. "Financialization and Economic Development: A Debate on the Social Efficiency of Modern Finance." *Development and Change* 49, no. 2 (January 2018): 302–329. https://doi .org/10.1111/dech.12385.

Stuckler, David, and Sanjay Basu. *The Body Economic: Why Austerity Kills: Recessions, Budget Battles, and the Politics of Life and Death*. Toronto: HarperCollins, 2013.

Summers, Larry. "Pandemic Bonds Have Potential to Be Win-Win." *Financial Times*, October 14, 2015. https://www.ft.com/content/00784360-52d1-3104-9e3f-56987e3defcd.

Swiss Re. *Resilience in Action: 2017 Financial Report*. Zurich: Swiss Re, 2018. https://reports
.swissre.com/2017/servicepages/downloads/files/2017_financial_report_swissre_ar17.pdf.

Szymanski, Anna. "Breakingviews—Pandemic Bonds Are the Sick Man of Finance." *Reuters*, February 26, 2020. https://www.reuters.com/article/us-china-health-breakingviews-idINKCN20K350.

Tett, Gillian. *Anthro-Vision: How Anthropology Can Explain Business and Life*. New York: Random House Business, 2021.

Tett, Gillian. "Blended Finance, the Spinach of Investing, Will Make Us Stronger." *Financial Times*, February 25, 2021. https://www.ft.com/content/16885bf1-b172-4dcc-b7f8-0b32798563c6.

Tett, Gillian. *Fool's Gold: How Unrestrained Greed Corrupted a Dream, Shattered Global Markets and Unleashed a Catastrophe*. New York: Abacus, 2009.

Tett, Gillian. "A Little Market Medicine to Prevent the Next Pandemic." *Financial Times*, January 22, 2015. https://www.ft.com/content/114a5aa2-a21f-11e4-bbb8-00144feab7de.

Thomas, Landon. "The World Bank Is Remaking Itself as a Creature of Wall Street." *New York Times*, January 28, 2018. https://www.nytimes.com/2018/01/25/business/world-bank-jim-yong-kim.html.

Tooze, Adam. *Crashed: How a Decade of Financial Crises Changed the World*. New York: Viking, 2018.

Tronto, Joan. *Caring Democracy: Markets, Equality, Justice*. New York: New York University Press, 2013.

Tyson, Jeff. "Why the World Bank's Staff Survey Is Delayed." *Devex*, December 23, 2014. https://www.devex.com/news/why-the-world-bank-s-staff-survey-is-delayed-85111.

Tyson, Jeff. "World Bank Staff Survey Highlights Discontent with Senior Management." *Devex*, June 22, 2015. https://www.devex.com/news/world-bank-staff-survey-highlights-discontent-with-senior-management-86384.

UNCTAD. "Developing Countries Face $2.5 Trillion Annual Investment Gap in Key Sustainable Development Sectors, UNCTAD Report Estimates." *UNCTAD*, June 24, 2014. https://unctad.org/press-material/developing-countries-face-25-trillion-annual-investment-gap-key-sustainable.

United Nations. "Universal Declaration of Human Rights." Accessed October 31, 2023. https://www.un.org/en/about-us/universal-declaration-of-human-rights.

Unruh, Lynn, Sara Allin, Greg Marchildon, Sara Burke, Sarah Barry, Rikke Siersbaek, Steve Thomas, et al. "A Comparison of 2020 Health Policy Responses to the COVID-19 Pandemic in Canada, Ireland, the United Kingdom, and the United States of America." *Health Policy* 126, no. 5 (May 2022): 427–437. https://doi.org/10.1016/j.healthpol.2021.06.012.

Urban Dictionary, s.v. "world bank." By Luther Bliss, January 29, 2018. https://www.urbandictionary.com/define.php?term=world%20bank.

USAspending.gov. "The Federal Response to COVID-19, Data through 1/31/2023." Accessed March 23, 2023. https://www.usaspending.gov/disaster/covid-19?publicLaw=all/.

US Bureau of Labor Statistics. "CPI Inflation Calculator." Accessed July 23, 2023. https://www.bls.gov/data/inflation_calculator.htm.

US Securities and Exchange Commission. "Accredited Investors—Updated Investor Bulletin." Last modified March 1, 2022. Accessed May 25, 2023. https://www.sec.gov/node/172921.

US Securities and Exchange Commission. "What We Do." Last modified December 29, 2023. https://www.sec.gov/about/what-we-do.

Vecchi, Veronica, Niccolò Cusumano, and Eric J. Boyer. "Medical Supply Acquisition in Italy and the United States in the Era of COVID-19: The Case for Strategic Procurement and Public–Private Partnerships." *American Review of Public Administration* 50, nos. 6–7 (July 2020): 642–649. https://doi.org/10.1177/0275074020942061.

Wade, Robert H. "US Keeps Control of the World Bank." *Le Monde Diplomatique*, October 24, 2012. https://mondediplo.com/outsidein/us-keeps-control-of-the-world-bank.

Wallace, Lauren J., Irene Agyepong, Sushil Baral, Deepa Barua, Mahua Das, Rumana Huque, Deepak Joshi, et al. "The Role of the Private Sector in the COVID-19 Pandemic: Experiences from Four Health Systems." *Frontiers in Public Health* 10, no. 878225 (May 2022): 1–16. https://doi.org/10.3389/fpubh.2022.878225.

Wallich, Christine I. "The World Bank's Currency Swaps." *Finance & Development* 21, no. 2 (June 1984): 15–19. https://www.elibrary.imf.org/view/journals/022/0021/002/article-A004-en.xml.

Weisenthal, Joe, and Tracy Alloway. "What the Coronavirus Means for Pandemic Bonds." *Odd Lots*, February 16, 2020. Podcast, transcript. https://www.transcriptforest.com/en/odd-lots/12041-what-the-coronavirus-means-for-pandemic-bonds-2020-02-17.

Wendland, Claire L. *Partial Stories: Maternal Death from Six Angles.* Chicago: University of Chicago Press, 2022.

Wielawski, Irene M. "Taking Charge." *Dartmouth Alumni Magazine*, September 2009. https://dartmouthalumnimagazine.com/articles/taking-charge.

Wikipedia. "British West African Pound." Last modified February 14, 2024. https://en.wikipedia.org/wiki/British_West_African_pound.

Winters, Janelle, and Devi Sridhar. "Earmarking for Global Health: Benefits and Perils of the World Bank's Trust Fund Model." *BMJ* 358, no. j3394 (August 2017): 1–5. https://doi.org/10.1136/bmj.j3394.

Woodly, Deva, Rachel H. Brown, Mara Marin, Shatema Threadcraft, Christopher Paul Harris, Jasmine Syedullah, and Miriam Ticktin. "The Politics of Care." *Contemporary Political Theory* 20, no. 4 (August 2021): 890–925. https://doi.org/10.1057/s41296-021-00515-8.

Woods, Ngaire. *The Globalizers: The IMF, the World Bank, and their Borrowers.* Ithaca, NY: Cornell University Press, 2006.

World Bank. *70 Years: Connecting Capital Markets to Development.* 2018. https://thedocs.worldbank.org/en/doc/905031541023749461-0340022018/original/70yearsconnectingcapitalmarketstodevelopment.pdf.

World Bank. "Building Human Capital Starts with Health." *World Bank Blogs*, December 12, 2018. https://blogs.worldbank.org/health/building-human-capital-starts-health.

World Bank. "Development Finance (DFi)." Accessed July 25, 2023. https://www.worldbank.org/en/about/unit/dfi.

World Bank. *From Billions to Trillions: MDB [Multilateral Development Bank] Contributions to Financing for Development.* July 2015. https://documents1.worldbank.org/curated/en/602761467999349576/pdf/98023-BR-SecM2015-0233-IDA-SecM2015-0147-IFC-SecM2015-0105-MIGA-SecM2015-0061-Box391499B-OUO-9.pdf.

World Bank. "IDA Borrowing Countries." Accessed April 27, 2023. https://ida.worldbank.org/en/about/borrowing-countries.

World Bank. "IDA Member Countries." Last modified November 9, 2023. https://www.worldbank.org/en/about/leadership/members#ida.

World Bank. *Loans to Kingdom of Belgium and to the Belgian Congo.* September 13, 1951. https://documents1.worldbank.org/curated/en/353751468003920929/pdf/Loan-0048-Belgium-Belgian-Congo-Development-Plan-Project-Loan-Agreement.pdf.

World Bank. "Maximizing Finance for Development." Infographic. April 10, 2018. https://www.worldbank.org/en/news/infographic/2018/04/10/maximizing-finance-for-development.

World Bank. "Maximizing Finance for Development." YouTube video, April 11, 2018. https://www.youtube.com/watch?v=sdzttzJphsE.

World Bank. *Operations Manual: Pandemic Emergency Financing Facility.* October 15, 2019. https://thedocs.worldbank.org/en/doc/842101571243529089-0090022019/original/PEFOperationsManualapproved10.15.18.pdf.

World Bank. "Over 70 Years of Innovation in the Global Capital Markets." Accessed February 24, 2024. https://treasury.worldbank.org/en/about/unit/treasury/about#2.

World Bank. *The Pandemic Emergency Financing Facility.* 2018. Accessed May 4, 2023. https://thedocs.worldbank.org/en/doc/763521516900352855-0090022018/original/EnglishPEFBrochure.pdf.

World Bank. *Pandemic Emergency Financing Facility Financial Report.* December 31, 2019. https://fiftrustee.worldbank.org/content/dam/fif/funds/pef/TrusteeReports/PEF_TR_12_19.pdf.

World Bank. *Pandemic Emergency Financing Facility Financial Report.* April 30, 2021. https://fiftrustee.worldbank.org/content/dam/fif/funds/pef/TrusteeReports/PEF_TF_04_30_2021.pdf.

World Bank. *Pandemic Emergency Financing Facility—Global Pandemic Response through a Financial Intermediary Fund.* May 3, 2016. https://documents1.worldbank.org/curated/en/354341467990992248/pdf/104838-BR-R2016-0071-Box394885B-OUO-9.pdf.

World Bank. *Pandemic Emergency Financing Facility: Operational Brief for Eligible Countries.* February 2019. http://pubdocs.worldbank.org/en/478271550071105640/PEF-Operational-Brief-Feb-2019.pdf.

World Bank. *Pandemic Emergency Financing Facility (PEF) Country Allocations*. February 2021. https://pubdocs.worldbank.org/en/140481591710249514/pdf/PEF-country-allocations-table.pdf.

World Bank. "Projects." Project List. Accessed July 22, 2023. https://projects.worldbank.org/en/projects-operations/projects-list.

World Bank. *Prospectus Supplement*. June 28, 2017. https://thedocs.worldbank.org/en/doc/f355aa56988e258a350942240872e3c5-0240012017/original/PEF-Final-Prospectus-PEF.pdf.

World Bank. "World Bank Group President: No More Business as Usual." October 11, 2013. https://www.worldbank.org/en/news/press-release/2013/10/11/world-bank-group-president-annual-meetings-plenary.

World Bank. "World Bank Issues Its First Ever Catastrophe Bond Linked to Natural Hazard Risks in Sixteen Caribbean Countries." *World Bank*, June 30, 2014. https://www.worldbank.org/en/news/press-release/2014/06/30/world bank-issues-its-first-ever-catastrophe-bond-linked-to-natural-hazard-risks-in-sixteen-caribbean-countries.

World Bank. "World Bank Launches First Ever Pandemic Bonds to Support PEF." World Bank Treasury. June 28, 2017. YouTube video, 3:48. https://www.youtube.com/watch?v=RgmBjDGHAAI.

World Bank. "World Bank Sustainable Development Bond Raises Awareness for Women and Girls' Empowerment." *World Bank*, January 9, 2018. https://www.worldbank.org/en/news/press-release/2018/01/09/world-bank-sustainable-development-bond-raises-awareness-for-women-and-girls-empowerment.

World Bank Group. *2013 Employee Engagement Survey Summary of Results*. 2013. https://www.brettonwoodsproject.org/wp-content/uploads/2014/03/EES2013_WBG_SummaryReport-staff-survey.pdf.

World Bank Group. *2014 Staff Survey*. 2014. https://s3.documentcloud.org/documents/2107735/world-bank-2014-sraff-survey.pdf.

World Bank Group. *Engagement Survey 2015*. 2015. https://www.documentcloud.org/documents/2119278-world-bank-staff-survey-comments.html.

World Bank Group. "Open Learning Campus Public Private Partnership." Accessed August 5, 2021. https://ppp.worldbank.org/public-private-partnership/library/world-bank-group-open-learning-campus-olc.

World Bank Group. "Public-Private Partnerships." Accessed March 7, 2024. https://ppp.worldbank.org/public-private-partnership/PPP_Online_Reference_Guide/Introduction.

World Bank Group. "Who We Are." Accessed July 23, 2023. https://www.worldbank.org/en/who-we-are.

World Bank Group. "World Bank Group." Accessed July 18, 2023. https://www.worldbank.org/en/home.

World Bank Group. *World Bank Group Archives Exhibit Series: Bretton Woods Monetary Conference, July 1–22, 1944*. January 2016. https://documents1.worldbank.org/curated/en/538791468000 300309/pdf/104697-WP-PUBLIC-2008-07-Bretton-Woods-Monetary-Conf.pdf.

World Bank Group. "World Bank Group Launches Groundbreaking Financing Facility to Protect Poorest Countries against Pandemics." May 21, 2016. https://www.worldbank.org/en/news /press-release/2016/05/21/world-bank-group-launches-groundbreaking-financing-facility-to -protect-poorest-countries-against-pandemics.

World Bank Group. "World Bank Launches First-Ever Pandemic Bonds to Support $500 Million Pandemic Emergency Financing Facility." June 28, 2017. https://www.worldbank.org/en/news /press-release/2017/06/28/world-bank-launches-first-ever-pandemic-bonds-to-support-500 -million-pandemic-emergency-financing-facility.

World Bank Group. "World Bank Group President Calls for New Global Pandemic Emergency Facility." October 10, 2014. https://www.worldbank.org/en/news/press-release/2014/10/10 /world-bank-group-president-calls-new-global-pandemic-emergency-facility.

World Bank Open Knowledge Repository. "Search Results." Open Knowledge Repository Beta. Accessed August 5, 2021. https://openknowledge.worldbank.org/home.

World Bank Treasury. "About." Accessed July 25, 2023. https://treasury.worldbank.org/en/about /unit/treasury/about.

World Bank Treasury. "Create, Don't Just Participate. The World Bank Student Careers." August 25, 2020, YouTube video, 1:57. https://youtu.be/RdLvR0mfMPk?si=ErQw5i453uRBojZ6.

World Bank Treasury. "Milestones in World Bank Bonds History: 1947–2017." October 16, 2017, YouTube video, 2:57. https://www.youtube.com/watch?v=TAJOZEaPJoA.

World Health Organization. *Coronavirus Disease (COVID-19): Situation Report—116*. May 15, 2020. https://www.who.int/docs/default-source/coronaviruse/situation-reports/20200515-covid -19-sitrep-116.pdf?sfvrsn=8dd60956_2.

World Health Organization. "Influenza (Avian and Other Zoonotic)." Accessed October 31, 2023. https://www.who.int/europe/health-topics/Influenza-avian-and-other-zoonotic.

World Health Organization. *What Worked? What Didn't? What's Next? 2023 Progress Report on the Global Action Plan for Healthy Lives and Well-Being for All*. 2023. https://iris.who.int/bitstream /handle/10665/367422/9789240073371-eng.pdf.

Ying Li, Thomas Hills, and Ralph Hertwig. "A Brief History of Risk." *Cognition* 203, no. 104344 (October 2020): 1–11. https://doi.org/10.1016/j.cognition.2020.104344.

Zack-Williams, A. B. "Crisis and Structural Adjustment in Sierra Leone: Implications for Women." In *Women Pay the Price: Structural Adjustment in Africa and the Caribbean*, edited by Gloria Thomas-Emeagwali, 53–61. Trenton, NJ: Africa World Press, 1995.

Zack-Williams, A. B. "Sierra Leone: Crisis and Despair." *Review of African Political Economy*, no. 49 (Winter 1990): 22–33. https://www.jstor.org/stable/4005975.

Zack-Williams, A. B, ed. *When the State Fails: Studies on Intervention in the Sierra Leone Civil War.* London: Pluto Press, 2012.

Zaloom, Caitlin. *Out of the Pits: Traders and Technology from Chicago to London.* Chicago: University of Chicago Press, 2010.

Zarocostas, John. "Jim Yong Kim Steps Down from the World Bank." *Lancet* 393, no. 10169 (January 2019): 305–306. https://doi.org/10.1016/S0140-6736(19)30155-2.

Zhu, Hengbo, Li Wei, and Ping Niu. "The Novel Coronavirus Outbreak in Wuhan, China." *Global Health Research and Policy* 5, no. 6 (March 2020): 1–3. https://doi.org/10.1186/s41256-020-00135-6.

# Index

Page numbers in italics refer to figures.